DARK SÉANCE

THE FABULOUS DAVENPORT BROTHERS: MOST FAMOUS MEDIUMS OF ALL TIME OR THE GREATEST FRAUDS?

Timothy Green Beckley

Aditional material by Sir Arthur Conan Doyle

TESTIMONY OF ROBERT COOPER

The sincere but disinterested investigator who accompanied the Davenports to Ireland, Scotland, Belgium and Germany, solely in the pursuit of truth, writes as follows:

"I have been intimately associated with the Davenports for seven months. I have witnessed the manifestations under a variety of circumstances — in the dark and in the light, in public and in private — and I have never seen any indication whatever of the slightest approach to trickery. On the contrary, I have seen much to convince me of the absence of anything of the kind. For instance, I have seen lights struck, contrary to regulations, when the instruments were sounding and floating in the air; but no one was discovered out of his place, the only result being the falling of the guitars to the ground."

Timothy Green Beckley, Publisher
Inner Light – Global Communications

GLOBAL COMMUNICATIONS
EST 1965

POST OFFICE BOX 753
NEW BRUNSWICK, NJ 08903

Dark Séance—The Fabulous Davenport Brothers

Timothy Green Beckley
Aditional material by Sir Arthur Conan Doyle

Revised Edition

Published in the United States of America By
Global Communications/Conspiracy Journal
Box 753 · New Brunswick, NJ 08903

Staff Members
Timothy G. Beckley, Publisher
Carol Ann Rodriguez, Assistant to the Publisher
Sean Casteel, General Associate Editor
Tim R. Swartz, Graphics and Editorial Consultant
William Kern, Editorial and Art Consultant

Sign Up On The Web For Our Free Weekly Newsletter
and Mail Order Version of Conspiracy Journal
and Bizarre Bazaar
www.Conspiracy Journal.com

Order Hot Line: 1-732-602-3407
PayPal: MrUFO8@hotmail.com

CONTENTS

The Fabulous DAVENPORT BROTHERS

THE BROTHERS DAVENPORT: AN EARLY BIOGRAPHY

In 1864 a biography of two prominent brothers involved with public displays of unexplained phenomena was published in London: **A Biography of The Brothers Davenport** by T. L. Nichols, M.D. The book was subtitled: "With some account of the physical and psychical phenomena which have occurred in their presence, in America and Europe." The book also chronicles the reactions of people confronted with displays of unexplained phenomena beyond their previous common life experiences.

The father worked in the police department and Nichols learned that "in the families of both father and mother had been observed many of those events which are considered supernatural by some persons . . . and which are both common and inexplicable."

Thus Mrs. Davenport, while a girl, heard, or imagined she heard, one day, a voice directing her to observe the time as marked upon a clock standing near her, which proved to be the moment of her mother's death at a distance. The female relations of Mr. Davenport are said to have possessed extraordinary gifts of healing, similar to those formerly attributed to the sovereigns of England, and something of the second-sight, or prevision, which many believe to have formerly been common in Scotland.

The first unusual incident recalled by the Davenport family is a phenomenon that has been reported in many other "paranormal" case studies: "In 1846 the family was disturbed by what they described as 'raps, thumps, loud noises, snaps, cracking noises, in the dead of the night' . . . but what could they do?"

In 1850, when knockings and other strange occurrences in the lives of the Fox Sisters in New York became the subject of newspaper articles, the marvels were discussed by the Davenport family residing in Buffalo of the same state with ten-year-old Elizabeth Davenport declaring her belief that if such things happened to anybody, they might just as well as happen to them.

The result was that in the evening the father, mother and three children sol-

DARK SÉANCE—THE DAVENPORT BROTHERS

emnly seated themselves round a table, placed their hands upon it, as they had read was done at Rochester, and waited further developments.

After a few moments a movement as of swelling or bulging was felt in the table; then cracking noises, tippings, raps, and finally very loud and violent noises.

They had prudently agreed to keep the matter a profound secret, not wishing to incur obloquy or ridicule; but Mr. Davenport's mind was too full of the matter, and, under an injunction of secrecy, he told a friend, who told it to another. Of course it spread like wildfire. "Knockings at the Davenports!" Hundreds flocked to the house.

Five years older than Elizabeth, her brother Ira "was taken with a violent propensity to write, his hand becoming subject to extraordinary gyrations . . . These messages were believed to be quite beyond either his mental or physical powers, and contained matters known only to the persons to whom they were addressed, and quite beyond his possible knowledge." Messages were also rapped out on the table by the method of "calling over the alphabet and having each letter designated." Visitors to the house witnessed the Davenport children levitating, among other strange occurrences.

On one morning, at this early period, the family was sitting around the breakfast table when the knives, forks, and dishes began to dance around as if suddenly endued with vitality. In a few moments the table began to move, tipping up sideways, balancing itself on one leg; and, finally, rising clear from the floor, floating in the air without the least support, and moving in such a way that it was wonderful that the dishes upon it did not slide off and come crashing upon the floor.

As the incident continued, brother William exclaimed that he saw a stranger "so tall that he can scarcely stand up in this room." William also heard him speak and reported, "He says he is not of this earth; his name is William E. Richards . . ." A message written by a levitating pencil directed the family to procure a large table for the better accommodation of those who were coming from far and near to see these wonders.

At the séances, which now began to be held regularly, the manifestations already described were repeated. Loud raps were heard; the table answered questions; spectral forms were seen in the flash of a pistol; lights appeared in the upper parts of the room; musical instruments floated in the air, while being played upon, above the heads of the company.

One day, at a private séance to which Mr. Davenport had invited several of his friends and persons well known to him, the table, by tippings and rappings, spelled out a message, which purported to come from one "George Brown," who described himself as a Canadian farmer who had resided at Waterloo, W. C., where his family still lived, and who had been robbed and murdered, in a place which he described, by members of a notorious gang of robbers on both sides of the

DARK SÉANCE—THE DAVENPORT BROTHERS

border known as the Townsend gang. These particulars were given by one of the boys, speaking in a sort of cataleptic or trance state, in which he became, apparently, the proxy of "George Brown." He named the sum of money – fifty-two dollars, the price of a yoke of oxen he had intended to purchase.

The boy in a trance also made known other circumstances that soon were confirmed as accurate by the county sheriff. After Mr. Davenport hesitated to make further investigations in Waterloo, although people offered to pay the expenses, "George Brown" announced that he intended to take Ira to the murder scene.

Not much attention was paid to what was considered an absurd threat; but the boy, a few evenings after, while engaged in his daily task of delivering evening papers, first felt "queer," then lost his consciousness and found himself standing in the snow with no tracks around him to show how he had come there, in a solitary place, a mile and a half from home, on the right bank of the Niagara river. "George Brown" at his next visit, declared that he had carried him across the river, which is half-a-mile wide, and brought him back again, just as an experiment . . .

The Davenports' home continued to offer displays of marvels to visitors. The public interest in the occurrences is reminiscent of what occurred earlier that century in the Bell Witch case in Tennessee, where the haunting presence is reported to have been nicknamed "Kate" by local witnesses who flocked to the Bells' home. However, some in the Davenports' community were displeased by the events. When the family began receiving hostile threats, the boys had to relinquish their paper-carrying occupation.

At the morning and evening parties of curious investigators into these strange phenomena, there were now not only heard the ringing of bells, thrumming of musical instruments, movements of various objects without apparent cause, including the three Davenport children, but hands, seemingly human, were both felt and seen. A hand and part of an arm would rise above the table, plainly visible, and allow itself to be felt for a moment, when it would dissolve, melt into air in the very grasp and under the eyes of the spectator. Then a voice, coming out of space, at first inarticulate, but later condensed as it would seem in a large horn or trumpet provided for the purpose, spoke distinctly to them, conversed with them, answered their questions, and advised or directed their proceedings.

The voice was asked, among other things, what was its name. It replied that names were of no consequence – one would do as well as another, and they might call it "John King," which they do to this day, or familiarly "John." This "John," the name of a voice, said to the father of the Davenports that he must take his two sons away from Buffalo, that it was dangerous for them to stay and that they were needed elsewhere.

During winter 1853-54, when Ira was 14 and William was 12, another transporting event was described where the brothers suddenly found themselves near their grandfather's house at Mayville, sixty miles from Buffalo. Nichols related:

... when Mr. Davenport had seen and felt signs and wonders enough to satisfy him that he could no longer oppose the desire of the mysterious intelligence to give the people of other regions similar opportunities, the two Brothers Davenport, accompanied first by their father, and afterwards by other persons who acted as their friends or agents, commenced the journeyings which have now continued nearly ten years, in which they have visited most of the important towns of one Continent and have begun a similar mission in another hemisphere.

The experience of one town or city was generally repeated in another, though the manifestations were varied, and new and more severe tests were proposed as old ones failed to detect what people thought **must** be imposture.

The brothers' exhibition show evolved during the course of two years of appearances in towns throughout Maine. A newspaper piece by Swedenborgian carpenter/inventor Mr. Darling denounced the Davenport manifestations and challenged them to submit to a test in Bangor that he would provide without them having any knowledge about the circumstances. When the appointed night came, Mr. Darling and six associates brought to the stage of a crowded concert hall an apparatus of wooden tubes and ropes for binding and securing the brothers so that they would not be able to move once they were seated and enclosed inside their cabinet. The cabinet featured openings in the walls where during a typical show mysterious arms and hands would commonly appear while inside the cabinet were placed a selection of musical instruments. There was also a bolt for the inside door. When the preparations for the test were completed, members of the audience examined the fixtures. The brothers were declared to be "in a tight place" and the announcement was received with immense applause.

"Now, ladies and gentlemen," said the agitated Mr. Darling, "they are secure." The house was hushed to silence. The two side-doors were closed and fastened, shutting in two-thirds of the cabinet, then the center door was shut **and instantly bolted on the inside – by whom**?

Mr. Darling heard the sound with a consternation he could not conceal but began to seal up the doors with sealing-wax, as if anyone could open them unobserved, under his eyes and the eyes of the whole assembly. Directly the instruments in the cabinet began to be played, hands and arms were displayed at an opening near the top of the center door, the trumpet was thrown out of the cabinet, and then the doors suddenly opened and the boys found as firmly secured as ever. The doors were closed again. A great rattling and whisking of ropes was heard for a few minutes; the doors were opened, and the brothers stood up as free as when they had walked into the cabinet.

Now the applause came from the other side, with mocking cries of "Darling,

DARK SÉANCE—THE DAVENPORT BROTHERS

Darling!" Mr. Darling gave it up like a man. He had done his best. If anybody could do better, he was welcome to try.

Their success in Bangor was of course triumphant, as it was generally throughout the State and wherever the people gave the phenomena a fair, or even unfair, examination.

Despite the success of the Davenport Brothers at their exhibitions, there were people who confronted them with what Nichols called "more or less violent opposition": "In large and orderly towns, the brothers were only denounced as charlatans, jugglers and humbugs generally; in the smaller ones, and among ruder communities, they were sometimes assailed with open violence."

On one occasion, after "a rabble of drunken sailors and fisherman" was overcome, Ira Davenport was asked by Nichols if the brothers had gone away to "try some less belligerent neighborhood." Ira was quoted in response:

"No; we stayed there. 'Morgan' told us to go on."

"But a while ago it was 'John,' or 'John King,' who seemed to have the direction of your affairs."

"Yes, but at this time it was Henry Morgan, the buccaneer."

Here is one of the anecdotes about the voice of "John."

At Cleveland, a beautiful city on Lake Erie, a very obstinate sceptic, watching narrowly to detect some jugglery or imposture, was very suddenly and drolly converted to a belief in the genuineness of the manifestations. He was sitting in the midst of the audience when the voice which sometimes accompanies the manifestations was heard to say with emphasis, "No, I don't want any of that"; at which the sceptic burst into laughter, which he afterwards explained. Taking a chew of tobacco, in a sort of bravado he held out the paper, mentally offering some to the voice or its owner — to "John." The words heard by the audience were the instantaneous answer.

A "visit or mission to the state of Maine was made in 1857." The brothers became acquainted with Luke P. Rand, who accompanied them for a period. Rand later published a pamphlet about his observations and experiences, "*A Sketch of the History of the Davenport Boys, Their Mediumship, Journeyings, and the Manifestations and Tests Given in Their Presence by the Spirits*" (1859). Nichols commented: "I think Mr. Rand would have done better to have kept to his facts, of which he seems to have witnessed an abundance, and to have left alone both theories and Scripture."

Mr. Rand, writing with great earnestness, and as far as I can judge with entire sincerity, says that "scores and hundreds were permitted to feel the kindly and intelligent clasp" of a large and strong hand, growing out of space, or coming out of darkness, which he believed to be the hand of "Henry Morgan," and of other hands similarly produced . . .

DARK SÉANCE—THE DAVENPORT BROTHERS

"Often, within three seconds from the time we have seen the boys pinioned to their seats, beyond the possibility of release by themselves, has that hand, at a distance beyond their possible reach, clasped my own with a firm grasp, and thus been thrust forth into the full gaze of the audience. And many scores of others have felt the same grasp and had the same experience . . . The facts are so astonishing that we often find persons who are not only incapable of receiving the testimony of others, but unable also to rely upon the evidences of their own senses."

When the brothers were in Oswego, they were joined by William M. Fay, who would continue to be associated with them. He was around the same age as the brothers. Nichols wrote: "He was born in Buffalo, of German parents, and one of the first evidences he gave of being attended by extraordinary manifestations was, when playing with other boys, being raised bodily from the ground, and lodged in a neighboring tree, in sight of his companions."

In Oswego, the Davenport brothers accepted an invitation to visit Phoenix, a nearby village. There, while giving a private séance, they were arrested and charged with violating a municipal law requiring persons exhibiting shows to procure a license. They were fined thirteen dollars and thirty-nine cents or in default to suffer one month's imprisonment at the county jail in Oswego. Nichols related that they opted to remain in jail for the period as "the intelligences who directed their movements . . . told them not to pay a farthing."

Nichols reported that there were eleven prosecutions in all – "a few of which resulted in small fines, and when these were resisted, in imprisonment." As the brothers continued touring the United States, they were occasionally confronted with opposition yet always managed to avoid harm.

Voyaging eastward to the Atlantic seaboard, the Brothers Davenport visited Philadelphia, in Pennsylvania, the second city in the United States. Here they met with violent opposition from several quarters – from the philosophers, from the religious bigots, the spiritualists and the rabble who cared for nothing but to make a row. It required fifty policemen to keep order. In spite of this, the most extraordinary manifestations were given and many curious tests were resorted to. One night a famous sceptic, in whose sagacity the people seemed to have great confidence, was chosen with remarkable unanimity as one of a committee to examine and report on the manifestations. He had come fully prepared. He tied them with the greatest care, and then, to make his knots secure, wound them with annealed wire, which he made fast by twisting with a pair of forceps.

"Are you satisfied?" asked Ira.

"Yes, perfectly satisfied."

"Will you be satisfied if the manifestations take place as usual?"

"Oh, yes, certainly."

"No, you will not; or if you are your friends will not, and before you leave this room somebody will charge you with being our confederate."

The man was indignant at such a supposition. He knew his popularity and believed that if he could be satisfied everybody who knew him would be also. He was not long in finding the contrary. When the audience was passing out, Mr. Ira heard him having high words and almost coming to blows with a man who accused him of having aided in what he believed to be an imposture.

In 1864 the brothers went to England, with Nichols appraising, "After the ten years of strange and wonderful experiences in America, here truthfully but briefly and imperfectly recorded, and while a sanguinary war is raging over their native land, the Brothers Davenport . . . received and obeyed the direction given them to cross the Atlantic . . . to continue in Britain and in Europe a mission in whose beneficent purposes they have an undoubting faith and which may carry them around the world."

Nichols identified the men accompanying the brothers in addition to William M. Fay: Mr. Palmer, an experienced agent who handled the business portion of the undertaking; and Mr. J. B. Ferguson, "a gentleman of education and position, formerly a clergyman of Nashville, the capital of Tennessee." Ferguson was further described as "the intellectual manager of the séances, in which powers and forces unknown to and unrecognized by science are demonstrated by incontrovertible facts."

The group arrived at Glasgow on September 9, and the first séance was given on the 28th, "attended by several gentlemen connected with the leading daily newspapers of London, and other distinguished men of science and letters . . . every daily newspaper excepting the 'Morning Post' published the accounts which were given as anonymous communications." Nichols considered public incredulity to find it "wonderful that the editors of these leading organs of public opinion published them at all." The following are excerpts from the London *Morning Post* account of the event. The article apparently had been written by a staff journalist.

"*Extraordinary Manifestations*

"Yesterday evening, in the front drawing-room of a house in the immediate neighborhood of Portland-place, a select number of persons were invited to witness some strange manifestations which took place in the presence, if not by the agency, of three gentlemen lately arrived from America. The party consists of two brothers named Davenport, twenty-four and twenty-five years of age, and a Mr. Fay, a gentleman born in the States but we believe of German origin. They are accompanied by Mr. H. D. Palmer, a gentleman long and favorably known in New York in connection with operatic matters, and by a Dr. Ferguson, who explains the nature of the manifestations about to be presented but who does not venture to give any explanation of them. It should be stated at the outset that the trio, who appear to be gifted in so extraordinary a manner, do not lay claim to any particu-

DARK SÉANCE—THE DAVENPORT BROTHERS

lar physical, psychological or moral power. All they assert is that in their presence certain physical manifestations take place. The spectator is, of course, at liberty to draw any inference he pleases. They invite the most critical examination (compatible with certain conditions to be observed), and those who witness the manifestations are at liberty to take all needful precautions against fraud or deception.

"A gentleman sits in the cabinet with his hands tied to the knees of the two Davenports, whose hands were bound behind their backs, and to the bench, and their feet securely fastened. The gentleman stated that 'the instant the door was closed, hands were passed over his face and head, his hair was gently pulled, and the whole of the musical instruments played upon, the bells violently rung close to his face, and the tambourine beat time on his head. Eventually the instruments were thrown behind him and rested between his shoulders and the back of the cabinet."

Here are the facts – two Davenports and a witness in a box scarcely larger than needed to contain them, and all securely bound – yet observe what happened:

A dark circle was then formed, the Brothers bound to chairs, and the whole company, including Mr. Ferguson and Mr. Fay, taking hold of hands. "***The instant*** the lights were extinguished, the musical instruments appeared to be carried all about the room. The currents of air which they occasioned in their rapid transit were felt upon the faces of all present. The bells were loudly rung; the trumpet made knocks on the floor, and the tambourine seemed to be running round the room jingling with all its might. At the same time, tiny sparks were observed, as if passing from south to west." Several persons were lightly, and one (the representative of the 'Times,') severely struck with the passing instruments. Lights were struck from time to time, and the Brothers always found securely bound.

Mr. Fay was now bound to one of the chairs, with his hands firmly tied behind him. As soon as the light was extinguished, a whizzing noise was heard. "It's off," said Mr. Fay, meaning his coat, and on striking a light, his coat was no longer on, but lying on the floor, and his hands were still tied together behind him! "Astonishing though this appeared to be, what followed was more extraordinary still. Dr. Ferguson requested a gentleman present to take off his coat and place it on the table. This was done, the light was extinguished, a repetition of the whizzing noise was heard, and the strange coat was found upon Mr. Fay, whose hands and feet were still securely bound, and his body tied almost immovably to the chair." Several other manifestations were made, and some while the Davenport Brothers and Mr. Fay, instead of being bound, were held by those present, and all with similar results.

This manifestation of the taking off a man's coat, and putting on another man's, both garments being intact, with the wrists closely bound together behind the back, and the person securely tied to a chair, is undoubtedly one of the most astounding ever given. It is simply what is called a physical impossibility. It is as if two links of a chain should be separated without a fracture and then restored to their places. That it was done on this occasion, and has been done scores, perhaps hundreds of times, there is no doubt whatever.

All this was done, it will also be observed, not in the presence of ignorant and credulous persons, but in a select company, which included some of the sharpest minds in England; not in a prepared theatre, but in a gentleman's drawing-room, where there could have been no deception had it been in any case possible.

The writer in the "Morning Post" makes the following observations:

"The séance lasted more than two hours, during which time the cabinet was minutely inspected, the coats examined to ascertain whether they were fashioned so as to favor a trick, and every possible precaution taken to bind the hands and feet of the persons whose presence appeared to be essential to the development of the manifestations.

"It may be asserted that all the illustrations above enumerated can be traced to clever conjuring. *Possibly they may or it is possible that some new physical force can be engendered at will to account for what appears on the face of it absolutely unaccountable.* All that can be asserted is that the displays to which we have referred took place on the present occasion *under conditions and circumstances that preclude the presumption of fraud*. It is true that darkness is in *some cases* an essential condition, but darkness does not necessarily imply deception. But, putting aside the cabinet manifestations, there is abundance left to excite curiosity and challenge the attention of the scientific. Learning, we know, is not a limited quantity; it is inexhaustible for all mankind, *and here is a field for the investigation of the scientific world.*

"In a little time we believe it is their intention to give séances at the Egyptian Hall or some other suitable place, when the public will be afforded an opportunity of witnessing some of the astonishing feats of which we have given an outline. For the present it is sufficient to say that they invite the strictest scrutiny on the part of men of science, and that, whatever be the theory involved, they repudiate any active agency in the production of the extraordinary manifestations which take place in their presence. It is perhaps well for them that they were not in the flesh a century and a half ago, as, in the then state of human knowledge and social enlightenment, they would unquestionably have been conducted to Smithfield and burnt as necromancers of the most dangerous type."

A Biography of The Brothers Davenport includes "The Testimony of Mr. Ferguson." The director and lecturer of the England séances contributed an account of his experiences, commenting: "I had been for years familiar with phenomena and experiences of a similar character of those represented as attending the Brothers . . ."

Here are some excerpts from the statement by Ferguson, beginning with a description of his first experience attending an exhibition of the brothers among an audience of thousands at the largest lecture hall in New York City.

The entertainment – for such it may properly be called – opened, and a committee was chosen to secure the young men in the cabinet and report to the audience what occurred.

It is enough to say that I was convinced that the Davenports were no jugglers, and that the displays of power through them admitted of no explanation according to any known estimate of natural laws. I called upon the Davenports in private and attended their public entertainments for eleven days and nights.

When the Davenports appeared at Brooklyn, near New York, it happened that their representative before the public was absent; and they, through their friends, invited me to introduce them to the public of the city of Brooklyn. In that city, at the time, I was solicited to meet the representatives of a highly respectable religious society, with a view to becoming their pastor. I, however, consented to introduce the Davenports in "the City of Churches." I did this in a spirit of candid enquiry and experiment, respecting a subject which I hoped might prove of interest. I did so knowing that, however desirable it might be that I should become the pastor of the church above mentioned, my action in this matter would put an end to all hope of such pastoral charge being entrusted to me. I did so because I was fully convinced that the phenomena which occurred in the presence of the Brothers was a part of the supra-mundane evidence given to this age – evidence not to be measured by the conventional restrictions of time and men, however respectable the time or however religious the men.

When I saw and knew, for myself and not by another, that the evidences given through the Davenports were true, I accepted a proposition to accompany them to England and Europe – if, after three or four months' experience with them before the public, I should find the work such as I could perform without detriment to them or to myself. Accordingly, I spent three months in the interior towns and cities of New York state and New England and a month in the chief cities of Canada.

During this time I resided with them at the same hotels, and we often occupied the same suite of apartments.

When they were, to all appearances, sound asleep, some of the most marked of the manifestations have occurred.

On extinguishing the light in my room, I have had my chair instantly lifted and placed upon my head, with the legs upward, and the cushion resting on the top of my head. A voice – not mine, not that of anyone present – has directed me to feel the position of those present. I did so, while the chair held itself, or was held, firmly

DARK SÉANCE—THE DAVENPORT BROTHERS

where it was placed. In distinct vocal tones I was invited to be seated, the chair being at the same time taken from my head and placed properly that I might comply with the invitation.

I might record a volume of such and similar manifestations. But with respect to all these evidences, expressions, or demonstrations from the invisible world, I would have one remark to make; I wish it to sink deep into the minds of my readers. These are not given in response to mere curiosity, idle wish or selfish desire. They have come when and where they were needed, and where there was a degree of good faith in the individual to use the evidence for universal good.

For six months I have travelled with the Davenports, and in various conditions, advantageous and disadvantageous, I have witnessed the evidence of the power that attends them.

Many of my own friends, utterly unconvinced, and looking upon me with profound astonishment that I should be so duped as to become insensible to the charms of respectability and, I may add, to the attraction and use of the "almighty dollar," have witnessed these evidences and have either become silent or have acknowledged that no duty could be more sacred than the one I have assumed.

These evidences are entirely above and beyond the capacity of those through whom or by whom they are given, physically, intellectually and morally.

It has of course been said that the Davenports have descended to tricks. I can only speak for the time I have known them. Since my connection with them I know that they have not so descended, nor needed to descend. It is to the fact of entire sincerity that I attribute their untarnished success in the New World and in London and England. They are mortal, and subject to temptation, like all of us; but as regards these evidences they can have no inducement to fraud any more than a man with a million of pounds has occasion to steal. They need not to invent tricks when genuine phenomena constantly attend them.

The year after his biography of the Davenport brothers was released, a biographical book about Ferguson was published: **Supra-Mundane Facts in the Life of Rev. Jesse Babcock Ferguson, A.M., LL.D., Including Twenty Years' Observations of Preternatural Phenomena (1865),** edited by T. L. Nichols, M.D.

A Biography of the Brothers Davenport also includes a description of a conversation with "John King" that occurred at a private séance where Benjamin Coleman – "a careful observer of extra-natural phenomena in both hemispheres" – sat with the Davenport Brothers and Ferguson. Here is an excerpt from Coleman's statement:

The lights being extinguished, we sat a short time in silence, when a startling bang was made upon the tambourine, which instrument, with the guitar, were instantly placed upon my knees. A hand gently caressed me on the head, and a stream of phosphoric light passed across the spacious room, which was succeeded by another rising from the floor to the ceiling. A voice then spoke to me through a trumpet which was brought within a few inches of my face; and in a clear, distinct and sonorous voice, I was thus addressed:

"How are you, Coleman?"

"Oh!" exclaimed both of the Davenports, "that's 'John' – that's 'John,' – we have not heard him speak for a long time. Keep him in conversation, Mr. Coleman."

I then said, "You appear to know me, John."

"Yes, I know you in spirit."

"Have you ever seen me before?"

"Yes; I saw you in America."

"Do you think, John, that you will be able to convince the skeptics in this country?"

"Yes; we have power enough to make them surrender. There is a lady standing by your side."

"What is her name?"

"Kate."

At this moment, one of the Davenports said, "I hope you will be with us tomorrow night, John (the night of the press séance)."

"Certainly, certainly!"—then turning in an opposite direction, as I could easily detect by the sound, the voice said, "How are *you*, Ferguson?"

After a few words more, the voice turned again to Mr. Coleman, a hand passed over his head and patted him kindly on the shoulder, and the voice said, "I must go now; good night."

In later firsthand testimonials of séance room phenomena, John King would be associated with Katie King. The pair were alternately known as Sir Henry Morgan and his daughter Annie Morgan (a topic of February 2015 blog articles).

Coleman also described incidents of phenomena involving clothing similar to occurrences that were seen as a regular feature of the public exhibitions —

At a séance at the house of a friend, the coat of Mr. Fay was removed from his back in an instant, and my friend's coat put upon him in the same space of time, Mr. Fay's hands being firmly tied together behind him, and the knots of the cord sealed. On the same occasion, the still more bewildering fact occurred of Mr. Ira Davenport's waistcoat being removed while his coat remained, his hands being bound behind his back. The waistcoat lay at our feet, with his watch in the pocket and the chain hooked in the button-hole, just as he had worn it a moment previously, the waistcoat remaining buttoned.

On another evening, the lights being extinguished, Sir Henry de Hoghton asked that Mr. Fay's coat should be taken off. He had scarcely uttered the words when Mr. Ferguson struck a brilliant light, and *I saw the coat leaving the body of Mr.*

DARK SÉANCE—THE DAVENPORT BROTHERS

Fay, and all could see it in its flight in the air, until it reached and rested on the knees of Sir Henry, who was sitting in the center of a large semicircle some ten or fifteen feet from either Mr. Faye or Mr. Ira Davenport, who were both tied hands and feet to their chairs. Sir Henry de Hoghton then took off his own coat, and, placing it on his knee, asked that it should be put upon Mr. Fay. We instantly heard a rushing sound, and in less time than it takes me to say it – in fact not more than a second or two – Sir Henry's coat was found not on Mr. Fay, but on Mr. Davenport, over his own coat, which had not been removed.

T. L. Nichols concluded:

If they are ever so coarse manifestations of the existence of intelligences ordinarily hidden from our senses, their use in overthrowing a coarser materialism is evident; if they give us palpable evidence of the existence of a universe of which we were in doubt, and of a life in the future, in which millions have no faith whatever, they are not useless.

These and similar manifestations seem to me to be rude and elementary lessons, adapted to ignorance and false science worse than ignorance; the first steps to the recognition of a higher life.

Another book available to be read online with anecdotes about the Brothers Davenport is **Spiritual Experiences, Including Seven Months with the Brothers Davenport** by Robert Cooper (1867). Here are some of Cooper's concluding statements.

It will of course be urged that these things are physical impossibilities. Such they undoubtedly are; they nevertheless take place; how they are accomplished we cannot, with our present knowledge of the properties of matter, even begin to understand. They of course involve the passage of matter through matter and therefore seem to favor a theory that has been recently put forth that what we regard as matter is only force.

My own belief is that these manifestations are the work of disembodied human intelligences, and that they are made for some great purpose; and though such work for spiritual beings may not be in accordance with our preconceived notions of such beings, or the evidence afforded by the manifestations of such a description as their alleged purpose would seem to warrant, still it is questionable whether a more effectual and suitable method could be devised of combating the hard-headed materialism of the times and convincing men that there is something in the universe besides matter.

DARK SÉANCE: REMEMBERING THE DAVENPORT BROTHERS

By Timothy Green Beckley

Ira Erastus Davenport (September 17, 1839 – July 8, 1911)
William Henry Davenport (February 1, 1841 – July 1, 1877)

The Davenport Brothers were an international sensation everywhere they toured!

Their performances were said to be utterly spellbinding. Some said they acted as a bridge to loved ones and friends who had passed away, while the disenchanted called them pathetic hoaxers out to fleece those "sad fools" among the public who did not seem to realize that the dead were dead and there was no way of contacting them for now and forever.

Why? Because men of science and medicine simply said so!

There is no doubt, regardless of your tendencies to believe or disbelieve, that their public séances could only be categorized as amazing. Supposedly, everything was done which would make it nearly impossible under "ordinary circumstances" for them to be involved in any form of misrepresentation. This included the brothers being bound hand and foot so that they theoretically could not move about in order to cause deception and give the appearance that they were legitimately in contact with the spirit realm. Once bound, they were placed inside a locked cabinet of extremely limited proportions. And this is where their very theatrical demonstration would begin – first with disembodied voices being heard throughout the room or theater. Then musical instruments began sounding loudly and eventually emerged from out of the upper portion of the spirit cabinet, flying about the room and in general causing quite a visual spectacle in the darkened quarters.

Thus the directive of the term Dark Séance – though the name also became intimately associated with the chaos and mayhem which seemed to follow them around from town to town, causing them to flee from their performances for fear of bodily harm and even death.

For even though the Brothers were honored and revered by thousands of devoted followers who believed they were truly manifesting supernatural phenomena directed from those residing in what Spiritualists called the Summerland (a paradise where we go when we die), there were those who loudly denounced them as frauds – nothing more than simple magicians, illusionists and conjurors. These skeptics – much like those of today – saw Ira and William as preying on the gullible, the weak minded, and those seeking proof, at any cost, that their loved ones were not truly "dead" but lived on in the afterlife. The fact that much of this "purported chicanery" took place around the time of the most disruptive and tumultuous period in American history – the Civil War – did not fail to register in the minds of both supporters and disbelievers alike.

WOMEN ALMOST DISMEMBERED AT PERFORMANCE

If anyone has ever attended an Extreme Wrestling match (ECW originated this action brand of grappling in the Philadelphia Armory several decades ago), you will know what I'm talking about. The fans literally hang from the rafters off of second and third floor balconies as they watch their fav bad guys and baby faces jump from ladders and toss each other out of the ring as if they mean to kill each other, although the civilized attending will realize it is only an act and everyone goes home pretty much the same way as when they slipped into their tights, trunks and masks – if you happen to be a luchador performing in a Mexican freestyle wrestling bout complete with a colorful disguise which hides one's identity.

Well, something may have gone desperately wrong when the Davenport Brothers set up shop in Liverpool. They were booked there for two weeks and from all indications the nightly performances attracted SRO throngs who had come to see what all the media hype was about. They were getting front page attention, and there was an extreme buzz like you might get when the Beatles rolled into town when you were a kid (if you are in my age group that is).

Apparently, one prideful woman named Lady Arthur Noyes Woodhull was utterly enthralled by the activities of the brothers and reported on what must have been a very DARK SÉANCE indeed!

"It could have been caused by a sudden manifestation of spirits, or it could also have not; a lady's arm may or may not have been dismembered in the ensuing stampede (God please have mercy on her social standing should it be true) but it pays us no end to speculate. Rather, it is but two weeks until the Brothers Davenport tread the boards of our very own Lyceum theatre, and, if indeed spirits do abound, then we shall scrutinize them with our own cerebella. We do not under any circumstances wish to resort to the barbarism demonstrated by our Liverpudlian cousins."

DARK SÉANCE—THE DAVENPORT BROTHERS

One gets the impression that the Lady, known to be a socialite and Victorian-era philanthropist, was called to emotional arms because of a rather dramatic incident involving someone in the employment of the Davenports' rather bloated entourage, said to be much like what a celebrity would have today following them around and taking care of incidental matters – like hiring plants in the audience and making sure the wires were positioned properly so that the instruments would move about overhead freely? Or so the skeptics claimed.

"At The Ravenous Donkey in Carlisle (where the party takes their rest before completing their journey north), the Davenports' very own valet has been startled to death. That is correct, startled to death. His final words before passing told of how he was shaken into waking by a mysterious young girl standing over him and screaming, but, when the room was quickly illuminated, no such girl could be found and the entire house remained fast asleep. By all accounts, the man, though wretched, was as far from a half-wit as you or I. Yet nobody can fathom just how a girl came to be in a room at one moment and then the next moment very much out of it."

Now, two possible meanings of "startled to death" exist . . . one being that the valet was merely frightened out of his PJs, or that possibly he had a heart attack, which would certainly have a menacing impact on their roving dark séances.

One wonders silently if this Victorian socialite wasn't somehow in the pocket of the Davenports, if one wants to think negatively about them, of course. She seemed to intend to enthrall her audience about the Brothers upcoming local appearance.

"So it is with careful consideration that I must advise anybody who may feel in any way uncertain about the prospect of journeying into a world of spirits to remain in their houses. If anybody has a tendency to shriek uncontrollably or lose bodily control suddenly and without warning, thus drawing attention to themselves – again, stay away. This show is not for you. And if you choose not to heed these warnings yet are insistent on a somewhat enthusiastic disposition then, please, for the sake of the rest, remember to bring your smelling salts."

THE BROTHERS RUN FOR THEIR LIVES

One would have hoped that the Davenports would bring more than smelling salts with them on tour, because, as history tells it, things got more than "desperate" as the crowds of the unsympathetic grew into mob proportions.

They were attacked on a number of occasions, chased down the streets, and ended up in the hospital with the police asking them to please leave during the night should they be set upon again.

It was, we are told, on Sunday, November 11, 1861, that, unknown to the brothers, a large number of men, intent on mob violence, came to their rooms. "As usual, they suffered themselves to be tied; which, having been done, some of the men searched them, ostensibly to see if they had false arms and trick-apparatus about them, but in reality to ascertain if they were armed, and how safe an operation it would be to attack them. They were not aware that the ever-watchful John King, the brothers' mentor in the spirit world, had already revealed their plot to an extent sufficient to cause Ira to arm himself and conceal his weapon so safely that the men failed to find out where or what. The séance began; and, at a concerted signal, the mob, armed to the teeth, rushed for the stage and attacked the cabinet with the utmost fury.

It instantly became apparent that the wretches meant nothing less than murder and would have carried their point, but for a Dr. Collins, who threw himself before the brothers and succeeded in releasing them from the ropes. No sooner was this done than a giant of a fellow seized Ira, to dash his brains out. The young man drew his knife. "Stand back!" cried he, his temper for once getting the mastery over him. "Stand back, or I will strike the first man who assaults me." But the giant would not stand back; for a second scoundrel made a dastardly attack from behind, seized Ira's arms, and for a moment they thought they had him at their mercy.

In order to prove that no deceptiveness was being incorporated into their performance, often members of the audience – including those who claimed academic training – were allowed into the spirit cabinet to make certain that the duo were securely enchained and unable to toss the instruments inside the cabinet about. (How could anyone even try to explain the fact that the stringed instruments, the tambourines and the horns were not tossed about but floated and spiraled around those seated in the theater outside the secured article of furniture?)

"It was reported that, on two occasions, persons in the spirit box with them have drawn pistols upon them, and in both instances were severely punished by their invisible guardians." Who says spirits can't take up arms when pressed by the wailing and flailing of members of the sometimes mean and hostile physical world in which we find ourselves residing?

There was another incident in Yonkers, New York, where one of the brothers almost had his skull crushed in when he was hit over the head with a heavy metal object.

No wonder most mediums have given up on physical mediumship. There are very few stage performances of this type today – in fact, we don't know of any. The Scole séances in the UK might come close, but the apparitions were limited to a small, private, hand-selected audience. Somehow we can't imagine the Amazing Kreskin being chased around the Johnny Carson show having hid a check under someone's seat in the audience. But, hey, you never know, there are plenty of wackos on the loose out there.

Probably we will never see a return to physical mediumship. Ectoplasm hardly ever gets regurgitated nowadays. And levitation is thought of as a parlor trick. But, as you turn the pages, the supernatural phenomena of the heyday of Spiritualism live on for you, if only vicariously, through the Davenport Brothers.

The price of admission?

An open mind!

USEFUL RESOURCES

Timothy Green Beckley, publisher/author

mrufo8@hotmail.com

Check out Tim's Author's Page on Amazon.com

Mr. UFOs Secret Files – YouTube Channel

Podcast Exploring The Bizarre – KCOR Digital Network

Web Addresses

http://www.ConspiracyJournal.com/

MR IRA DAVENPORT.   MR FAY.   MR COOPER.   MR WM DAVENPORT.

The Fabulous DAVENPORT BROTHERS

THE DAVENPORT BROTHERS – PROOF OF THE AFTERLIFE OR MERELY AN ILLUSION TO CON THE GULLIBLE?

By Timothy Green Beckley

I have always been intrigued by the history of spiritualism. To me, it is a fascinating part of Americana which grew out of the two Fox sisters communicating with a spirit through simple rappings on the walls of a rural Albany, New York, home and led to a spiritual movement with millions of followers in its heyday.

As an investigator and experiencer of the paranormal most of my life, I have found that many physical phenomena said to take place in the séance room closely parallel what might transpire at a UFO landing site or to an individual supposedly being abducted by Ultra-Terrestrials – my term for "aliens" since we do not know from where these entities might be arriving.

You have, for example, multiple cases where . . .

** – Individuals have passed through solid walls in order to be transported onboard a hovering or landed UFO, much like spirits can pass through any solid object and just as the Davenport Brothers were said to have done when the cosmic currents were flowing just right.

** – Abductees have reported floating through the air only to find themselves inside a spaceship, where, as in a séance room, tables and chairs and even mediums go aloft as if they were of featherweight. This is especially true, as we shall find out, in the case of the Davenport Brothers.

** – Weird lights and glowing objects dance about the séance room, much as objects called "orbs" do at the scene of many a UFO incident. One such case happened in Marley Woods, Missouri, investigated by researcher Ted Phillips, where "spook lights" of various sizes and dimensions floated above the ground and have lately been observed inside the homes of nearby residents who live on the perimeter of the woods where the lights first materialized.

DARK SÉANCE—THE DAVENPORT BROTHERS

** – Spirit photography has always been a crucial part of the spiritualist trappings. Take a photo in the séance room and presto! When developed, it's likely to show some sort of spirit dancing around in midair. Of course, the "spirit" has often turned out to be an associate covered in cheese cloth and "standing in" for an apparition that might have found it difficult to transport itself on a minute's notice from the next world. In comparison, UFO photos have become commonplace, with hundreds filling up pages on YouTube. Pictures of aliens have replaced spirit guides, the end result being that there are probably as many kooky UFO photos around today – thanks to smart phones and digital devices – as there were of spirits posing with some pride in front of bulky box cameras in the golden days of Spiritualism.

** – Certainly we can't forget about the teleportation of objects associated with ETs and mediums alike. Known as "apports," a variety of objects, including rocks, arrowheads and roses, have frequently dropped down from the ceiling and landed without making any sort of commotion at the feet of those seated in a circular pattern waiting for the appearance of loved ones from the dark oasis. In modern UFOlogy, inside the homes of witnesses, objects disappear and show up later in the most unlikely places, sometimes landing with a thud but mostly floating down silently. Israeli spoon-bender Uri Geller has a reputation for being present when things mysteriously flop down nearby. On one occasion, a stone statue came crashing through a patio screen door from out of nowhere, landing on an enclosed porch. Plus, money has drifted down from the sky, pelting the roof of the place where Geller was staying. In another incident, an astronaut who had left his pen on the moon found it in his home back on Earth in a place where he least expected it.

** – And hey, hey, lest we forget, several researchers, including former Mutual UFO Network investigator and author of Alien Agenda Diane Tessman, have commented on what is best described as gossamer-like "angel's hair" emanating from UFOs. The substance has fallen to Earth in a number of cases.

"Sometimes it drapes itself over fences, utility lines, trees, and, in a few cases, entire towns," notes Tessman, who has reportedly had repeated contact with human-looking beings from other realms starting when she was four or five years of age.

"Frequently, strands of the bizarre substance range from a few inches to more than one hundred feet long," she continues. "It is white, sometimes sticky, and usually evaporates entirely. One horrified researcher   watched it disappear as he raced toward his lab."

Those who have studied the history of spiritualism will realize without being prompted that angel hair closely resembles what is known as "ectoplasm," a stringy spider web-like substance created during the transmutation of spirits attempting to take on physical form in the presence of sitters during a séance who are looking for a dose of sensationalism and not content with just a recognizable voice emanating out of a drifting trumpet hovering over their heads.

In a reprint of the classic UFO contactee book, **Over The Threshold**, by Dana Howard (edited by Sean Casteel), I did my best to explain that, although of a controversial nature, there are literally hundreds of so-called spirit photographs in which the images of the dearly beloved seem to be materializing out of this substance in either a darkened or dimly lit séance room. Sometimes "half-formed," sometimes appearing about as "human" as possible, the ectoplasm is like a second skin, as if the soul were being encased in a cocoon and about ready to be newly birthed.

In Dana Howard's work – available from Amazon.com – she describes how, in the course of a spiritualistic service, a spacewoman seemed to be in the middle of her materialization and connected to the ceiling of the church building by this web-like substance. Howard fully well realized, being involved in mediumship for many years, that this ectoplasm forms the building blocks of what was soon to be a flesh-and-blood spaceperson standing before everyone in attendance.

THE DAVENPORT'S MATERIALIZE INTO AMERICAN HISTORY

To set the stage for what lies ahead and give readers a bit of background, but not wanting to go on and on about material you will find freely shared elsewhere within these pages, the Davenport Brothers – William Henry and Ira Erastus – produced spiritualistic phenomena during a time when physical mediumship was the order of the day.

According to magician and escape artist Harry Houdini, the "performance" the brothers gave was not to be taken at face value because he "knew" that what they were doing was a matter of stage configuration, an illusion just like one of the famous magicians you might see on TV is capable of performing – like making an elephant or the Statue of Liberty seemingly disappear in front of a vast audience. It's all a matter of misdirection, of having nothing up your sleeve but hiding something behind your back, so to speak.

The Davenport Brothers, however, never really declaimed themselves to be masters of stage magic. They kind of left it up to their immense following to decide if they were consorting with spirits or simply fooling those gullible enough to be hooked on the quasi-theological doctrine of spiritualism and the shenanigans of fraudulent mediums.

But if you were in the first ten rows, center stage, and caught their performance with an open mind – and scrutinizing eyes – you might not have been so easily convinced that what they did was not legitimately on the up and up.

Outside of Sir Arthur Conan Doyle, who fully vetted the Brothers Davenport, one of the primary writers on their extraordinary abilities is, as far as I am con-

DARK SÉANCE—THE DAVENPORT BROTHERS

cerned, the late Dr. Nandor Fodor, whose writings on the paranormal fascinated me so much when I was still in my early teens that I must have devoured his book Between Two Worlds three times. And, believe me, I seldom read anything all the way through even once these days. As a bit of background, Fodor was born in Beregszasz, Hungary. A one-time assistant to Dr. Sigmund Freud, Dr. Fodor received a doctorate in law from the Royal Hungarian University of Science in Budapest. He moved to New York to work as a journalist and relocated to Britain in 1929, where he worked for a newspaper.

Fodor was one of the leading authorities on poltergeists, haunting and the paranormal during a span of several decades that ended with his death in the 1960s. Freud's associate wrote on subjects like prenatal development and dream interpretation but is credited mostly for his magnum opus, Encyclopedia of Psychic Science, first published in 1934. Fodor was the London correspondent for the American Society for Psychical Research (1935-1939). He worked as an editor for the Psychoanalytic Review and was a member of the New York Academy of Sciences. He is still highly regarded to this day – including by this writer, who would like very much to interview his surviving daughter, Andrea Fodor Litkei.

The eminent parapsychologist – in an era when the pursuit was hardly known outside the academic arena – rightfully notes that at the height of the Davenport Brothers' career, there were few others who ventured to put on a public display in full view of such large audiences.

Apparently, the Brothers grew up with the supernatural all around them, notes Dr. Fodor, who did a good job of tracing their paranormal heritage.

"Their father was a police official in Buffalo. In 1846, two years before the outbreak at Hydesville (Fox Sisters), raps, thumps, loud noises, snaps, and crackling noises were heard at their home in the night. In 1850, the two boys and their younger sister, Elisabeth, tried table turning. The table soon moved, raps were heard, messages were spelt out, Ira's hand was seized to write automatically, and, a little later, the marvel of a simultaneous levitation of the three children was witnessed by all present. On the fifth night of the experiments, in compliance with rapping directions, a pistol was fired by Ira in a vacant corner of the room. At the instant of firing, it was taken from his hand by the flash of a human figure that was seen holding it and smiling at the company. This was the first appearance of John King, their self-constituted control. It lasted for an instant only. With the extinction of the flash, the figure vanished and the pistol fell on the floor. The rope-tying performance for which the brothers became famous was also instituted on spirit direction. From the most complicated knots they were released in a remarkably short time. In due course, direct writing and direct voice developed and the boys were soon on the road, holding séances amid trying circumstances."

It should be noted that the researchers of that period were keen on trying to uncover deception. If they found a hint of fraud, they would bring it to the public's attention, and often it would end the career of an up and coming, enterprising spiritualist who now found his name and reputation being dragged through the mud.

"Public committees were set up to examine their phenomena and rope-tying was developed to an art of torture. In 1857, the Boston Courier offered a reward of $500 for the production of genuine physical phenomena. Dr. H. F. Gardner of Boston accepted the challenge and arranged, before a committee of Harvard Professors (Benjamin Pierce, Louis Agassiz, B. A. Gould and E. N. Horsford), a series of séances with the Misses Kate and Leah Fox, J. W. Mansfield, Dr. G. A. Redman and the Davenport Brothers. When the turn of the latter came, they were tied in the most brutal manner; the ropes were drawn through holes bored in the cabinet and firmly knotted outside so as to make a network. The knots were tied with linen and Prof. Pierce sat in the cabinet between the mediums. As soon as he entered, an invisible hand shut the bolt, the din of musical instruments immediately began, a phantom hand was thrust out through a small opening, curtains opened near the top of the middle door of the wardrobe-like cabinet, and the professor felt it about his head and face. At the end, the mediums were found released and, according to Dr. Nichols' biography, "the ropes were found twisted around the neck of Prof. Pierce."

The latter statement, however, was pronounced "shamelessly false" by the Boston Courier. Yet it is a fact that the results of the Harvard investigation, with the exception a short preliminary negative report, were never published. On the other hand, Dr. Loomis, Professor of Chemistry and Toxicology in the Georgetown Medical College, who also made an investigation, stated in a long report that the manifestations were produced through some new unknown force with which he was unacquainted. A Professor Mapes also had interesting experiences in Buffalo. He conversed with the spirit control, John King, in the direct voice for half an hour; his hand was seized in a powerful grasp and, when it was taken again, the invisible hand increased in size and was covered with hair. A large table on the elevated platform where the mediums were sitting was carried in an instant over the heads of the sitters and deposited in the most distant part of the room.

Throughout their careers, the Davenport Brothers were met with outrage, consternation, criticism and downright hostility. It's as if it were – pardon the pun – a matter of life or death to determine how "genuine" their conjurations were.

"Were we mere jugglers," write the Davenports of these experiences to the Rev. J.B. Ferguson, "we should meet with no violence or we should find protection. Could we declare that these things done in our presence were deception of the senses, we should, no doubt, reap a plentiful harvest of money and applause. As tricks they would transcend, according to the testimony of experienced observers, any ever exhibited in Occident or Orient. The wonders of the cabinet, or still more, of the dark séance, surpass all pretensions of conjurers. We should safely defy the world to equal them and be honored for our dexterity. But we are not jugglers, and truthfully declare that we are not, and we are mobbed from town to town, our property destroyed and our lives imperiled."

HALLELUIAH! That's probably the best that can be said in their defense.

That is not to say that the Davenports couldn't stoop to perform an actual bit of magic just like a stage magician when their actual, supposed powers failed them. They had been caught with their pants down on several occasions. (Probably literally, as every medium of the day was thoroughly searched before going into their secluded spirit cabinet.)

A letter from Dr. John F. Gray, a well-known New York Spiritualist, to Epes Sargent, dated June 7, 1864, says: "I have not seen the Davenports this time here but I entertain no doubt of the genuineness of the manifestations made in their presence. When they were here some years ago they were detected in making spurious manifestations when the genuine failed."

In his phenomenal An Encyclopedia of Psychic Science, Dr. Fodor is quick to point out that there were almost always rigid scientific protocols in place. Says he: "As a means of control, the hands of the mediums were often filled with flour or pennies were placed on their shoes after carefully drawing the outline of the shoes on a piece of paper beneath. When the door of the cabinet was opened, the flour was found in their hands as before without white spots on their evening dress and the pennies in their place. The performance while sitting in the cabinet was called the light séance. There was a second part, the dark séance, in which the lights in the room were extinguished and, dispensing with the cabinet, the mediums sat between the other sitters, tightly bound to their chairs. The tying and releasing occurred as in the cabinet. The swishing of the rope was heard. The knots presented no obstacle. Sometimes every intermediate one was left undone with the seal at the end, yet the mediums were found free. As an additional amusement, the rope was often coiled around the neck of some sitter and through the ropes, in some mysterious way, the coats of the mediums, or their waistcoat underneath, with watch and chair undisturbed, were whisked off and on again. Those who entered the cabinet in the light séance to sit with the Brothers were usually victims of strange pranks. Their handkerchiefs were taken, their breast pin removed and stuck into the coat behind and their spectacles, if they wore any, were transferred to the face of one of the mediums."

"I have, at different times," writes Robert Cooper, who spent seven months with the Davenport Brothers in Britain and on the Continent, "seen at least three hundred persons enter the cabinet, all of whom certified that there was no movement on the part of the Brothers."

DARK SÉANCE—THE DAVENPORT BROTHERS

We are told that as mediums the Davenport Brothers were unique in several respects. "In the Winter Palace in Russia," it was reported, "they held a séance before a thousand people in the presence of the Czar. Indeed, as many as two thousand were known to participate in England. They never asked for music. The phenomena were instantaneous. It is almost impossible to imagine that in a career of almost thirty years (William Davenport died in Sydney in 1877), their secret, if they had one, would not have been discovered."

Always one to get in on the act, Harry Houdini publicly declared that the Davenport Brothers were in the same business he was – i.e. "stage magician-ship." But in a note to Arthur Conan Doyle, he made a strange confession which leaves the entire issue of fact or fiction open to continued debate after almost two centuries.

"I was an intimate friend of Ira Erastus Davenport. I can make positive assertion that the Davenport Brothers were never exposed . . . I know more about the Davenport Brothers than anyone living."

Whatever he might have known – Houdini wasn't telling!

The Davenport Brothers.

DARK SÉANCE—THE DAVENPORT BROTHERS

The Fabulous DAVENPORT BROTHERS

SHERLOCK HOLMES' CREATOR EXAMINES
THE DAVENPORTS' PSYCHIC MANIFESTATIONS

By Sir Arthur Conan Doyle

In order to present a consecutive story, the career of D. D. Home has been traced in its entirety. It is necessary now to return to earlier days in America and consider the development of the two Davenports. Home and the Davenports both played an international part, and their history helps to cover the movement both in England and in the States. The Davenports worked upon a far lower level than Home, making a profession of their remarkable gifts, and yet by their crude methods they got their results across to the multitude in a way which a more refined mediumship could not have done. If one considers this whole train of events as having been engineered by a wise but by no means infallible or omnipotent force upon the Other Side, one observes how each occasion is met by the appropriate instrument, and how as one demonstration fails to impress some other one is substituted.

The Davenports have been fortunate in their chroniclers. Two writers have published books describing the events of their life, and the periodical literature of the time is full of their exploits.

Ira Erastus Davenport and William Henry Davenport were born at Buffalo in the State of New York, the former on September 17, 1839, and the latter on February 1, 1841. Their father, who was descended from the early English settlers in America, occupied a position in the police department of Buffalo. Their mother was born in Kent, England, and went to America when a child. Some indications of psychic gifts were observed in the mother's life. In 1846 the family were disturbed in the middle of the night by what they described as "raps, thumps, loud noises, snaps, crackling noises." This was two years before the outbreak in the Fox family. But it was the Fox manifestations which, in this case as in so many others, led them to investigate and discover their mediumistic powers.

DARK SÉANCE—THE DAVENPORT BROTHERS

* "A Biography of the Brothers Davenport." By T. L. Nichols, M.D., London, 1864. "Supra-Mundane Facts in the Life of Rev. J. B. Ferguson, LL.D." By T. L. Nichols, M.D., London, 1865. "Spiritual Experiences: Including Seven Months with the Brothers Davenport." By Robert Cooper, London, 1867.

The two Davenport boys and their sister Elizabeth, the youngest of the three, experimented by placing their hands on a table. Loud and violent noises were heard and messages were spelt out. The news leaked abroad, and, as with the Fox girls, hundreds of curious and incredulous people flocked to the house. Ira developed automatic writing, and handed to those present messages written with extraordinary rapidity and containing information he could not have known. Levitation quickly followed, and the boy was floated in the air above the heads of those in the room at a distance of nine feet from the floor. Next, the brother and sister were influenced in the same way, and the three children floated high up in the room. Hundreds of respectable citizens of Buffalo are reported to have seen these occurrences. Once, when the family was at breakfast, the knives, forks, and dishes danced about and the table was raised in the air. At a sitting soon after this a lead pencil was seen to write in broad daylight, with no human contact. Séances were now held regularly, lights began to appear, and musical instruments floated and played above the heads of the company. The Direct Voice and other extraordinary manifestations too numerous to mention followed. Yielding to requests from the communicating intelligences, the brothers started journeying to various places and holding public séances. Among strangers, tests were insisted upon. At first the boys were held by persons selected from those present, but this being found unsatisfactory because it was thought that those holding them were confederates, the plan of tying them with ropes was adopted. To read the list of ingenious tests successively proposed, and put into operation without interfering with the manifestations, shows how almost impossible it is to convince resolute skeptics. As soon as one test succeeded another was proposed, and so on. The professors of Harvard University in 1857 conducted an examination of the boys and their phenomena. Their biographer writes*:

* "A Biography of the Brothers Davenport." By T. L. Nichols, M.D., pp. 87-8.

The professors exercised their ingenuity in proposing tests. Would they submit to be handcuffed? Yes. Would they allow men to hold them? Yes. A dozen propositions were made, accepted, and then rejected by those who made them. If any test was adopted by the brothers, that was reason enough for not trying it. They were supposed to be prepared for that, so some other must be found.

Finally, the professors bought five hundred feet of new rope, bored with holes the cabinet set up in one of their rooms, and trussed the boys in what is described as a brutal manner. All the knots in the rope were tied with linen thread, and one of their number, Professor Pierce, took his place in the cabinet between the two brothers. At once a phantom hand was shown, instruments were rattled and were felt by the professor about his head and face. At every movement he felt for the boys with his hands, only to find them still securely bound. The unseen operators at last released the boys from their bindings, and when the cabinet was opened the ropes were found twisted round the neck of the professor! After all this, the Harvard professors made no report. It is instructive also to read the account of the really ingenious test-apparatus consisting of what may be described as wooden sleeves and trousers, securely fastened, devised by a man named Darling, in Bangor (U.S.A.). Like other tests, it proved incapable of preventing instant manifestations. It is to be remembered that many of these tests were applied at a time when the brothers were mere boys, too young to have learned any elaborate means of deception.

It is not strange to read that the phenomena raised violent opposition almost everywhere, and the brothers were frequently denounced as jugglers and humbugs. It was after ten years of public work in the largest cities and towns in the United States that the Davenport Brothers came to England. They had submitted successfully to every test that human ingenuity could devise, and no one had been able to say how their results were obtained. They had won for themselves a great reputation. Now they had to begin all over again.

The two brothers, Ira and William, at this time were aged twenty-five and twenty-three years respectively. The NEW YORK WORLD thus describes them:

They looked remarkably like each other in almost every particular, both quite handsome with rather long, curly black hair, broad, but not high foreheads, dark keen eyes, heavy eyebrows, moustache and "goatee," firm-set lips, muscular though well-proportioned frame. They were dressed in black with dress-coats, one wearing a watch-chain.

Dr. Nichols, their biographer, gives this first impression of them:

The young men, with whom I have had but a brief personal acquaintance, and whom I never saw until their arrival in London, appear to me to be in intellect and character above the average of their young countrymen; they are not remarkable for cleverness, though of fair abilities, and Ira has some artistic talent. The young men seem entirely honest and singularly disinterested and unmercenary – far more anxious to have people satisfied of their integrity and the reality of their manifestations than to make money. They have an ambition, without doubt, which is gratified in their having been selected as the instruments of what they believe will be some great good to mankind.

They were accompanied to England by the Rev. Dr. Ferguson, formerly pastor of a large church at Nashville, Tennessee, at which Abraham Lincoln attended; Mr. D. Palmer, a well-known operatic manager, who acted as secretary; and Mr. William M. Fay, who was also a medium.

DARK SÉANCE—THE DAVENPORT BROTHERS

Mr. P. B. Randall, in his biography of the Davenports (Boston 1869, published anonymously), points out that their mission to England was "to meet on its own low ground and conquer, by appropriate means, the hard materialism and skepticism of England." The first step to knowledge, he says, is to be convinced of ignorance, and adds:

If the manifestations given by the aid of the Brothers Davenport can prove to the intellectual and scientific classes that there are forces – and intelligent forces, or powerful intelligences – beyond the range of their philosophies, and that what they consider physical impossibilities are readily accomplished by invisible, and to them unknown, intelligences, a new universe will be open to human thought and investigation.

There is little doubt that the mediums had this effect on many minds.

The manifestations of Mrs. Hayden's mediumship were quiet and unobtrusive, and while those of D. D. Home were more remarkable, they were confined entirely to exclusive sets of people to whom no fees were charged. Now these two brothers hired public halls and challenged the world at large to come and witness phenomena which passed the bounds of all ordinary belief. It needed no foresight to predict for them a strenuous time of opposition, and so it proved. But they attained the end which the unseen directors undoubtedly had in view. They roused public attention as it had never been roused before in England on this subject. No better testimony in proof of that could be had than that of their strongest opponent, Mr. J. N. Maskelyne, the celebrated conjurer.

He writes*: "Certain it is, England was completely taken aback for a time by the wonders presented by these jugglers." He further adds:

* "Modern Spiritualism," p. 65.

The Brothers did more than all other men to familiarize England with the so-called Spiritualism, and, before crowded audiences and under varied conditions, they produced really wonderful feats. The hole-and-corner séances of other media, where with darkness or semi-darkness, and a pliant, or frequently a devoted assembly, manifestations are occasionally said to occur, cannot be compared with the Davenport exhibitions in their effect upon the public mind.

Their first séance in London, a private one, was held on September 28, 1864, at the residence in Regent Street of Mr. Dion Boucicault, the famous actor and author, in the presence of leading newspaper men and distinguished men of science. The press reports of the séance were remarkably full and, for a wonder, fair.

The account in the Morning Post the next day says that the guests were invited to make the most critical examination and to take all needful precautions against fraud or deception, and continues:

The party invited to witness the manifestations last night consisted of some twelve or fourteen individuals, all of whom are admitted to be of considerable distinction in the various professions with which they are connected. The majority have never previously witnessed anything of the kind. All, however, were determined to detect and if possible expose any attempt at deception. The Brothers Davenport are slightly built, gentleman-like in appearance, and about the last persons in the world from whom any great muscular performances might be expected. Mr. Fay is apparently a few years older and of more robust constitution.

After describing what occurred, the writer goes on:

All that can be asserted is that the displays to which we have referred took place on the present occasion under conditions and circumstances that preclude the presumption of fraud.

THE TIMES, the DAILY TELEGRAPH, and other newspapers published long and honest reports. We omit quotations from them because the following important statement from Mr. Dion Boucicault, which appeared in the Daily News as well as in many other London journals, covers all the facts. It describes a later séance at Mr. Boucicault's house on October 11, 1864, at which were present, among others, Viscount Bury, M.P., Sir Charles Wyke, Sir Charles Nicholson, the Chancellor of the University of Sydney, Mr. Robert Chambers, Charles Reade, the novelist, and Captain Inglefield, the Arctic explorer.

SIR,

A séance by the Brothers Davenport and Mr. W. Fay took place in my house yesterday in the presence of (here he mentions twenty-four names, including all those already quoted).

At three o'clock, our party was fully assembled. We sent to a neighboring music-seller for six guitars and two tambourines so that the implements to be used should not be those with which the operators were familiar.

At half-past three, the Davenport Brothers and Mr. Fay arrived and found that we had altered their arrangements by changing the room which they had previously selected for their manifestations.

The séance then began by an examination of the dress and persons of the Brothers Davenport, and it was certified that no apparatus or other contrivance was concealed on or about their persons. They entered the cabinet and sat facing each other. Captain Inglefield then, with a new rope provided by ourselves, tied Mr. W. Davenport hand and foot, with his hands behind his back, and then bound him firmly to the seat where he sat. Lord Bury, in like manner, secured Mr. I. Davenport. The knots on these ligatures were then fastened with sealing-wax, and a seal was affixed. A guitar, violin, tambourine, two bells and a brass trumpet were placed on the floor of the cabinet. The doors were then closed, and a sufficient light was permitted in the room to enable us to see what followed.

DARK SÉANCE—THE DAVENPORT BROTHERS

I shall omit any detailed account of the babel of sounds which arose in the cabinet, and the violence with which the doors were repeatedly burst open and the instruments expelled; the hands appearing, as usual, at a lozenge-shaped orifice in the center door of the cabinet. The following incidents seem to us particularly worthy of note:

While Lord Bury was stooping inside the cabinet, the door being open and the two operators seen to be sealed and bound, a detached hand was clearly observed to descend upon him, and he started back, remarking that a hand had struck him. Again, in the full light of the gas chandelier and during an interval in the séance, the doors of the cabinet being open, and while the ligatures of the Brothers Davenport were being examined, a very white, thin, female hand and wrist quivered for several seconds in the air above. This appearance drew a general exclamation from all the party.

Sir Charles Wyke now entered the cabinet and sat between the two young men, his hands being right and left on each and secured to them. The doors were then closed, and the babel of sounds recommenced. Several hands appeared at the orifice, among them the hand of a child. After a space, Sir Charles returned amongst us and stated that while he held the two brothers, several hands touched his face and pulled his hair; the instruments at his feet crept up, played round his body and over his head, one of them lodging eventually on his shoulders. During the foregoing incidents, the hands which appeared were touched and grasped by Captain Inglefield, and he stated that to the touch they were apparently human hands, though they passed away from his grasp.

I omit mentioning other phenomena, an account of which has already been rendered elsewhere.

The next part of the séance was performed in the dark. One of the Messrs. Davenport and Mr. Fay seated themselves amongst us. Two ropes were thrown at their feet, and in two minutes and a half they were tied hand and foot, their hands behind their backs bound tightly to their chairs, and their chairs bound to an adjacent table. While this process was going on, the guitar rose from the table and swung or floated round the room and over the heads of the party and slightly touching some. Now a phosphoric light shot from side to side over our heads; the laps and hands and shoulders of several were simultaneously touched, struck, or pawed by hands, the guitar meanwhile sailing round the room, now near the ceiling, and then scuffling on the head and shoulders of some luck less Wight. The bells whisked here and there, and a light thrumming was maintained on the violin. The two tambourines seemed to roll hither and thither on the floor, now shaking violently, and now visiting the knees and hands of our circle – all these foregoing actions, audible or tangible, being simultaneous. Mr. Rideout, holding a tambourine, requested it might be plucked from his hand; it was almost instantaneously taken from him. At the same time, Lord Bury made a similar request, and a forcible attempt to pluck a tambourine from his grasp was made which he resisted. Mr. Fay then asked that his coat should be removed. We heard instantly a violent twitch, and here occurred the most remarkable fact. A light was struck before the coat had quite left Mr. Fay's person, and it was seen quitting him, plucked off him upwards. It flew up to the chandelier, where it hung for a moment and then fell to the ground. Mr. Fay was seen meanwhile bound hand and foot as before. One of our party now divested himself of his coat, and it was placed on the table. The light was extinguished and this coat was rushed on to Mr. Fay's back with equal rapidity. During the above occurrences in the dark, we placed a sheet of paper under the feet of these two operators and drew with a pencil an outline around them, to the end that if they moved it might be detected. They of their own accord offered to have their hands filled with flour, or any other similar substance, to prove they made no use of them, but this precaution was deemed unnecessary; we required them, however, to count from one to twelve repeatedly, that their voices constantly heard might certify to us that they were in the places where they were tied. Each of our own party held his neighbor firmly, so that no one could move without two adjacent neighbors being aware of it.

At the termination of this séance, a general conversation took place on the subject of what we had heard and witnessed. Lord Bury suggested that the general opinion seemed to be that we should assure the Brothers Davenport and Mr. W. Fay that after a very stringent trial and strict scrutiny of their proceedings, the gentlemen present could arrive at no other conclusion than that there was no trace of trickery in any form, and certainly there were neither confederates nor machinery, and that all those who had witnessed the results would freely state in the society in which they moved that, so far as their investigations enabled them to form an opinion, the phenomena which had taken place in their presence were not the product of legerdemain. This suggestion was promptly acceded to by all present.

There is a concluding paragraph in which Mr. Dion Boucicault states that he is not a Spiritualist, and at the close of the report his name and the date are affixed.

This wonderfully full and lucid account is given without abbreviation because it supplies the answer to many objections, and because the character of the narrator and the witnesses cannot be questioned. It surely must be accepted as quite final so far as honesty is concerned. All subsequent objections are mere ignorance of the facts.

In October, 1864, the Davenports began to give public séances at the Queen's Concert Rooms, Hanover Square. Committees were appointed from the audience, and every effort made to detect how it was all done, but without avail. These séances, interspersed with private ones, were continued almost nightly until the close of the year. The daily press was full of accounts of them, and the brothers' names were on everyone's lips. Early in 1865 they toured the English provinces, and in Liverpool, Huddersfield and Leeds they suffered violence at the hands of excited mobs. At Liverpool, in February, two members of the audience tied their hands so brutally that blood flowed, and Mr. Ferguson cut the rope and released them. The Davenports refused to continue, and the mob rushed the platform and smashed up the cabinet. The same tactics were resorted to at Huddersfield on February 21, and then at Leeds with increased violence, the result of organized opposition. These riots led to the Davenports cancelling any other engagements in England. They next went to Paris, where they received a summons to appear at the Palace of St. Cloud, where the Emperor and Empress and a party of about forty witnessed a séance. While in Paris, Hamilton, the successor of the celebrated conjurer, Robert Houdin, visited them, and in a letter to a Paris newspaper, he said: "The phenomena surpassed my expectations, and the experiments are full of interest for me. I consider it my duty to add they are inexplicable." After a return visit to London, Ireland was visited at the beginning of 1866. In Dublin they had many influential sitters, including the editor of the IRISH TIMES and the Rev. Dr. Tisdal, who publicly proclaimed his belief in the manifestations.

In April of the same year the Davenports went to Hamburg and then to Berlin, but the expected war (which their guides told them would come about) made the trip un-remunerative. Theatre managers offered them liberal terms for exhibitions, but, heeding the advice of their ever-present spirit monitor, who said that their manifestations, being supernatural, should be kept above the level of theatrical entertainments, they declined, though much against the wish of their business manager. During their month's stay in Berlin they were visited by members of the Royal family. After three weeks in Hamburg they proceeded to Belgium, where considerable success was attained in Brussels and all the principal towns. They next went to Russia, arriving in St. Petersburg on December 27, 1866. On January 7, 1867, they gave their first public séance to an audience numbering one thousand. The next séance was at the residence of the French Ambassador to a gathering of about fifty people, including officers of the Imperial Court, and on January 9 they gave a séance in the Winter Palace to the Emperor and the Imperial family. They afterwards visited Poland and Sweden. On April 11, 1868, they reappeared in London at the Hanover Square Rooms and received an enthusiastic welcome from a crowded audience. Mr. Benjamin Coleman, a prominent Spiritualist, who arranged their first public séances in London, writing at this time of their stay of close on four years in Europe, says*:

* SPIRITUAL MAGAZINE, 1868, p. 321.

I desire to convey to those of my friends in America who introduced them to me, the assurance of my conviction that the Brothers' mission to Europe has been of great service to Spiritualism; that their public conduct as mediums – in which relation I alone know them – has been steady and unexceptionable.

He adds that he knows no form of mediumship better adapted for a large audience than theirs. After this visit to London the Davenports returned home to America. The brothers visited Australia in 1876, and on August 24 gave their first public séance in Melbourne. William died in Sydney in July, 1877.

Throughout their career the Davenport Brothers excited the deep envy and malice of the conjuring fraternity. Maskelyne, with amazing effrontery, pretended to have exposed them in England. His claims in this direction have been well answered by Dr. George Sexton, a former editor of the SPIRITUAL MAGAZINE, who described in public, in the presence of Mr. Maskelyne, how his tricks were done, and comparing them with the results achieved by the Davenports, said: "The two bear about as much resemblance to each other as the productions of the poet Close to the sublime and glorious dramas of the immortal bard of Avon."* Still the conjurers made more noise in public than the Spiritualists, and, with the press to support them, they made the general public believe that the Davenport Brothers had been exposed.

* Address at Cavendish Rooms, London, June 15, 1873.

In announcing the death in America of Ira Davenport in 1911, LIGHT comments on the outpouring of journalistic ignorance for which it furnished the opportunity. The Daily News is quoted as saying of the brothers: "They made the mistake of appearing as sorcerers instead of as honest conjurers. If, like their conqueror, Maskelyne, they had thought of saying, 'It's so simple,' the brethren might have achieved not only fortune but respectability." In reply to this, LIGHT asks why, if they were mere conjurers and not honest believers in their mediumship, did the Davenport Brothers endure hardships, insults and injuries and suffer the indignities that were put upon them, when by renouncing their claims to mediumship they might have been "respectable" and rich?

An inevitable remark on the part of those who are not able to detect trickery is to ask what elevating purpose can be furthered by phenomena such as those observed with the Davenports. The well-known author and sturdy Spiritualist, William Howitt, has given a good answer:

Are these who play tricks and fling about instruments spirits from Heaven? Can God really send such? Yes, God sends them, to teach us this, if nothing more: that He has servants of all grades and tastes ready to do all kinds of work, and He has here sent what you call low and harlequin spirits to a low and very sensual age. Had He sent anything higher it would have gone right over the heads of their audiences. As it is, nine-tenths cannot take in what they see.

It is a sad reflection that the Davenports – probably the greatest mediums of their kind that the world has ever seen – suffered throughout their lives from brutal opposition and even persecution. Many times they were in danger of their lives.

DARK SÉANCE—THE DAVENPORT BROTHERS

One is forced to think that there could be no clearer evidence of the influence of the dark forces of evil than the prevailing hostility to all spiritual manifestations.

Touching this aspect, Mr. Randall says*:

* "Biography," p. 82.

There seems to be a sort of chronic dislike, almost hatred, in the minds of some persons toward any and everything spiritual. It seems as if it were a vapor floating in the air – a kind of mental spore flowing through the spaces and breathed in by the great multitude of humankind which kindles a rankly poisonous fire in their hearts against all those whose mission it is to bring peace on earth and good will to men. The future men and women of the world will marvel greatly at those now living, when they shall, as they will, read that the Davenports and all other mediums were forced to encounter the most inveterate hostility; that they, and the writer among them, were compelled to endure horrors baffling description, for no other offense than trying to convince the multitude that they were not beasts that perish and leave no sign, but immortal, deathless, grave-surviving souls.

Mediums ALONE are capable of DEMONSTRATING the fact of man's continued existence after death; and yet (strange inconsistency of human nature) the very people who persecute these, their truest and best friends, and fairly hound them to premature death or despair, are the very ones who freely lavish all that wealth can give upon those whose office it is merely to GUESS at human immortality.

In discussing the claims of various professional magicians to have exposed or imitated the Davenports, Sir Richard Burton said:

I have spent a great part of my life in Oriental lands and have seen their many magicians. Lately I have been permitted to see and be present at the performances of Messrs. Anderson and Tolmaque. The latter showed, as they profess, clever conjuring, but they do not even attempt what the Messrs. Davenport and Fay succeed in doing: for instance, the beautiful management of the musical instruments. Finally, I have read and listened to every explanation of the Davenport "tricks" hitherto placed before the English public, and, believe me, if anything would make me take that tremendous jump "from matter to spirit," it is the utter and complete unreason of the reasons by which the "manifestations" are explained.

It is to be remarked that the Davenports themselves, as contrasted with their friends and travelling companions, never claimed any preternatural origin for their results. The reason for this may have been that as an entertainment it was more piquant and less provocative when every member of the audience could form his own solution. Writing to the American conjurer Houdini, Ira Davenport said in his old age, "We never in public affirmed our belief in Spiritualism. That we regarded as no business of the public, nor did we offer our entertainment as the result of sleight-of-hand, or, on the other hand, as Spiritualism. We let our friends and foes settle that as best they could between themselves, but, unfortunately, we were often the victims of their disagreements.''

Houdini further claimed that Davenport admitted that his results were normally effected, but Houdini has himself stuffed so many errors of fact into his book, **A Magician Among the Spirits,** and has shown such extraordinary bias on the whole question that his statement carries no weight. The letter which he produces makes no such admission. A further statement quoted as being made by Ira Davenport is demonstrably false. It is that the instruments never left the cabinet. As a matter of fact, The Times representative was severely struck in the face by a floating guitar, his brow being cut, and on several occasions when a light was struck instruments dropped all over the room. If Houdini has completely misunderstood this latter statement, it is not likely that he is very accurate upon the former.

It may be urged, and has been urged, by Spiritualists as well as by skeptics that such mountebank psychic exhibitions are undignified and unworthy. There are many of us who think so, and yet there are many others who would echo these words of Mr. P. B. Randall:

The fault lies not with the immortals, but in us; for, as is the demand, so is the supply. If we cannot be reached in one way, we must be, and are, reached in another; and the wisdom of the eternal world gives the blind race just as much as it can bear and no more. If we are intellectual babes, we must put up with mental pap till our digestive capacities warrant and demand stronger food; and, if people can best be convinced of immortality by spiritual pranks and antics, the ends resorted to justify the means. The sight of a spectral arm in an audience of three thousand persons will appeal to more hearts, make a deeper impression, and convert more people to a belief in their hereafter, in ten minutes, than a whole regiment of preachers, no matter how eloquent, could in five years.

—Sir Arthur Conan Doyle

DARK SÉANCE—THE DAVENPORT BROTHERS

Utter confusion and chaos ensues as patrons at one of the Dark Séances of the Davenport Brothers appear to arm themselves and are about to storm the stage. Rumors persisted that one woman in the audience was tossed about and lost an arm in the melee.

MEDIUMS DAVENPORT BROTHERS
Ira Erastus Davenport Medium
William Henry Davenport Medium

Ira Erastus Davenport (1839-1911) and William Henry Davenport (1841-1877) were born in Buffalo, New York State. From an early age the Davenport Brothers experimented as Physical Mediums, producing automatic writing, manifestations and also sitting around a table placing their hands upon it in what was probably one of the earliest séances, a couple of years before the Fox Sisters experienced the Hydesville Rappings.

Instances of direct voice and levitation of objects and the Davenport Brothers themselves were also witnessed. As news spread of their abilities, the brothers embarked upon a tour of demonstrations around the world, using a cabinet to demonstrate their physical mediumship. Many tests were carried out to establish the cause of the physical phenomena, most notably by professors from Harvard University in 1857. Despite various elaborate methods of restraints, no scientific explanation could be found.

The Davenport Brothers continued to demonstrate their Physical Mediumship in America, Europe and Australia despite suffering some hostility and persecution from the skeptics of their day. Later they were placed in the annals of history of being show people.

The Spirit Guide of the Davenports claimed to have been Henry Owen Morgan, the buccaneer, who was knighted by Charles II and was appointed Governor of Jamaica. He first appeared with the Davenport Brothers in 1850 and was first seen in the flash of a pistol fired by Ira Davenport in the dark. He remained as Spirit manager with the Davenports throughout their career and in typtology or direct voice gave them sound advice in difficult positions. His activity was multifarious. While faithfully serving the Davenport Brothers, he took charge of the performances in the Koon log house in the wilds of Ohio. Here he assumed an august mien. As the head of a band of 160 Spirits he claimed descent from a race of men known by the generic title Adam, and having as leaders "the most ancient

DARK SÉANCE—THE DAVENPORT BROTHERS

Angels." They signed their communications as King No. 1, No. 2., etc., and some-times: Servant and Scholar of God. In his last incarnation, he strayed from the path of virtue and became a redoubtable pirate. He communicated in direct voice through a trumpet, his own invention, and through direct scripts. The tone of these writings was sanctimonious and upbraiding, i.e.: "We know that our work will be rejected by many and condemned as the production of their King Devil, whom they profess to repudiate, but do so constantly serve by crucifying truth and rejecting all that is contrary to their own narrow pride and vain imaginings."

The Davenport Brothers were instrumental in building the popularity of the American Spiritualist movement prior to the Civil War. They created a sensation all over the country and in Europe and continued mystifying audiences for years. William Henry and Ira Erastas Davenport introduced the Spirit cabinet for Mediums to use during a séance. These cabinets, or enclosures, would section the Medium off from view while they were producing their strange phenomena. This would prove to be both popular and astounding to audiences as the Mediums were usually bound hand and foot in the cabinet while the seemingly impossible phenomena manifested about them.

Ira Davenport was born in 1839 and his brother William came along two years later in 1841. Their father, a Buffalo, New York, policeman, was intrigued by the stories of the Spirit rappings in Hydesville, so the family decided to try their own sittings at home. Immediately, they got chilling results and Ira would later tell friends that his younger sister, Elizabeth, actually levitated about the room.

Soon after, the family got in touch with what would become the Davenports' Spirit Guide, a phantom named John King (who would go on to become the busiest Spirit Guide in the Spiritualist movement). King allegedly told the family to begin renting a hall and giving public performances of the Davenport brothers reputed powers. The boys were only 16 and 14 when they went on stage for the first time in 1855. The initial performances contained tricks. But soon the Davenport brothers began to introduce other phenomena into the act, like musical instruments which floated in the air, playing under their own power, and Spirit Hands that touched and pulled at sitters and audience members.

By the end of the year, they were performing in New York City and had introduced not only the Spirit Cabinet into their séances but complicated escapes from ropes and knots as well. This would become a signature for their act.

At the suggestion of an audience member during a performance, a box similar to a small closet was assembled on stage. The brothers would now be able to work, not only in total darkness, but away from prying eyes as well. Part of the brothers' act was to look for volunteers from the audience who would then tie them up inside of the cabinet. Overeager skeptics often tied the Davenports with elaborate and painful knots that sometimes drew blood. In spite of this, once the

DARK SÉANCE—THE DAVENPORT BROTHERS

cabinet doors were closed, wondrous Spirit Music filled the air from inside and disembodied hands would appear through apertures that had been left open on the exterior walls.

On occasion, a spectator from the audience would be invited on stage and would be seated between the brothers in the cabinet. A few moments after the doors were closed, the man in the center would be often tossed out of the box with his coat gone, his necktie around his leg and a tambourine seated on his head. Someone would fling open the doors and the Davenports would be found tied up, just as they were before.

The Davenports also performed a dark séance on stage, asking members of the audience to be present to ensure that no trickery was involved. The brothers were securely tied to a table on the stage and the lights were turned out. Soon after, ghostly forms began to float about on the stage. Of course, when the lights were raised again, the brothers would still be bound.

Now, treat the following with a bit of logic, as it comes from a cunning, calculating and jealous conjurer, Houdini.

Their act created a sensation. Spiritualists hailed it as genuine proof of Spirit Phenomena, while critics regarded the brothers as mere stage magicians. Interestingly, neither brother ever claimed to be a Medium, leaving that up to the audience to decide. They did, however, bill the act as a séance, and most Spiritualists believed their manifestations to be genuine. The men began as entertainers and allowed a gullible public to think them to be more than that. Harry Kellar, the master magician, was employed by the Davenports for a time and afterwards learned to do tricks that altogether surpassed even the brothers' skills at rope-tying and escapes.

The great secret of the Davenports' success lay in their uncanny (albeit natural) ability to extricate themselves from complex knots and ties and then return to them in record time. The most important part of the procedure took place during the binding, when they managed to obtain plenty of slack in the ropes by twisting, flexing and contorting their limbs. Once they relaxed, the ropes could be easily slipped out of.

Years after they retired from the business, surviving brother Ira was interviewed and befriended by magician Harry Houdini. Davenport told Houdini that they never intended to become known as Mediums, but their almost supernatural powers came along during the early heyday of the Spiritualist movement, and, rather than turn down the money and appearances, they allowed the public to think whatever they wanted to about them. Davenport taught Houdini some of their best escapes and Houdini later used them and found them to be very effective and clever. He also discovered that the brothers rubbed oil into their hands so that they could slip out of the ropes more easily.

DARK SÉANCE—THE DAVENPORT BROTHERS

They also employed as many as ten accomplices at a time and took great pains to hinder investigators and debunkers by placing traps in the aisles of the theatre. That way, no one could sneak onto the stage during their séance and surprise them. One of the tricks that they used during private performances was to run a string through the buttonholes of the sitters. The reason for this, they said, was to "prevent collusion," but, in reality, it prevented anyone from approaching the Davenport's Spirit Cabinet.

In spite of this, many people refused to believe that the brothers could be anything other than Spirit Mediums. Even newspaper accounts gave them credit for producing miracles. This report appeared in the conservative **London Post**:

"The musical instruments, bells, etc., were placed on the table; the Davenport Brothers were then manacled, hands and feet, and securely bound to the chairs by ropes. A chain of communication (though not a circular one) was formed, and the instant the lights were extinguished the musical instruments appeared to be carried about the room. The current of air, which they occasioned in their rapid transit, was felt upon the faces of all present.

"The bells were loudly rung; the trumpets made knocks upon the floor, and the tambourine appeared running around the room, jingling with all its might. At the same time sparks were observed as if passing from south to west. Several persons exclaimed that they were touched by the instruments, which on occasion became so demonstrative that one gentleman received a knock on the nasal organ which broke the skin and caused a few drops of blood to flow."

With the press taking such a remarkable view of the brothers, it's no wonder that spectators were even more impressed and amazed. And while the Davenports never made any claims of being Mediums, they continued to thwart investigators until the end of their careers. In all of those years, they were never caught cheating!

The Davenports' careers came to an end in 1877 when William died suddenly. In honor of his brother, Ira ordered a magnificent memorial for him on which was carved a representation of their ropes, cabinet and other séance props. William had died in Australia and cemetery officials in Sydney would not allow the monument within the cemetery grounds. It was placed outside instead. Ira himself died in 1911.

The Exposure of the Davenport Brothers by John Hulley and Robert Cummins

Ira Erastus Davenport (1839-1911) and William Henry Davenport (1841-1877), known as the Davenport Brothers, were American magicians in the mid-1800s, sons of a Buffalo, New York, policeman. The brothers presented illusions claimed to be supernatural.

The Davenports' most famous effect was the box illusion. The brothers were tied inside a box which contained musical instruments. Once the box was closed, the instruments would sound. Upon opening the box, the brothers were tied in the positions in which they had started the illusion. Those who witnessed the effect were made to believe supernatural forces had caused the trick to work. They toured the United States for 10 years and then travelled to England where spiritualism was beginning to become popular.

The Davenport public séances began in October 1864 at the Queen's Court Concert Rooms, Hanover Square, London. They continued almost nightly until the end of the year. No committee could pinpoint the brothers' fraud, though a group of stage magicians attempted to prove that the performance was fraudulent.

Although their stay in London was somewhat successful, the Davenports met with open hostility in the countryside. In Liverpool, for example, two members selected from the audience tied the mediums with a peculiarly intricate knot. The mediums protested that it was unfairly tight and injured their circulation. A doctor from the audience made an examination and pronounced against them. The Davenports refused to sit and asked Ferguson to cut the knot. The next night a riot broke out and the party left town. At Hull, Huddersfield and Leeds they found a hostile public inclined to lynch them. Since they did not find the police protection sufficient, they broke off their engagements and returned to America.

The two members selected from the audience in Liverpool were John Hulley, the famous gymnast, and Robert B. Cummins. Their confrontation with, and eventual exposure of, the Davenport Brothers filled many column inches of both local and national newspapers for several weeks after the event, most of which are reproduced below. Included in the reports are several from the Porcupine magazine, a 19th century fortnightly journal of current events – social, political and satirical in Liverpool.

The Davenports' exposure also led to a County Court action being brought by Cummins to recover the entrance fee of five shillings paid to see a séance which did not come off. The judge found against Mr. Hime, the Liverpool agent of the Davenports who agreed to repay all persons affected.

A dramatic illustration of Home's feat
of levitation. Did he accomplish
that which was thought impossible?

The Fabulous DAVENPORT BROTHERS

THE BROTHERS DAVENPORT
By Dr. H. L. Nichols

CHAPTER ONE
AN INTRODUCTION

The Motive and Method of this Book – The Possible and the Actual – Facts and Theories.

It is my purpose, in the following pages, to give as clear, full and truthful a narrative of the lives of the two young Americans, known to the world as the Brothers Davenport, and of the remarkable physical and psychical phenomena which have for eleven years been witnessed, in their presence, by multitudes of people, as I am able to write. The account is substantially taken from the lips of the two brothers, especially from those of Mr. Ira E. Davenport, the eldest brother, whose story of the experience of his whole life has, in my judgment, every mark of simple truthfulness. His account is confirmed by the reports of American newspapers in sixteen States which they have visited, by several pamphlets and biographical sketches, and by the testimony of various persons, both Englishmen and Americans, who have been witnesses of the extraordinary manifestations with which they have been accompanied and some of whose testimonies will be found in the following pages.

In writing this narrative, I do little more than to set down in order what has been told me by those in whose veracity I place entire confidence, and reduce to a moderate compass the testimony of "a cloud of witnesses." I wish to present the facts connected with these young men, separated, as far as possible, from any theory held by themselves or others in regard to them.

The reader will be left, as he must and ought to be, to draw his own conclusions. I have no interest to deceive any one or to distort or exaggerate a single fact in the narrative. It will be admitted that these facts are sufficiently wonderful without the least exaggeration. From first to last they seem, to those who have only observed the ordinary occurrences of life, incredible.

The word is not strong enough. They are what most people will consider impossible. To a similar objection to an extraordinary fact, someone has replied, "I did not say it was possible; I only said it was true."

It is not well, however, to be hasty in asserting that anything is impossible. Many things, once deemed impossible, are now matters of daily observation. It is not long since millions of people would have considered crossing the ocean by steam, traveling eighty miles an hour on a railway and sending messages by electricity physical impossibilities.

The first photographs were great marvels. Many facts in geology, natural history and physiology are marvelous and inexplicable, or unexplained. It is not known how a broken bone is repaired or blood sent to a limb deprived of the use of its large arteries.

We are all accustomed to many things which, but for their being common, would seem marvelous and be thought impossible. At the same time, I do not pretend for a moment that the cases I have mentioned are parallel to this of the phenomena produced in presence of the Brothers Davenport. I wish to say only that the first question in regard to phenomena is not one of probability, or even of what is called possibility, but always a question of fact. It is not, is it likely; but is it true?

If, in describing these phenomena, I do not attempt to account for them, and offer no theory in regard to them, it would be a mere affectation for me to ignore the theories held by others. These are two in number only.

The first is that the Davenports are simply magicians, or prestidigitators, like Houdin, Anderson, and many others, who by their own skill and the aid of confederates produce their manifestations; and that they are impostors and knaves in solemnly denying that they use any such means, or any means whatever, to produce them.

The second theory is that the manifestations are genuine and effected by the aid of some usually invisible intelligences, supposed by some to be demons, and by others the spirits of human beings who have departed from this life.

Besides these, there have been vague suggestions of unknown elements, electrical action, odic forces and hidden powers appertaining to the human organism which may be unconsciously exercised. These are vague suggestions, and have not the consistency of developed theories, and are unsupported by any basis of observation or experiment. I mention them now only that the reader, in perusing the statement of facts, may try, if he wishes to do so, to account for them upon any hypothesis he may prefer. I shall revert again to these theories; but it will be evident to everyone that the great question first of all to be settled is whether the manifestations are what they are represented to be – that is, produced by some power other than the Davenports and their associates; or, whether the Davenports are impostors who have for eleven years been deceiving vast multitudes, and all this time liable to punishment, and worthy of punishment and execration, as the meanest, basest – the most audacious and most atrocious of cheats and humbugs.

The Brothers Davenport, from the ages of twelve and fourteen to the present time, have stood before the world charged by multitudes with this imposture. They have been brought to public trial many hundreds of times, and in the presence of hundreds of thousands of people; and the charge of collusion, trick, or deception of any kind has never been proved against them.

What has happened in this long scene of trials and triumphs will be found in the following chapters, which will be read with interest, I am certain, and I hope also with candor and profit.

Ira Davenport (left) pictured with Harry Houdini
shortly before Ira's death.

The Fabulous DAVENPORT BROTHERS

CHAPTER TWO
BIRTH AND PARENTAGE

Born, where, when, and of whom – Family Characteristics – Monitions and Prevision – Childhood – Startling Manifestations – Boyish Occupation.

Ira Erastus Davenport and William Henry Davenport, who are known as the Brothers Davenport, were born in Buffalo, State of New York, United States of America; the former September 17, 1839, the latter February 1, 1841. Their only sister, Elizabeth Louisa Davenport, was born December 23, 1844.

Ira Davenport, the father, was born at Skeneatales, New York, in 1816. He is descended from early English settlers in America. His wife, Virtue Honeysett, was born in the county of Kent, England, in 1819, and was taken to America in her childhood.

Buffalo, the residence of the Davenports, situated at the outlet of Lake Erie by the Niagara River, and twenty miles south of the famous cataract, was, at the period of the birth of the Brothers Davenport, an enterprising city of some twenty thousand inhabitants and has since increased to a population of more than a hundred thousand. Mr. Davenport, senior, had a place under the city government, in the department of police; and though in moderate circumstances, was widely known and appears to have deserved and enjoyed the confidence of his fellow-citizens. His wife's father and other relations resided at Mayville, in Chautauque County, about sixty miles southwest of Buffalo. I mention this circumstance for a reason that will appear in the course of the narrative.

I find nothing in the characters of the progenitors of the Davenports which would account for the extraordinary phenomena which have occurred for eleven years past in the presence of the subjects of this biography by the laws of hereditary descent. It is related, indeed, that in the families of both father and mother had been observed many of those events which are considered supernatural by some persons, and imaginations and coincidences by others, and which are both common and inexplicable. Thus Mrs. Davenport, while a girl, heard, or imagined she heard, one day, a voice directing her to observe the time as marked upon a

51

clock standing near her, which proved to be the moment of her mother's death at a distance. The female relations of Mr. Davenport are said to have possessed extraordinary gifts of healing, similar to those formerly attributed to the sovereigns of England, and something of the second-sight, or prevision, which many believe to have formerly been common in Scotland.

I mention these matters, not as attaching weight to them, but because they are among the family traditions. It is proper to say, however, that Mr. Ira Davenport, senior, in early life, had minute and circumstantial previsions of events, places, persons and many of the circumstances of his future life; but this is not, I suspect, so uncommon an experience as many persons imagine.

During the childhood of the Brothers Davenport but few events occurred worthy of recital. Ira remembers, when very young, that his mother was alarmed by loud knockings in the house, that she called in a neighbor, and that they pursued from room to room and were followed by knockings which they did not know how to question and which soon subsided. These disturbances were coincident with a severe, and, as it seemed, dangerous illness of Mr. Davenport, then absent on a journey.

In 1846, the family was disturbed by what they described as "raps, thumps, loud noises, snaps and cracking noises in the dead of the night." They were startling and annoying, but what could they do? Disconnected from the subsequent events, they were scarcely worthy of remembrance.

The two boys, born so near each other, had, and still have, a striking resemblance to each other. They are somewhat below the medium size and have a strongly marked and handsome physiognomy, more English, perhaps, than American. They received the common school education free to every boy in America, and are, I think, in thought and conversation rather above the average of young men brought up in similar conditions. Their earliest and only employment, by which they assisted their parents in their boyhood, was in the delivery of newspapers from one of the several newspaper offices in Buffalo.

The Fabulous DAVENPORT BROTHERS

CHAPTER THREE
THE BEGINNING OF THE MANIFESTATIONS

The Rochester Knockings – First Séance of the Davenport Family – Great Excitement – The Pistol-Flash and Specter – Sharpshooting in the Dark – Floating in the Air – Analogies and Explanations.

About the year 1850, the western part of New York was greatly excited by accounts of what were called the Rochester Knockings. Rochester is a city of New York somewhat less in size than Buffalo, and distant some ninety miles, on the borders of Lake Ontario. The knockings occurred in a family of a mother and three daughters, who became known as the Fox Girls. Their furniture was shaken, doors violently opened and shut, drawers opened, articles thrown about, and finally questions were answered and messages spelled out by raps or detonations which appeared to be made on or in the tables, floors, doors, and similar objects.

Naturally, these strange occurrences were noised abroad, published in the newspapers, and became a subject of general conversation. Mr. Davenport was a sturdy unbeliever in the rappings; but the marvels were talked about in the family. One evening Miss Elizabeth, then ten years old, declared her belief that if such things happened to anybody, they might just as well happen to them. Whether this was childish bravado, or the result of some internal conviction, it is needless to enquire. The result was that in the evening the father, mother, and three children solemnly seated themselves round a table, placed their hands upon it, as they had read was done at Rochester, and waited further developments.

After a few moments a movement as of swelling or bulging was felt in the table; then crackling noises, tippings, raps, and finally very loud and violent noises. At first Mr. Davenport suspected the children were "having a lark," but when the noises came to be quite beyond their power to make, and messages were spelled out beyond their power to manufacture – for the oldest boy was now only in his fifteenth year – he was convinced that whatever the agency might be, it was no deception practiced by any member of his family. It is easy to conceive that their first experiences were of absorbing interest. They sat around the table from seven

DARK SÉANCE—THE DAVENPORT BROTHERS

o'clock in the evening until daylight next morning.

They had prudently agreed to keep the matter a profound secret, not wishing to incur obloquy or ridicule; but Mr. Davenport's mind was too full of the matter, and, under an injunction of secrecy, he told a friend, who told it to another. Of course it spread like wildfire.

"Knockings at the Davenports!"

Hundreds flocked to the house. It was not only filled but surrounded. The yard and even the street were full. The thumpings, knockings, messages, and so on, were repeated. On the third evening, editors, lawyers, preachers, bankers, merchants, all classes of people, crowded the house; and amid the manifestations such as had been previously given, Master Ira was taken with a violent propensity to write, his hand becoming subject to extraordinary gyrations. An effort was made by several strong men to hold his hands, but without success. On being furnished with paper and a pencil, he wrote with extraordinary rapidity a series of brief messages, which he distributed to various persons in the company. These messages were believed to be quite beyond both his mental and physical powers and contained matters known only to the persons to whom they were addressed and quite beyond his possible knowledge.

On the fifth evening there was witnessed a new and surprising, or perhaps I should say more surprising, manifestation. In compliance with a direction rapped out on the table, by the now familiar method of calling over the alphabet and having each letter designated, a pistol was procured, and capped, but not loaded. One of the boys was then directed to go to a vacant corner of the room and fire it. At the instant that he fired, the pistol was taken from his hand, and by its flash was plainly seen by every person in the room held by a human figure, looking smilingly at the company. The light and the form vanished together, as when we see a landscape in a flash of lightning, and the pistol fell upon the floor. It was a very impressive scene and, if so explained, a striking optical illusion – if a whole company can be supposed to be affected by an illusion; while, if a deception, it was remarkably well managed and might put the patent for Professor Pepper's ghosts in peril.

Among the pistol experiments at Buffalo, somewhat later was one which may be of interest to sportsmen and the rifle volunteers. Visitors brought their own loaded pistols, which were laid upon the table. A mark was placed upon the wall at the opposite extremity of the room. The light was then blown out, leaving the room in perfect darkness. In this darkness, the pistol, untouched by any one present, would be fired. Often a spectral figure was seen or imagined in the flash of the pistol. But the mark was always hit. Sometimes the ball cut out the designated spot in a playing card, sometimes it passed through the core of an apple. These tests were so common that there must be hundreds of witnesses to testify to

DARK SÉANCE—THE DAVENPORT BROTHERS

their reality.

On the next night the manifestations were varied again, the house being as crowded as ever; and neither the idea of illusion or delusion seems to account satisfactorily for the phenomena witnessed by credible people, who were probably as much in their senses as people can be expected to be under such circumstances. A request was made by means of the rappings that the room should be partially darkened. It is, perhaps, useless to ask why. In Nature and in Art some operations require light, and some its absence. Most flowers bloom by day – some open only in the night. But I have only to relate what happened on this memorable evening.

The boy Ira was seated at the table, by the side of his father, and scarcely had the light been dimmed when he was taken from his side by some resistless force, laid upon the table, and floated in the air over the heads of all the people, and from one end of the room to the other, at a height of nine feet from the floor, every person in the room having the opportunity of feeling him as he floated in the air above them. While they were watching this marvel, someone cried, "William is flying, too!" The two brothers were found to be alike defying the laws of gravitation, or borne up by some force, the nature of which we need not stop to enquire. Stranger still – if one such fact can be stranger than another, or if one more adds to the marvel – the little sister joined her two brothers in the air, and all three floated about over the heads of the people.

I am aware that natural philosophers may give an explanation of this phenomenon, or, what answers often for an explanation, an analogy; if, indeed, it may not be considered less troublesome to deny the fact. It may be said that showers of fishes, frogs, etc., which must have been for days sustained in high regions of the atmosphere, prove that there are forces in nature which overcome or suspend gravitation, and that the three Davenport children may have been sustained and floated about in the air in the same manner. I freely admit the force of the suggestion. The believers in animal magnetism will contend that they were borne up and kept up by the united and excited will-power of the assembly. This is also a hypothesis of some plausibility; but, as I have said before, my business is with the facts rather than with possible or impossible reasons.

The facts which I have narrated became known to all Buffalo and the region round about. They were witnessed by hundreds of as respectable people as live anywhere. There are many persons still living there – for these events occurred scarcely eleven years ago – who could testify to every fact I have here given. There was very ocular evidence of the force with which Ira was raised up into the air, by a repulsion perhaps as strong as the usual attraction which brings us down, for his head bulged through the plaster of the ceiling. At another time, and in the full sight of many persons, Ira was carried through the air, not only about the room, but through the hall, across the yard, and landed beyond a fence in the street, a distance, by measurement, of seventy feet.*

   *I ought, perhaps, to say that this phenomenon of levitation is not peculiar to the Davenports, nor to this age. It has been witnessed in this country, in the case of Mr. Home, and is related of many persons in the last eight hundred years. Any industrious reader in the library of the British Museum will be able to find a multitude of well-authenticated cases, some of which have been judicially examined and proven by a host of witnesses. It may be doubted, however, if they can find, in any of the numerous cases, any philosophical explanation of the phenomenon.

Glowing orbs abd anomolous forms
were common sights at many Dark Séances.

The Fabulous DAVENPORT BROTHERS

CHAPTER FOUR
ASTOUNDING PHENOMENA

Excitement and Persecution – Dance of Breakfast Dishes – A Gigantic Apparition – An Invisible Scribe – An Astonished Furniture Dealer – A Self-Writing Pencil.

I am unable to give the particulars of many wonderful occurrences of this early period, because there were so many, and because the memory of many of them has been obscured by the events of more than ten years. I give those which, from some peculiar feature, were recorded at the time or have been best remembered.

It cannot be supposed that the excitement caused by events of so remarkable a character, witnessed by so many persons, was entirely of an agreeable character. Neither the probity of the father, the blameless character of the mother, nor the innocence of the children, the oldest of whom was only in his fifteenth year, saved them from reproach, slanders, hatred and persecution. Perhaps the only matter of astonishment is that, in a frontier town, which had at that time a considerable population of a wild and lawless character, there was not more of violence and outrage. It needed no little firmness on the part of Mr. Davenport to go quietly on the even tenor of his way, amid ridicule, charges of fraud and imposture, threats of prosecution and imprisonment, mob outrage and Lynch law, and attempts at personal violence and clandestine murder. His natural firmness of character, the consciousness of entire honesty and good motives, and the sympathy of many of the best men in Buffalo, sustained him. They were as interested in the matter as he could be. Furthermore, these marvels had come to him unsought and unexpected.

He naturally believed they had some purpose, which he trusted was a good one. He and his family seemed set apart for a peculiar work. It is not strange that he bore obloquy with calmness and met threats with courage. He was in just the condition to have become a martyr.

On one morning, at this early period, the family was sitting around the breakfast table when the knives, forks, and dishes began to dance around, as if suddenly endowed with vitality. In a few moments, the table began to move, tipping up sideways, balancing itself on one leg; and, finally, rising clear from the floor, floating in the air without the least support, and moving in such a way that it was wonderful that the dishes upon it did not slide off* and come crashing upon the floor. While the table was displaying these curious antics, William, the younger of the two brothers, exclaimed, "There is the biggest man I ever saw; what a large man!" As no one else saw any one in the room who did not belong to the family, we are obliged to take the word of Master William for what he saw, or imagined he saw. The father interfered in his usual sensible way, saying, "William, my son, keep still. Perhaps this big man may have something to say to us."

He may have read that it was the correct thing to speak to an apparition; it was, at least, but common politeness to give him a chance to speak, if disposed to do so. His voice came from empty space; but William seemed moved to speak, and said, "This stranger is so tall that he can scarcely stand up in this room; and he is large in proportion. He is a real giant."

"Will he tell who he is; where he came from; and what he wants of us?" asked the father.

The answer, still given by the boy, seems very absurd; but I give it as it is reported, notwithstanding. The boy said, "He says he is not of this earth; his name is William E. Richards; and that he wishes to give us, and those who meet with us, important instructions, on which much will depend in the future." Obviously, all this may have come from the boy's excited imagination, though that would not account for the dance of the breakfast dishes or the flight of the table with the breakfast upon it, phenomena witnessed by the whole family; and which naturally predisposed them to believe in other and greater marvels.

At two o'clock, P.M., according to the request of the imaginary or otherwise tall personage, not of this world, but bearing or assuming for the time the very sublunary name of "Richards," the party assembled, including the Davenport family and the friends they selected for so interesting and important a séance. In the room were two tables. The company sat around one. On the other had been placed, by direction, writing paper and pencils.

They sat silently some two minutes, when, in the broad light of day, they all saw a lead pencil rise from the table, take a nearly perpendicular position, as if held by some invisible being, and commence writing rapidly upon the paper, while the paper itself seemed to be alive and to move under the pencil.

It is not in my power to give a copy of the document so curiously written. It consisted, in part, of directions for preparing a room, and procuring a large table, for the better accommodation of those who were coming from far and near to see these wonders. "Go," said the paper, or pencil, or the invisible, supposed by

William to be the giant he saw, or imagined he saw, "and I will go with you and assist in making a proper selection. When you come to a suitable table I will rap my approval."

They started immediately for a large furniture establishment, kept by Mr. Taunton Baldwin, and, after looking at several tables, waiting for the promised sign, they came to one, and were all startled, and especially the furniture dealer, by a loud and very emphatic detonation. Mr. Baldwin, unaccustomed to that mode of selecting furniture, enquired into the matter and soon became satisfied that something made noises on or in his table.

The most noticeable phenomenon described in the last portion of this chapter, that of a pencil writing without visible control, is a fact which does not rest upon the testimony alone of the Davenports or those who saw it at their house in Buffalo. There have been many similar cases, related upon unimpeachable testimony. One that occurs to me was that of Senator Simmons, of Rhode Island. Wishing to see a certain name written by a pencil while he sat at the table and watched the proceeding, he saw the pencil move, rise, and make an ineffective effort to write, and then topple over as if the weight were too much for the force.

He then took a pair of scissors, and, holding one of the bows over the paper, placed the pencil within it, in a perpendicular position. Then he distinctly saw the pencil, of itself, write out the name desired, and then, raising itself from the paper, go back and dot an i. There were other circumstances more important, perhaps, than the writing; but I have preferred to mention only the physical phenomena.

It was not uncommon for the spirits to emerge from a sealed spirit cabinet
and walk amongst the audience.

The Fabulous DAVENPORT BROTHERS

CHAPTER FIVE
ORGANIZATION OF REGULAR SÉANCES

An Apology or Explanation – Marvelous Manifestations – Tests applied – Boys floating in the Air – A striking Test – March of the Family Crockery – Upheld by a Specter – A Balancing Feat – "George Brown" – A Murdered Man's Story – A Boy carried off by a Ghost.

The purchase of the large table, as narrated in the last chapter, was the beginning of a new series of manifestations. The friends of Mr. Baldwin, the furniture dealer, were curious to see the wonders he had witnessed, and the home of the Davenports was filled, day and night, with eager enquirers. It was very repugnant to Mr. Davenport to receive money from those whose curiosity was gratified, and he steadily refused for many months to do so. His time was occupied, his business deranged and his family burdened with expenses. It was only when he left home to take charge of the boys in their early journeyings that he consented to receive some compensation. It became necessary, moreover, to fix a price, if only as a means of excluding an idle and perhaps mischievous crowd that would otherwise have claimed admission.

I do not know that there is any need of this explanation, or for any apology. Authors, artists, poets, statesmen, and ministers of religion all live and all receive money for their work. He that serves the altar must live by the altar. The laborer is worthy of his hire. Every laborer – everyone who renders a service – everyone whose time we occupy deserves payment unless he obtains money under false pretenses. The fraudulent, of course, have no claim whatever.

Nor does the receipt of money afford a presumption of fraud, but rather the contrary. It is always to be presumed that the man who wants our money wishes to render some equivalent. We are not to assume hastily that any man – much less a man of unblemished reputation – is an impostor and a scoundrel.

At the séances, which now began to be held regularly, the manifestations already described were repeated. Loud raps were heard; the table answered questions; spectral forms were seen in the flash of a pistol; lights appeared in the upper parts of the room; musical instruments floated in the air, while being played upon, above the heads of the company. It would be too much to expect of human nature to suppose that all these things were witnessed with simple faith and open-mouthed credulity. There were enough to say it was a trick and to be determined to detect it. Probably nine out of ten, when told of what occurred, declared it all a humbug and that they could detect and expose it. Consequently, a close watch was kept upon the Davenports. Persons were appointed to hold them. The whole company took hold of hands when the room was darkened that each might vouch for the two next him.

On one occasion, four persons selected for the purpose held the two boys; four others securely grappled Mr. and Mrs. Davenport; and even the little Elizabeth was held by two others. Every possible precaution was taken.

When all this had been arranged, Ira was lifted bodily into the air, until he rose above the heads of those who held him, and floated away close to the ceiling. Then both boys, Ira and William, were laid upon the table, and Mr. Plympton, a well-known auctioneer of Buffalo, was requested to hold them firmly by the feet. He seized their ankles when Ira was raised bodily into the air, followed by William. Not succeeding in holding both, he next tried the youngest, who, in spite of his added weight, was raised up with such force that his head broke through the ceiling of lath and plaster. Mr. Plympton had held to the boy with all his strength, but letting go, to prevent being himself drawn he knew not where, the boy, suddenly freed, went up – by lunar attraction, let us say, or terrene repulsion – with the result to his skull and the plastering already stated. The people who heard the crash thought the boy was killed and called for a light; but he was found to be quite unhurt. There was no mistake, however, about the hole in the ceiling.

Another manifestation, to use a convenient word in describing what we have perhaps no proper name for, was on this wise: The company was seated around two tables, and the room quite darkened.

Why darkened? it will be asked. Why not darkened? might be asked as readily. It is a mystery, no doubt; but the whole matter is equally mysterious. While every person in the room was sitting by the tables, in the darkness, the door of a pantry was flung violently open, and the entire stock of family crockery and glassware taken from the shelves and piled upon the tables. I say "taken" and "piled" as I do not know how it was done, or who did it; it is better, perhaps, to say merely that the whole stock was found to be heaped upon the tables, which had been placed together. Then the boys were raised up and placed upon the dishes, and all the chairs heaped upon the whole, without the agency of any mortal hand that could be discovered. All this was done without the fracture of a single article and in total darkness. Lights were struck, and with great care the boys and chairs were taken down. The lights were again extinguished, and every article was restored to its proper place in the pantry, without the slightest mishap or accident.

I am "free to confess" that if I were inventing facts, or manifestations, or phenomena, I should choose something more dignified than the displacement and placement of shelf, china, and glass; but a scene which was witnessed the next day, at a two o'clock matinee, may perhaps be more satisfactory. The room was not darkened, only obscured to a pleasant twilight. After several of the usual phenomena were exhibited, the two boys were raised from their chairs, carried across the room and held up with their heads downward before a window,

"We distinctly saw," says an eyewitness, "two gigantic hands attached to about three-fifths of a monstrous arm; and those hands grasped the ankles of the two boys and thus held the lads, heels up and heads downward, before the window: now raising, now lowering there, till their heads bade fair to make acquaintance with the carpet on the floor."

This curious, but assuredly not dignified, exhibition was several times repeated and was plainly seen by every person present. Among these persons was an eminent physician, Dr. Blanchard, then of Buffalo, now of Chicago, Illinois, who was sitting in a chair by the side of Elizabeth Davenport; and all present saw an immense arm, attached to no apparent body – growing, as it were, out of space – glide along near the floor till it reached around Dr. Blanchard's chair, when the hand grasped the lower back round of Elizabeth's chair, raised it from the floor, with the child upon it, balanced it, and then raised it to the ceiling. The chair and child remained in the air, without contact with any person or thing, for a space of time estimated to be a minute, and then descended gradually to the place it first occupied.

In the midst of a series of similar manifestations, too numerous and too much alike in their general characteristics to be recorded, there came one of a novel and startling character, which was destined to separate the family and start the two brothers upon that extraordinary tour around the world, which in ten years has brought them to the confines of Europe and the center of one of its most powerful kingdoms.

One day, at a private séance to which Mr. Davenport had invited several of his friends and persons well known to him, the table, by tippings and rappings, spelled out a message which purported to come from one "George Brown," who described himself as a Canadian farmer who had resided at Waterloo, W.C., where his family still lived, and who had been robbed and murdered, in a place which he described, by members of a notorious gang of robbers on both sides of the border known as the Townsend gang.

These particulars were given by one of the boys, speaking in a sort of cataleptic or trance state, in which he became, apparently, the proxy of "George Brown." He named the sum of money – fifty-two dollars, the price of a yoke of oxen he had intended to purchase. He, that is the boy, his spokesman, was cross-examined by a lawyer who was present, but he adhered to his story; gave the name and residence of his wife, the number of his children and other particulars.

Mr. Davenport was much impressed with the story and went with a friend across the Niagara River to Waterloo the next day, where, after due enquiry, he found that no such man as the "George Brown" had ever lived there. There was a rascal named Townsend, and a gang called by his name, but he could find no clue to the robbed and murdered farmer.

Returning home crestfallen, it may be presumed, they met the sheriff of the county and asked him if he had ever heard of a George Brown, of Waterloo.

"Yes," said the officer, "but not this Waterloo; a George Brown used to live at the other Waterloo, sixty miles away. I used to know him well, but he disappeared some time ago and was supposed to have been robbed and murdered by some of the Townsend gang. I know his wife and family well."

The circumstances related by the sheriff agreed perfectly with the account the boy in the trance had given.

On the return of the delegates to Canada, and before they could report proceedings, young Ira fell into the "state," took up the ghostly tale of George Brown, the murdered man, and related everything that had happened to them, including the conversation with the sheriff.

Great as was the impression made upon Mr. Davenport, he could not overcome his natural skepticism and fear of ridicule enough to go to the Waterloo, to find the widow of poor Brown, and make further investigations, though several persons offered to subscribe the money for his expenses. He shirked the responsibility.

"George Brown," still enacted by Ira, or finding representations and spokesmen in tables, or otherwise, did not appear to be pleased with the little faith given to his story, and the manner in which his wishes were neglected, and announced that he intended to take Ira to the scene of his murder. Not much attention was paid to what was considered an absurd threat; but the boy, a few evenings after, while engaged in his daily task of delivering evening papers, first felt "queer," then lost his consciousness and found himself standing in the snow, with no tracks around him to show how he had come there, in a solitary place, a mile and a half from home, on the right bank of the Niagara river.

"George Brown," at his next visit, declared that he had carried him across the river, which is half-a-mile wide, and brought him back again, just as an experiment; but as the boy was unconscious all the time, until he found himself on the bank, while his family were getting alarmed at his absence, and as nobody saw him carried across the river, we have only "George Brown's" testimony on the subject, which we are not obliged to believe without a sufficient corroboration.

Of course, we cannot prove a negative. If the boy could be carried across the room and out into the street, why not across Niagara River? A feat beyond Blondin's, it must be confessed. If seventy feet, why not as many miles? If people lose their gravity, or are hurried away by their emotions, or other sufficiently powerful influences, who shall say how far they may be carried? I believe simply that Master Ira, as he then said and still says, in a manner that carries conviction with it, found himself standing in the snow on the bank of the Niagara, without knowing how he came there. As "we must draw the line somewhere," I propose to draw it there. "George Brown" may have wished to stretch it. Or he wished, it may be, to see his murderers stretching lines of a different description.

In any case, I think Mr. Davenport, Sr., ought to have gone to Waterloo, and he was soon very sorry that he did not.

DARK SÉANCE—THE DAVENPORT BROTHERS

The Fabulous DAVENPORT BROTHERS

CHAPTER SIX
"WE FLY BY NIGHT"

Hands and Voices – Advent of "John King" – Required to leave Buffalo – Refusal and the Consequences – A mysterious Night Trip of Sixty Miles – Manifestations in Mayville – Another Ghost and Murder.

Whatever opinion may be formed by the calm-judging reader of this matter of the murder of "George Brown," of Waterloo, Canada West, it soon became evident enough that the Davenports had incurred the animosity of somebody. There came to them dark threats of vengeance. The boys were warned to be on their guard. They were too brave to mind much about obscure hints of assassination, and, like nine American boys out of ten, Ira armed himself with a loaded pistol for their defense. One night the two boys found themselves waylaid and were fired at. Ira valorously fired in return, and then both took to their heels. The boys escaped without injury, except to their clothing; there was a rumor that Ira's bullet had been better sped. Not long after, some friends came with the story that the house was to be attacked at night and the children murdered, and several persons volunteered to watch over and defend them. The boys were required to forego their paper-carrying expeditions, which were their business, play and exercise.

At the morning and evening parties of curious investigators into these strange phenomena, there were now not only heard the ringing of bells, thrumming of musical instruments, movements of various objects without apparent cause, including the three Davenport children, but hands, seemingly human, were both felt and seen. A hand and part of an arm would rise above the table, plainly visible, and allow itself to be felt for a moment, when it would dissolve, melt into air in the very grasp and under the eyes of the spectator. Then a voice, coming out of space, at first inarticulate, but later condensed as it would seem in a large horn or trumpet provided for the purpose, spoke distinctly to them, conversed with them, answered their questions, and advised or directed their proceedings. I do not know that this voice was a greater marvel than many others that I have related.

DARK SÉANCE—THE DAVENPORT BROTHERS

The first thing that occurs to everyone is that it was the result of so common an art as ventriloquism. A ventriloquist has no difficulty in making a voice appear to come from up a chimney, or out of a box or from the cellar. Other illusions can be managed by tubes and reflectors, as in the "mysterious lady" exhibited some years ago, and the Anthropoglossos or "singing head" more recently. With a common speaking tube, a person a hundred feet distant, and in another part of a large building, seems to be speaking close to your ear. But Mr. Davenport and his family knew that they were not ventriloquists, and all who came to see them could easily satisfy themselves that there was no machinery. Besides, the voice was only one of so many "signs and wonders" that it was hardly worth trying to account for that, unless the others could be explained as easily.

The voice was asked, among other things, what was its name. It replied that names were of no consequence – one would do as well as another, and they might call it "John King," which they do to this day, or familiarly "John." This "John," the name of a voice, said to the father of the Davenports that he must take his two sons away from Buffalo, that it was dangerous for them to stay and that they were needed elsewhere. Mr. Davenport would not consent either to leave his family with them or allow them to go. He thought they were very well as they were. He had come to have some faith in the voice, and the things he saw and heard, but saw no sufficient reason why he should go about the world to give other people a chance of witnessing the same phenomena. If people wished to see them, let them come to the boys. Decidedly the boys should not go to them. The reply was that if they were not allowed to go, they could and would be taken.

The strange event which took place as the result, apparently, of this conversation, is variously vouched for; but I have preferred to take the facts from the lips of Mr. Ira Davenport, the elder of the two brothers. He says that he was walking one evening, at about nine o'clock, in the streets of Buffalo with his brother William, this being the winter of 1853-4, and the boys in their twelfth and fourteenth years. The next thing he knew he awoke in a field near his grandfather's house some sixty miles from Buffalo.

On waking up William, who had not returned to consciousness, they made their way to their grandfather's house, where they were received with surprise, and their story heard with astonishment. Their father was immediately informed by telegraph of their safety and whereabouts, and he, good obstinate man, set himself to find out how they got to Mayville. On enquiry, he found that no railway train could have taken them, after the hour they left home, more than a portion of the distance, and the conductors on the road knew the boys and had not seen them.

"John" declared through the trumpet, after their return home, that he had transported them, or caused them to be transported, simply to show Mr. Davenport that they could be taken to any distance as easily as they could be carried about the room, and to show him that it was useless for him to try to keep them in Buffalo. The boys, so far as I can judge from the manner in which the story was related to me by Ira, undoubtedly believe that they were taken by no ordinary means of conveyance, and that the difficulties of the journey were overcome for them in some unexplained and inexplicable manner by the same power, whatever that may be, which has for eleven years worked in their presence so many marvels, not less difficult of explanation than their little trip from Buffalo to Mayville. They do not say that they were carried all the way or part of the way. They think they must have walked a long distance, for their feet were blistered. They were there and knew not how.

During this visit to the residence of their grandfather, a circumstance occurred which made a strong impression upon the whole family, and especially upon the father of the young Davenports, who had come to bring them home. One night the whole house was alarmed by cries, slamming of doors, thumpings, rappings and other noises. The grandfather, a religious man, came from his room with his Bible, which failed to bring quiet. When the first consternation was over, a voice was heard trying to speak to them. It could not at first be understood; but a tin horn having been procured, the voice issued from it with sufficient distinctness to tell its story. It (the voice, let us say) declared itself to be "John Hicks," a brother-in-law of Mr. Davenport, who had some years ago lost his first wife, married another and died suddenly sometime after. The voice, coming out of the trumpet which had succeeded the racket, told a sad and startling story. It said "John Hicks" (whose voice it professed to be) had been poisoned by his wife; but it exacted a promise from Mr. Davenport that he would let his body and the whole matter rest and not seek for justice or vengeance against his murderess.

This, to a man full of the discipline and habits of the police department, was a hard promise to keep. Mr. Davenport related the matter to his friends, and their curiosity stimulated his sense of duty, and he proceeded to have the corpse of his brother-in-law disinterred and subjected to a post-mortem examination. The Dr. Blanchard already mentioned was one of the physicians. The details of the examination have not been submitted to the writer hereof – only the fact that the stomach and contents were found entire, with appearances to justify, to say the least, strong suspicion of foul play; but the evidence was not sufficient to convict the supposed offender.

All sorts of conjurers and tricksters tried
to duplicate the amazing Davenport Brothers.

The Fabulous DAVENPORT BROTHERS

CHAPTER SEVEN
STRIKING TESTS AT BUFFALO

Keeping to the Facts – J. B. Britain's Experience – Visit of Rev. B. F. Barrett – Statement of Stephen Albro and Mrs. Taylor – Most Surprising Wonders.

There remains little more that need be said of the lives and adventures of the Brothers Davenport in their native city. The father was at length brought to the belief that they had a wider mission and consented, for a time, to accompany them. I may, however, mention a few of the more striking and peculiar displays of the mysterious force and intelligence, or intelligent controlling force, which claimed to have produced the phenomena already described. It will be observed that I have ventured no opinion and offered no theory respecting the nature of this intelligent force. It called itself, in the first instance, "Richards;" then it adopted the name of "John," or "John King." It, or something, professed to be "George Brown of Waterloo," who had been murdered for his money; and it, or something else, declared itself to be "John Hicks," poisoned by his wife, like "Hamlet's father." It may be hard to believe that the voices were produced or the manifestations made by any of these persons; but it is also rather difficult to prove the contrary. Let us, then, like true Baconian philosophers, cling to our facts.

"How can we reason, but from what we know?" Let us have the facts first and inferences afterwards. We may not be able to impeach our only witness – a tipping table, a pencil writing without a hand, or a voice making itself audible or articulate by means of a tin trumpet; but I do not see that we are bound, on the other hand, to put implicit faith in their unsupported testimony.

Many persons went from New York to Buffalo, three hundred miles, to witness the manifestations. During a visit of J. B. Brittain, Esq., a well-known writer and public speaker, a number of photographic portraits were placed in his hands, which he knew to have been half-a-mile away when the séance commenced, while no one had entered the house to bring them. On this occasion the forms produced, as from space, seen and felt by all present, were those of young children of two years old; and as there were no such children in the house, there was no thought of imposture. Moreover, the three young Davenports were heard and felt floating in the air over the heads of the company, each holding some musical instrument and producing sounds which marked their progress. Mr. Brittain stood up and felt them in the air above him.

Another of these visitors was the Rev. Mr. Barrett, Swedenborgian clergyman at Brooklyn, near the city of New York. As a Swedenborgian he believed, of course, in common with all Christians, in the existence of beings separated from the common forms of material existence; but he did not believe that they had power to act upon matter, and of this, if true, he wished to be convinced.

As a test he brought with him a glass bottle of immense strength which he proposed should be broken by an invisible force. As a security against deception, he locked himself into a room with the two boys. He examined every part of it for trap-doors or means of concealment. He laid the bottle on a table and sat down, placing his hands and feet on both the boys, so as to feel the least motion they could make. Then he blew out the candle.

The first thing that occurred was sufficiently ludicrous. The just extinguished candle was rubbed all over his face. A voice, plainly heard by all three, for no others were present, informed him that it was a preparation to enable him to swallow the truth, of which he was to receive evidence. Then came a blow, an explosion or concussion that sounded like the stroke of a sledge-hammer, and the bottle flew across the room, broke the plastering on a brick wall, but was itself unbroken. It was replaced upon the table. A louder and heavier blow came with a similar result. This process was repeated seven times, each time with greater force, and the last time the bottle was shattered into a hundred pieces, flying all over the room, a piece grazing the face of Mr. Barrett. His hat, which he had placed upon the floor at one end of the room, was then plunged into a tub of water which happened to be standing at the other end, and in that state placed upon his head.

When the candle was lighted, Mr. Barrett began to gather up the pieces of the bottle. Ira asked him what he could want of them.

"When my friends, to whom I tell the story, say that I was 'psychologized' or hallucinated," said he, "I wish to show them these pieces of glass and ask them if they are also hallucinated when they believe they see and handle them."

Blowing out the candle again, Mr. Barrett was raised in his chair from the floor and received other tests of an equally convincing character.

Skeptics, then as now, often resorted to private tests, but never without being exposed, and sometimes in a ludicrous manner, worthy of the "tricksy spirits" of our great dramatist. One day a gentleman blacked the mouth of the trumpet through which the voice was heard to issue, supposing he could by that means detect whoever should use it. In the course of the conversation with the voice he asked that he might be touched. Instantly he felt a finger moving around his lips.

On a candle being lighted, he went eagerly to examine the mouths of the boys and others present, to see if they were blacked; but every one burst into a laugh at seeing a black circle, as if made with the mouth of the trumpet, around his own.

Of another séance given at this period, I find a circumstantial account published in a Buffalo weekly newspaper, The Age of Progress, describing a visit of the editor to the Davenports, dated October 13, 1855, and signed by the editor's name – Stephen Albro.

Mr. Albro had been requested to procure a séance for a lady, whom he accompanied to the room at 10 o'clock A.M. on the day appointed. He says:

"Mr. Davenport and his elder son were present, and we four locked ourselves in, that we might be entirely secluded and free from interruption. I then took particular note of everything in the room and saw that the only two ways of ingress were secured and that there was no possibility for anyone besides ourselves to be in the room or to get in without our knowledge. Then one of the two inside window-shutters was closed, and the other was partially closed, leaving an opening of about two inches in width, and consequently apertures above and below, through all of which a sufficiency of light was admitted to make a twilight in the room, by which I could plainly see everyone around the table; see both avenues of ingress and detect every motion of every hand in the room. When accustomed to the light, I read an advertisement which hung up against the wall, ten feet from me. Ira sat next me on my left, the lady on my right, and Mr. Davenport on the opposite side of the table."

After several manifestations, William came and knocked at the door and was admitted; then the manifestations became more powerful. After mentioning several incidents similar to those already described, Mr. Albro continues:

"The next manifestation was the appearance of human fingers from under the table [where bells had been rung, musical instruments played, etc., while the editor had carefully guarded against deception], reaching over the edge of the table and leaping upon it. Then whole hands appeared in the same manner. These fingers and hands were from the size of a large man's hand to that of a small child. [No children were present.] The largest ones were black, and all the others were white. [Observe that there were but five persons, including the Davenports, in the room, which was light enough for everything to be distinctly seen.] During the time of these exhibitions, I put my hand under the table. In a minute after, I felt the pressure of cold fingers on my thumb. Then it was grasped by a whole hand. I asked who it was that grasped my thumb and was told that it was the spirit of my father, the truth of which was soon made evident by my own vision. I then requested my father to grasp my whole hand, which he did with such power that it reminded me of the almost giant grip which he occasionally made me feel in urchin-hood. He had a large and very powerful hand; and the one which grasped mine was like it, both in size and power.

"By the raps an umbrella was called for, which was standing in a corner of the room. One of the boys brought it and put it under the table, closed. In a few moments it made its appearance from under the table, opened to its full extent. It came out at the end of the table, at the left hand of the elder of the two boys, and was raised up and held over his head, the lower end of the staff remaining below the table and between the boy's knees. It was moved up and down and twirled round one way and the other as it was held over his head. It immediately moved from him to me, the staff passing along against the edge of the table. My head being higher than that of the boy, it was necessary to elevate it to get it over my head. In doing this, a female hand and arm, of the most exquisite model, appeared from under the table – the beautiful hand grasping the staff of the umbrella and moving it up and down and turning it, as above related. To this narrative of facts, to which I append my signature, I am ready at any time to append my affidavit; and further, I am ready to testify, under oath, that none of these things which I have related were done by any of the five persons in the room, and that no other person belonging to this mundane sphere was in the room during their enactment."

(Signed) 'Stephen Albro.'

The above statement is slightly condensed from the original, but not altered in any essential particular. Mr. Albro, I am assured, was widely known in Buffalo and all that region as a man of high respectability and intelligence – one not likely to be deceived, and certainly not likely to deceive others.

The lady who accompanied Mr. Albro also furnished the following statement:

"To the Readers of the Age of Progress!

"Mr. Albro, having shown me the foregoing report in manuscript, and I being the lady referred to as accompanying him to Mr. Davenport's room, and witnessing the manifestations which he narrates, I hereby certify that this report is true in every particular – not including what he felt with his hands under the table. And I further certify that his account, instead of exceeding the truth, falls much short of the reality of what I witnessed."

(Signed) "Mary M. Taylor."

If it were considered worthwhile to do so, I could fill twenty volumes like this with similar statements, made under the solemnities of an oath if required, testifying to similar phenomena and given by honest and intelligent witnesses whose evidence would be taken by any court in Christendom in any case whatever.

Mr. Albro appears to have been convinced that the hand which grasped his was that of his father, long since dead. What he appears to have known as a fact was that it was not the hand of Mr. Davenport, or of the lady or the two boys, the only persons present. So of the hands that appeared at the end of the table, and the beautiful feminine hand and arm that held the umbrella. If the facts narrated by Mr. Albro stood alone, or if he and those with him were the only witnesses, we might throw them aside as a cheat or hallucination; but when there are hundreds of such facts and thousands of such witnesses, it becomes more difficult. Still, a man of strong will can refuse to believe almost anything.

The Fabulous DAVENPORT BROTHERS

CHAPTER EIGHT
THE BROTHERS DAVENPORT ON THEIR TRAVELS

Beginning of the Binding Tests – Judge Paine's ingenious Experiments – Thread and Sealing Wax — Sewed up in Sacks – Invincible Incredulity – Tobacco Test at Cleveland – Betting and Sailors' Tests at Toledo – A German Philosopher at Ann Arbor – Tarred Rope and Waxed Ends at Rochester – A Series of Trials.

When time enough had elapsed for the good people of Buffalo to be satisfied of the verity of the facts heretofore related, and when Mr. Davenport had seen and felt signs and wonders enough to satisfy him that he could no longer oppose the desire of the mysterious intelligence to give the people of other regions similar opportunities, the two Brothers Davenport, accompanied first by their father, and afterwards by other persons who acted as their friends or agents, commenced the journeyings which have now continued nearly ten years, in which they have visited most of the important towns on one Continent, and have begun a similar mission in another hemisphere.

It is impossible, in my brief limits, to fully describe the incidents of their long journeyings. The experience of one town or city was generally repeated in another, though the manifestations were varied, and new and more severe tests were proposed as old ones failed to detect what people thought must be imposture. The best I can do in this case is to keep as nearly as possible the order of time and select from the great mass of ever-occurring incidents those which seem most interesting in themselves and those which will give the reader the best idea of the nature of the phenomena involved, and the best means of judging, if such a judgment can be formed, of the cause and purpose of what was done, by whom and why. My own work in the matter, as far as I can now see, is pretty much confined to the what, or the first part of the subject. The rest may, I hope, be safely confided to the judgment of an enlightened public.

It was not long after the Davenport Brothers commenced to visit places where they were unknown, and where the wonders exhibited in their presence, and to which their presence seems to be in some way a necessary condition, created an intense and wild excitement, breaking out at times into blind and violent opposition and persecution, before tests began to be required to satisfy people more or less that they were not imposed upon by artful jugglers. They were first held by persons selected from the audience, two or more being appointed to hold each of the brothers while the manifestations were being accomplished. This process was found to be exhausting to the boys, perhaps from some adverse or antagonistic magnetism, and unsatisfactory to the public, who looked upon those selected to hold them as confederates. It was then proposed to bind them with ropes. When the ropes, though knotted in the most careful manner by the most skillful persons, were found to be untied in a few moments, the crowd asked, naturally enough, "Why don't you have handcuffs?" The handcuffs were procured; but they were no more satisfactory than the ropes, for the intelligent audience said, "You have got handcuffs made on purpose," but, as they seldom brought any themselves, it was difficult to satisfy their requirements.

At Painesville, a small town in Ohio, on Lake Erie, Judge Paine, who had given his name to the township, contrived, with several of his friends, a series of tests which showed no little ingenuity. These were men of the class who may be called invincibly incredulous. Neither seeing, hearing, nor feeling, with them was believing. They would have delighted a recent writer in the Cornhill Magazine, who has declared that no one ought to believe anything unusual on any amount of evidence – that of his own senses included.

After the brothers had been bound as securely as the Lake Erie sailors and riggers could tie them, and the manifestations had been made while they were thus bound, spectral hands shown, instruments played upon and thrown about, or they unbound by what appeared invisible agency, or the genii of Eastern story, the Judge proposed a test which, he said, would satisfy him and everybody. This, of course: nothing is more common than for a man to imagine that what satisfies him of the truth of something hard to believe must satisfy everybody else. The result is that each person who is satisfied is instantly denounced as a fool or a knave by all the remaining unbelievers.

The learned Judge said that if the boys were bound, not with rope, but with linen thread, and this sealed with sealing-wax, and then the trumpet blacked with printers' ink, so as to blacken any hand that touched it, he would be satisfied, and everybody else, of course. The test was accepted; the manifestations occurred as usual and the seals were unbroken. Was Judge Paine satisfied? Not in the least. The next day he was ready with a new test. This time, the boys were first tied with cords, then enclosed in sacks, and the sacks tacked to the floor. All the instruments were blacked, and every possible precaution taken. The hall and the streets were crowded with people. The hands were formed, the instruments whirled about in the air and beaten, and abundant evidence given that somebody or something was wide awake and active; but when lights were brought, the brothers were very safe in their sacks. When the Judge saw them secure, he said to his friends, "We've got to give in on this!" But the next day he had a new theory: the boys had untied themselves, ripped open the bags, made the manifestations and then got back again all safely sewed up and tied. Truly, there is no credulity like incredulity.

At Cleveland, a beautiful city on Lake Erie, a very obstinate skeptic, watching narrowly to detect some jugglery or imposture, was very suddenly and drolly converted to a belief in the genuineness of the manifestations. He was sitting in the midst of the audience when the voice which sometimes accompanies the manifestations was heard to say with emphasis, "No, I don't want any of that," at which the skeptic burst into laughter, which he afterwards explained.

Taking a chew of tobacco, in a sort of bravado he held out the paper, mentally offering some to the voice or its owner – to "John." The words heard by the audience were the instantaneous answer.

Toledo is a port on Lake Erie, at the extremity opposite to Buffalo, a town of considerable traffic, but having a population, it must be confessed, of a somewhat lawless character. The traveler who stops at a hotel at Toledo is likely enough to run against a Faro table, and will readily find men to bet on anything, from a trotting horse to a presidential election. Of course, a crowd assembled to see the now famous Brothers Davenport; and equally, of course, they began to lay heavy wagers on the success or non-success of the performance. A committee was selected to give the sporting men the fairest possible chance. It consisted of two sailors, two riggers, and two captains of vessels to direct operations. They brought their own rope, a sufficient quantity, and marlinspikes, to work with.

They not only tied the ropes about their heads, feet, arms, and bodies, in all the ingenious knots known to the craft, but spliced the ropes as well as tied them, and then wetted the knots, to make the rope swell. After three-quarters of an hour of hard work, the two captains declared themselves satisfied. It is doubtful if, without using their knives, they could have freed the boys in the time which had been taken to tie them. While thus bound, the usual manifestations, of which I need not repeat the description, were given, and the boys found bound as strongly as ever. Then the lights were turned down, and they were found with every knot untied, completely liberated, in the space of five minutes. The losing sportsmen paid their bets, and the audience went home astonished if not satisfied.

Not the least of the many difficulties and annoyances attendant upon the giving of such manifestations and tests as have been described was the conduct of the committees who stood between the brothers and the large assemblages who everywhere gathered to see them. Sometimes it was difficult to get persons willing to serve; at others they were prejudiced and unfair, or what theologians call "invincibly ignorant." For example, at Ann Arbor, in Michigan, a German, whose conceit and bad English made him a sort of favorite with the public, was selected to sit in the cabinet in which the two brothers were bound. He sat between them, so as to be able to tell at every moment whether they continued to be bound – whether they even stirred in the places to which they were firmly secured, and, above all, whether a concealed confederate exhibited phantom hands, played upon the instruments or threw them out upon the platform. The German was shut in the cabinet. The instruments climbed up his body, rested on his head and were played upon as usual. Hands and arms appeared at the openings of the closet. He was between the two brothers, where he could hear every breath and feel every motion. The doors were thrown open, and they were seen to be securely bound. Then the German gentleman gave his testimony.

"Were they fastened all the time?" he was asked.

"Yaas; dey vas fastened every minute."

"Did they make any movement?"

"No; dey never sdirred at all."

"Was there anybody else there but you three?"

"No; nobody else vas dere. How coult dey be? You could see dat yourselves."

"Well, then, whose were the hands, and who made the noises?"

"Oh, dey vas de poys."

"How do you know? You just said they were bound fast all the time, and didn't move."

"Yaas, dey vas fast enough; but it most have been dem, because dere vas nobody else to do it!"

The logic is perfect, of course, but not entirely satisfactory.

At Rochester, in New York, new methods of binding were tried. When fortifications were to be made for the defense of a town, and the council discussed the choice of the materials to be used, a man who owned a quarry was in favor of stone; the proprietor of a brickyard contended for the superiority of well-burnt bricks, and the tanner declared that "there was nothing like leather." Rochester, besides its millers and merchants, has a large population of canal boatmen and shoemakers. The canalers insisted on tarred ropes, while the shoemakers stuck to waxed-ends as the best means of tying the brothers securely. As a compromise, they used both, and the young men were first bound as fast as a sailor on "the raging Erie Canal" could devise, and then finished off with the tying of waxed thread by the shoemaker. It was of no use; rather, it was of just the same use as any other thorough and satisfactory test. All the manifestations were given, which the audience satisfied themselves there was nobody to give, and then the boys in a few moments were freed from their adhesive entanglements. Those who could be satisfied of the verity of what they saw were satisfied. Those who could not were content to call it a humbug and imposture, the nature and agencies of which, however, they were farther than ever from being able to explain.

While on a visit to London, a large flourishing town in Canada West, in 1857, a séance was attended by his Worship the Mayor and several members of the corporation. The mayor himself actively assisted in fastening the brothers with tarred ropes, and, as a private test, which it is believed he communicated to no one, he blacked some of the knots which were not in sight but which were afterwards found untied. When the doors of the cabinet had been closed, a voice from the trumpet said, "Mr. Mayor, why did you black the knots?" The result was that no visible hands were blackened.

In every such case, it is to be observed, these two boys are put on trial of honesty and veracity. They declare that certain manifestations of physical and intellectual power – force directed by intelligence – take place in their presence which neither they nor any other living person actively or consciously produce; every séance is a trial more or less perfectly conducted of this first question at issue. The first fact established, other questions may be in order.

SPIRITUALISM MADE USEFUL.

The Fabulous DAVENPORT BROTHERS

CHAPTER NINE
THE CAMBRIDGE PROFESSORS

'Old Harvard' – Scientific Incredulity – A University Commission – The Fox Girls – The Brothers examined – Plenty of Rope – Prof. Pierce in the Cabinet – Phosphorus – What came of it

It was at about this period that certain Professors of Harvard University undertook to investigate, explain, and abolish everything of a preter-or super-natural character. Old Harvard is the Oxford of the New World – the oldest university, and one which holds the highest rank. Its seat is Cambridge, a suburb of Boston, which claims to be the Athens of America and the "hub of the universe" beside. Thus; Boston is the most intelligent and scientific city in America, and America is the most intelligent country in the world; ergo, Boston in a literary and scientific way is the hub, focus, or pivotal center of the universe.

Q.E.D. (*quod erat demonstrandum*—proven by demonstration)

The parties arrayed in this contest were principally Dr. Gardner of Boston, who asserted that phenomena were exhibited above or beyond the ordinary operations of nature, and which could not be accounted for by physical laws as recognized by modern science; and Professors Agassiz, Pierce, and others, of Harvard, who denied the possibility as well as the fact of such manifestations. As a rule, men who have made a reputation in any science drive down a stake there — erect a barricade which no one must pass, and are ready to denounce all discoveries which go beyond their own. They deny every alleged fact which does not square with their theories. Showers of fish may fall upon a marching regiment in India, and be fried and eaten by the soldiers; toads may be seen coming alive from solid rocks blasted with gunpowder twenty feet below the surface in quarries or railway cuttings, and the toads, and the rocks where they had lain ever since the rocks were formed, with the holes in which they reposed split across by the explosion, preserved and seen by all who care to see them, and yet no Professor of Natural History will admit the fact until he has got a theory to fit it. It is a humbug, an imposture, and a delusion. 'So much the worse for the facts.'

DARK SÉANCE—THE DAVENPORT BROTHERS

Our Harvard Professors made or accepted the challenge to examine some of the preternatural phenomena — not that they had the least idea of finding and accepting truth, or advancing the cause or increasing the domain of science, but that they might expose and authoritatively denounce what they believed to be a great imposture or a great delusion. It was a very good thing to do, provided they had been as willing to accept an established fact as they were to denounce an established humbug.

Among the persons summoned to be tried before the Harvard Professors on the charge of falsely pretending that very unusual, or what may properly be called super- or preternatural phenomena occurred in, and seemingly by means of, their presence, were the Misses Fox, and the Brothers Davenport. The manifestations in the presence of the Fox girls were chiefly confined to loud explosive rappings or thumpings on tables, doors, or other vibratory substances, which raps manifested an intelligent source by answering questions, written or mental, and spelling out messages. Phenomena, force, intelligence. This is what the Harvard Professors had first to investigate, before going further. The raps or thumps were plain and loud enough. They seemed to come from the centre of doors or tables — the professors' doors or tables, which could not be suspected of jugglery.

The girls, who have been described to me as honest and simple-hearted, were subjected by the learned professors to a very severe ordeal. First, they were carefully examined for concealed machinery. Then it was a question whether they could not make loud thumpings, as with a mallet, seeming to come out of the centre of a mahogany table, with their knee joints or toes. So their limbs were confined, and their feet placed upon pillows. It was of no use. The sounds continued all the same, and the professors made no other discovery but that there were unaccountable noises.

The Brothers Davenport were reserved till the last. At the beginning, they were submitted to a cross-examination. The professors exercised their ingenuity in proposing tests.

"Would they submit to be handcuffed?"

"Yes."

"Would they allow men to hold them?"

"Yes."

A dozen propositions were made, accepted, and then rejected by those who made them. If any test was accepted by the brothers, that was reason enough for not trying it. They were supposed to be prepared for that, so some other must be found. It was of no use to put them to any test to which they were ready, and apparently eager, to submit. At last the ingenious professors fell back upon rope — their own rope, and plenty of it. They brought five hundred feet of new rope, selected for the purpose. They bored the cabinet, set up in one of their own rooms, and to which they had free access, full of holes. They tied the two boys in the most thorough and the most brutal manner. They have, as any one may see, or feel, small wrists, and hands large in proportion — good, solid hands which cannot be slipped through a ligature which fits even loosely on the wrists.

When they were tied hand and foot, arms, legs, and in every way, and with every kind of complicated knotting, the ropes were drawn through the holes bored in the cabinet, and firmly knotted outside, so as to make a network over the boys. After all, the knots were tied with linen thread.

Professor Pierce then took his place in the cabinet between the two brothers, who could scarcely breathe, so tightly were they secured. As he entered. Professor Agassiz was seen to put something in his hand. The side doors were closed and fastened. The centre door was no sooner shut than the bolt was shot on them inside, and Professor Pierce stretched out both hands to see which of the two firmly-bound boys had done it. The phantom hand was shown; the instruments were rattled; the professor felt them about his head and face; and at every movement kept pawing on each side with his hands, to find the boys both bound as firm as ever. Then the mysterious present of Professor Agassiz became apparent. The professor ignited some phosphorus by rubbing it between his hands, and half suffocated himself and the boys with its fumes, in trying to see the trick or the confederate. At last, both boys were untied from all the complicated fastenings without and within the cabinet, and the ropes were found twisted around the neck of the watchful Professor Pierce!

Well, and what came of it all? Did the professors of Harvard tell what they had seen? Not in the least. To this day they have made no report whatever of the result of their investigation, and are probably, to this day, denouncing it all as humbug, imposture, delusion, et cetera. What can a man of science do with a fact he cannot account for, except deny it?

It is the simplest way of overcoming a difficulty, and avoiding the confession that there is something in the world which he does not understand. Of all men in the world, men of science, and especially scientific professors, are the last to acknowledge that 'there are more things in heaven and earth, than are dreamt of in their philosophy.'

The cabinet trick offered by the Davenport Brothers. From an old print in the Harry Houdini Collection.

Instruments were a favorite item for spirits to move around; even extremely heavy grand pianos seemed to lift up off the floor.

Want a spirit cabinet of your very own? Such items could be ordered and shipped anywhere you wanted — but no two day delivery like Amazon Prime currently provides.

The Fabulous DAVENPORT BROTHERS

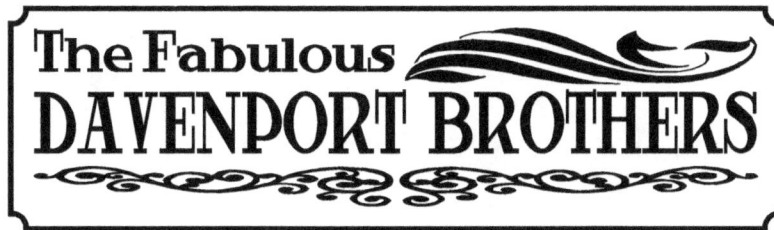

CHAPTER TEN
AMONG THE DOWN-EASTERS

Lola Montes – A Row in a Garret – A Storm of Feathers – A Scene at Portland – A Mad-house Test – Boxed up at Bangor – A Discomfited Darling – Seeing is not always believing.

Having got through with the Professors of Old Harvard, and passed through college, but without receiving the diploma to which they were entitled, the Brothers Davenport reposed at the Fountain House, in Boston, where they made the acquaintance of many distinguished personages in the literary emporium, of whom they pleasantly remember the pretty, eccentric, and kind-hearted Lola Montes, Countess of Landsfeld, who received what she believed to be communications from several of her departed friends, and notably from her last husband who had drowned himself on their voyage from Australia to California. There was, of course, no inquest, for the body was never found, but a jury could not have hesitated to return a charitable verdict. If not a case of mental alienation, they could not have made it worse than jelo de se (referred to probate), with extenuating circumstances. The beauteous Lola mourned for him sincerely, and was very generous to his family. Here, also, they became acquainted with Mr. F. Woodward, who, in the absence of their father, who returned to Buffalo, became for a time their agent.

(A Brief Sidebar):

Lola Montez c.1851
Born
Maria Dolores Eliza Rosanna Gilbert
17 February 1821
Grange, Sligo, Ireland
Died
17 January 1861 (age 39)

DARK SÉANCE—THE DAVENPORT BROTHERS

New York City, US
Nationality
Irish
Other names
Donna Lola Montez
Occupation
Dancer
Spouse(s)
Lieutenant Thomas James
George Trafford Heald
Patrick Hull
Partner(s)
Ludwig I of Bavaria

Marie Dolores Eliza Rosanna Gilbert, Countess of Landsfeld (17 February 1821 – 17 January 1861), better known by the stage name Lola Montez, was an Irish dancer and actress who became famous as a "Spanish dancer," courtesan, mistress of King Ludwig I of Bavaria, who made her Countess of Landsfeld. She used her influence to institute liberal reforms. At the start of the Revolutions of 1848 in the German states, she was forced to flee. She proceeded to the United States via Switzerland, France and London, returning to her work as an entertainer and lecturer.

Lola Montez portrait
by Josef Heigel before 1840

Lola Montez's
lithographie

DARK SÉANCE—THE DAVENPORT BROTHERS

Lola's mother, Eliza(beth) Oliver was the child of Charles Silver Oliver, a former High Sheriff of Cork and member of Parliament for Kilmallock in County Limerick. Their residence was Castle Oliver. In December 1818, Ensign Edward Gilbert met Eliza Oliver when he arrived with the 25th Regiment. They were married on 29 April 1820, and Lola was born the following February, refuting persistent rumors that her mother was pregnant with her at the time of the wedding. The young family made their residence at King House in Boyle, County Roscommon until early 1823, when they journeyed to Liverpool, thence departing for India on 14 March.

As with many other aspects of her life, discrepant reports of the birth of Eliza Gilbert have been published. For many years, it was accepted that she was born in the city of Limerick, as she herself claimed, possibly on 23 June 1818; this year was graven on her headstone, which seemed to make it the literal "last word". However, when her baptismal certificate came to light in the late 1990s, it was established that Eliza Rosanna Gilbert was actually born in Grange, County Sligo on 17 February 1821. She was baptized at St Peter's Church in Liverpool on 16 February 1823 while her family was en route to her father's post in India. As her mother's family was in County Limerick, it is not hard to see how little Eliza could have been told "We're from Limerick" and assumed that the city was meant.

Shortly after their arrival in India, Edward Gilbert died of cholera. Her mother, who was now 19, married another officer, Lieutenant Patrick Craigie, the following year. Craigie quickly came to care for little Eliza, but her spoiled and half-wild ways concerned him greatly.

Eventually, it was agreed she would be sent back to Britain to attend school, staying with Craigie's father in Montrose, Scotland, at first. But the "queer, wayward little Indian girl" quickly became known as a mischief-maker. On one occasion, she stuck flowers into the wig of an elderly man during a church service; on another, she ran through the streets naked.

At the age of ten, Eliza was moved on again – this time to Sunderland, England. When her stepfather's older sister, Catherine Rae, set up a boarding school in Monkwearmouth with her husband, Lola joined them to continue her education.[1]

Eliza's determination and temper were to become her trademarks. The little girl's stay in Sunderland lasted only a year, as she was then transferred to Bath for a more sophisticated education.

In 1837, 16-year-old Eliza eloped with Lieutenant Thomas James, and they married. The couple separated five years later, in Calcutta, and she became a professional dancer under a stage name.

She had her London debut as "Lola Montez, the Spanish dancer" in June 1843, but she had been recognized as Mrs. James. The resulting notoriety hampered her career in England and she departed for the Continent. At this time, she was almost certainly accepting favors from a few wealthy men, and was regarded by many as a courtesan.

Life as a courtesan.

Lola Montez (1847), painted by Joseph Karl Stieler for Ludwig I of Bavaria and his Schönheitengalerie

Lola Montez
(Gouache by Carl Buchner, 1847)

In 1844, Lola made an unsuccessful Parisian stage debut as a dancer in Fromental Halévy's opera, Le lazzarone. She met and had an affair with Franz Liszt, who introduced her to the circle of George Sand. After performing in various European capitals, she settled in Paris, where she was accepted in the rather Bohemian literary society of the time, being acquainted with Alexandre Dumas, père, with whom she was rumored to have had a dalliance. After the 1845 death of her lover, newspaperman Alexandre Dujarier, in a duel, unrelated to her, she left Paris.

In 1846, she arrived in Munich, where she was discovered by and became the mistress of, Ludwig I of Bavaria. The rumour was, at the time they met, Ludwig had asked her in public if her bosom was real. To which her response was to tear off enough of her garments to prove it. She soon began to use her influence on the king and this, coupled with her arrogant manner and outbursts of temper, made her unpopular with the local population (particularly after documents were made public showing that she was hoping to become a naturalized Bavarian citizen and be elevated to nobility). Despite the opposition, Ludwig made her Countess of Landsfeld on his next birthday, 25 August 1847. Along with her title, he granted her a large annuity.

For more than a year, she exercised great political power, which she directed in favor of liberalism, against the conservatives and the Jesuits. Her influence became so great that the ultramontane administration of Karl von Abel was dismissed because that minister objected to her being made Countess Landsfeld. The students of the university were divided in their sympathies, and conflicts arose shortly before the outbreak of the revolutions of 1848, which led the king, at Lola's instigation, to close the university. In March 1848, under pressure from a growing revolutionary movement, the university was re-opened, Ludwig abdicated, and Montez fled Bavaria, her career as a power behind the throne at an end. It seems likely that Ludwig's relationship with Montez contributed greatly to the fall from grace of the previously popular king.

After a sojourn in Switzerland, where she waited in vain for Ludwig to join her, she made one brief excursion to France and then removed to London in late 1848. There she met and quickly married George Trafford Heald, a young army cornet (cavalry officer) with a recent inheritance. But the terms of her divorce from Thomas James did not permit of either spouse's remarriage while the other was living, and the beleaguered newlyweds were forced to flee the country to escape a bigamy action brought by Heald's scandalized maiden aunt. The Healds resided for a time in France and Spain, but within two years, the tempestuous relationship was in tatters, and George reportedly drowned. In 1851 she set off to make a new start in the United States, where she was surprisingly successful at first in rehabilitating her image.

United States
Lola Montez in 1851, daguerreotype
by Southworth y Hawes

A caricature from the period showing Lola Montez leaving Europe for the United States.

From 1851 to 1853, she performed as a dancer and actress in the eastern United States, one of her offerings being a play called Lola Montez in Bavaria. In May 1853, she arrived at San Francisco. Her performances there created a sensation, but soon inspired a popular satire, Who's Got the Countess? She married Patrick Hull, a local newspaperman, in July and moved to Grass Valley, California, in August. This marriage soon failed; a doctor named as correspondent in the divorce suit brought against her was shortly after murdered. Montez remained in Grass Valley at her little house for nearly two years. The restored Home of Lola Montez went on to become California Historical Landmark No. 292. Montez served as an inspiration to another aspiring young entertainer, Lotta Crabtree. Lotta's parents ran a boarding house in Grass Valley, and Lotta soon attracted the attention of neighbor Montez, who encouraged Lotta's enthusiasm for performance.

Australia

In June 1855, Montez departed for a tour of Australia to resume her career by entertaining miners at the gold diggings during the gold-rush of the 1850s, arriving at Sydney on 16 August 1855.

Historian Michael Cannon claims that "In September 1855 she performed her erotic Spider Dance at the Theatre Royal in Melbourne, raising her skirts so high that the audience could see she wore no underclothing at all. Next day, the Argus thundered that her performance was 'utterly subversive to all ideas of public morality'. Respectable families ceased to attend the theatre, which began to show heavy losses." At Castlemaine in April 1856, she was "rapturously encored" after her Spider Dance in front of 400 diggers (including members of the Municipal Council who had adjourned their meeting early to attend the performance), but drew the wrath of the audience by insulting them following some mild heckling.

She earned further notoriety in Ballarat when, after reading a bad review in The Ballarat Times, she allegedly attacked the editor, Henry Seekamp with a whip. The "Lola Montes Polka" (composed by Albert Denning) is rumored to have been inspired by this event; however, the song was published in 1855 and the incident with Seekamp occurred months later in February 1856.

She departed for San Francisco on 22 May 1856[citation needed]. On the return voyage her manager was lost after going overboard.

Later life in the U.S.

Rapidly aging, Lola failed in attempts at a theatrical comeback in various American cities.

She arranged in 1857 to deliver a series of moral lectures in Britain and America written by Rev. Charles Chauncy Burr.

She spent her last days in rescue work among women. In November 1859, the Philadelphia Press reported that Lola Montez was living very quietly up town, and doesn't have much to do with the world's people. Some of her old friends, the

Bohemians, now and then drop in to have a little chat with her, and though she talks beautifully of her present feelings and way of life, she generally, by way of parenthesis, takes out her little tobacco pouch and makes a cigarette or two for self and friend, and then falls back upon old times with decided gusto and effect. But she doesn't tell anybody what she's going to do."

By then she was showing the tertiary effects of syphilis and her body began to waste away. At age 42 she died. She is buried in Green-Wood Cemetery, in Brooklyn, New York where her tombstone states: "Mrs. Eliza Gilbert / Died 17 January 1861"

Legacy

• Her life was portrayed in the 1922 German film Lola Montez, the King's Dancer. Montez is played by Ellen Richter.

• Lola Montez has been mentioned by several writers as a possible source of inspiration for the character Irene Adler in Arthur Conan Doyle's Sherlock Holmes story, "A Scandal in Bohemia". The character bears certain similarities to Montez in being a popular performer who influences national politics through her relationship with a powerful individual.

· Montez was portrayed by Martine Carol in the film Lola Montès (1955), based on the novel La Vie Extraordinaire de Lola Montès by Cecil Saint-Laurent, directed by Max Ophüls and co-starring Peter Ustinov and Oskar Werner.

· Montez was the last interpretation of Conchita Montenegro, in the film Lola Montes (1944), with a moralizing script, directed by Antonio Román.

· Montez's time in the Australian goldfields was the subject of the musical Lola Montez staged in Melbourne, Brisbane and Sydney in 1958 starring Mary Preston. The musical was liked by critics but did not become a commercial success. A recording of the musical was released on LP in 1958 in both mono and stereo versions.

    ·   Montez also appears in Royal Flash by George MacDonald Fraser, where she has a brief affair with Harry Flashman. She is also a character in the film of the same name, in which she is played by Florinda Bolkan.

    ·   Montez is featured prominently in Spider Dance by Carole Nelson Douglas, the last work in her Irene Adler mystery series. Montez is rumored to be the title character's mother.

    ·   She has been portrayed by Carmen D'Antonio in Golden Girl (1951), Sheila Darcy in Wells Fargo (1937), Yvonne De Carlo in Black Bart (1948), and Rita Moreno in an episode of the 1950s TV show Tales of Wells Fargo.

    ·   In one of J. B. Priestley's last fictional works, The Pavilion of Masks, she is unmistakably the original for Cleo Torres, Spanish dancer and mistress of a German prince.

    ·   Montez was allegedly the inspiration for Jennifer Wilde's historical romance novel Dare To Love (1978), whose protagonist Elena Lopez is also a British woman passing herself off as Spanish who becomes an exotic dancer. In the book, Elena has an affair with Franz Liszt, becomes friends with George Sand and has a friendship with the king of a small Germanic country obviously based on Ludwig I of Bavaria, then moves to California, all documented as having happened in Montez's life.

    ·   Montez is also the inspiration for Lola Montero in Edison Marshall's novel Infinite Woman.

    ·   In the 1983 television miniseries Wagner, Richard Wagner (Richard Burton), referring to the rumors surrounding his own relationship with Ludwig II, tells John Gielgud's character, "I am no Lola Montez!"

    ·   Trestle Theatre Company created a production entitled Lola about the life of Lola Montez.

    ·   Montez is described in Daughter of Fortune (original Spanish title Hija de la fortuna) by the Chilean-American author Isabel Allende.

DARK SÉANCE—THE DAVENPORT BROTHERS

· A feature film Spider Dance (2011) focuses on the latter years of Lola's life and her time in Australia.

· Musician Joanna Newsom's song and title track "Have One on Me" is about Lola Montez.

· The Danish band Volbeat has a song on their album Outlaw Gentlemen & Shady Ladies entitled Lola Montez. The lyrics reference the spider dance and the incident with Henry Seekamp.

· It has been asserted that the character "Lola" in the musical Damn Yankees was inspired by Lola Montez, but there is no evidence for this.

· The British/Irish writer Marion Urch based her epic historical novel An Invitation to Dance (Brandon 2009) on the life of Lola Montez. The novel has been published in the US, Russia (Arabesque) and Germany (Aufbau-Verlag).

• Lola Montez has two lakes (an upper and lower) named after her in the Tahoe National Forest in Nevada County, California.

• There is also a mountain named in her honor, Mount Lola. At 9,148 feet, it is the highest point in Nevada County, California.

(And now to continue):

Woodward entered upon this trust with very little, if any, faith in the reality of the manifestations. He presumed there was some trick about them; but as he could not discover it, he thought others would not, and so he consented to aid in what he thought must be a paying speculation.

On arriving at Newburyport, a beautiful seaport town of Massachusetts, north-east of Boston, the hotel at which they proposed to stop was so full that the only place they could get was a large attic, in which were a dozen or more double and single beds, arranged as in a ward in a hospital, a common enough thing in America, where the ball room of a tavern is filled with cot-beds, in crowded seasons.

In this large room, where there were already two lodgers, Mr. Woodward took one bed, and the two brothers another. Woodward, being purse-bearer, put the wallet containing his money under his pillow. When the light had been extinguished a little while, the bed on which the brothers reposed began to rock about like a boat on the waves, or jolted with the motion of a hard trotting horse. Woodward called out to know what was up. On being told, his curiosity was greatly excited, and he begged to be allowed to come to them, that he might feel, at least, what was being done.

He came, forgetting his wallet, but had no sooner laid down on the eccentric and demonstrative bed, than he heard his money jingling. He sprang to get it, but it was gone, and could nowhere be found. Then commenced a wild uproar in the room. Cords were broken, beds fell upon the floor, sheets and coverlids were torn in pieces, and the two strangers rose in a fright, dressed hastily, paid their bills, and went to find more quiet lodgings. The noise increased. Woodward felt strange hands seizing him. His wallet was restored as mysteriously as it had been taken. At last the landlord came up with a light, when everything became instantaneously as quiet as it had been tumultuous a moment before. He inquired the cause of the uproar. The young men could only protest that they had not made it. "Well, then," said the reasonable man, "I should like to know who did if you didn't. There is nobody else here, and this room is in a nice condition, I don't think."

"All we can say is that we have been perfectly quiet, and have not made the least noise or done any mischief."

As the two Davenports and Mr. Woodward gave the same assurance, the landlord was a little staggered, but returning common sense made him look about the room at his demolished furniture, and remark that they were, as far as he could see, the only persons who could have caused the damage he was already reckoning up to put in the bill, with serious doubts as to its speedy liquidation.

"We have told you all we know about the matter," said Ira, "but if you will blow out the candle, you may probably have a chance of judging for yourself."

Standing by the bed with the two boys and making sure of the presence of the equally astonished Woodward, the landlord blew out the light. The instant it was extinguished the contents of a feather bed were emptied over his head, and the hullaballoo began again worse than ever — ropes cracking, sheets tearing, and bedsteads crashing, until he felt his way to the door, escaped from the room, and rushed down stairs 'as if the devil was after him.'

When he had gone, things became peaceful, and the three companions were left to their repose. In the morning the great garret room was as fine a spectacle of a wreck as one could wish to see. The landlord's first impulse was to get his bill for damages paid, and then to get rid of his troublesome and alarming guests. Mr. Woodward paid the rather heavy bill — some sixty pounds for a night's lodging — and, at the urgent request of the landlord, they took their leave to another hotel. But the news spread, and the garret was visited that day by three or four hundred people.

Traveling eastward from Newburyport they came to Portland, the finest seaport in Maine, and one of the best on the Atlantic coast; a beautiful town, moreover, of 26,000 inhabitants, and the residence of John J. S.Teal, novelist and poet. Here the excitement and the interest to see them was very great, but they were not the less subjected to tests of an extraordinary character. To make sure that the phantom hands — I say phantom, though they are palpable as well as plainly visible — were not the hands of the Davenports (and it was made very certain that they could not be those of any other person) they were bound hand and foot, and to their seats, by two sea captains and two riggers, selected from the audience, who secured them with all the ingenuity and appliances of their craft. These adepts consumed not minutes merely but hours, at least hard upon two hours, in tying them. Their character was at stake, and they made very thorough work.

In spite of all this the manifestations proceeded as usual. While the two brothers were thus bound at each end of the cabinet as fast as human skill could bind, and the cabinet in which they were seated was watched on every side, above and beneath, by an eager crowd and a hard-headed committee, the doors were fastened on the inside not by a spring bolt, but by one that requires to be pushed by some force, and then began the ringing of bells, drumming on tambourine, tuning of violin and guitar, the appearance of hands and even of arms, and finally such a concert as could not have been played by less than three pairs of hands; at the end, or as a finale to which, the doors were suddenly thrown open, the instruments rolled and tumbled out upon the floor almost before the noises had ceased, and the committee and whole audience saw and felt that not a knot had been stirred, and that not one of the four hands of the two boys inside could by any possibility have been free for a moment, or have done any of the things that had been seen and heard.

In the audience was an officer of the State Lunatic Asylum, and when they were next to be secured, he proposed to do it, not by ropes, but by an apparatus he had brought with him for that purpose, and which was one for binding dangerous lunatics. This apparatus consisted in part of leather handcuffs, made so as to be as secure as those of steel, without being painful. As an additional security, the gentleman was allowed to be seated inside the cabinet between the boys, so that he could be sure, whatever was done, they had no hand in it. The doors closed — the centre-bolt shot of its own accord, and the instruments inside began their astonishing gyrations. I am not aware of what was done by the gentleman who was keeping watch and ward, but for some reason, or without a reason, he got a severe blow upon the nose, and came out very thoroughly convinced that neither of the boys had given it, and requiring no more striking proofs that there were forces, and perhaps beings in the universe, with which or whom he had not been previously acquainted.

Proceeding slowly through the state of Maine, in which they spent two years, visiting nearly every town of any importance, they came to Bangor, the great lumber mart and manufactory on the falls of the Penobscot river, at the head of navigation, a thriving, busy town, and full of the very cutest and smartest of down-east Yankees.

One of these, Mr. Darling, a prosperous master-carpenter, man of science, ingenious mechanic, who had made notable inventions, who was an energetic and leading man, and who, as a Swedenborgian, was well 'posted' in the matters not only of this world and its inhabitants, but of the 'heavens, and hells, and earths of the universe,' wrote a piece in a newspaper, denouncing the Davenport manifestations as utterly unworthy of any angels, demons, or spirits with whom he was acquainted, — and as a receiver of the faith and works of Swedenborg, he thought himself authorized to speak for them, — but an impudent and bungling piece of jugglery, which he engaged to expose, if they would submit to a test he would provide, without knowing it beforehand, so as to be able to circumvent it, under a penalty of three hundred dollars.

This challenge was at once accepted, and the town, of course, thrown into a fever of excitement. The newspapers took up the matter, as they must every matter which greatly interests the public, according to the great law of supply and demand. The town thought and talked of little else than the great match between the Swedenborgian master- carpenter and the Brothers Davenport. It may be doubted if even a presidential election would have made a greater excitement. There are usually two parties to an excitement, but I believe a majority of the people of Bangor expected to see the Davenports thoroughly exposed and put to open shame, and there v/as somewhat of the combined sensation of a trial and execution at the same time — as if the judge, after a conviction for murder, instead of drawing on the black cap and passing sentence, should call in the executioner and have the convict hanged, after the manner of Judge Lynch and drumhead courts-martial.

The night appointed came, and the hall was more than crowded — it was jammed. The brothers had no notion of the nature of the trial, and were, perhaps, as much astonished and as much amused as anybody, when Mr. Darling and his six confederates marched solemnly upon the stage, with a load of what seemed boxes, and ropes, which turned out, upon examination, to be really a very ingenious apparatus. The audience cheered as if the victory had been already won, and the few who believed in the manifestations were gloomy and perplexed. If they did not doubt, they feared.

Mr. Darling proceeded to adjust his apparatus. It consisted of long wooden tubes, two for the arms of each brother, fitting closely, and projecting three inches beyond the ends of their fingers. There were similar tubes for the legs. Holes had been bored in them, so that they could be fastened to the arms and legs, or otherwise secured. While Mr. Darling and his assistants were securing them, the Davenports aided them with suggestions, advising them to fasten the knots away from their teeth, and from experience instructing them how their limbs could be placed in more secure positions. This cool and quiet confidence greatly troubled Mr. Darling. He trembled with excitement. The perspiration rolled from his face. At last the operation was declared completed. Persons from the audience were invited to examine the fixtures.

DARK SÉANCE—THE DAVENPORT BROTHERS

They were decided to be "in a tight place" and the announcement was received with immense applause. Editors, preachers, and other skeptics, were in a state of ecstatic beatitude.

'Now, ladies and gentlemen,' said the agitated Mr. Darling, 'they are secure.' The house was hushed to silence. The two side-doors were closed and fastened, shutting in two-thirds of the cabinet, then the center door was shut, and instantly bolted on the inside — by whom?

Mr. Darling heard the sound with a consternation he could not conceal, but began to seal up the doors with sealing-wax, as if anyone could open them unobserved, under his eyes and the eyes of the whole assembly. Directly the instruments in the cabinet began to be played, hands and arms were displayed at an opening near the top of the centre door, the trumpet was thrown out of the cabinet, and then the doors suddenly opened, and the boys found as firmly secured as ever. The doors were closed again. A great rattling and whisking of ropes was heard for a few moments; the doors were opened, and the brothers stood up as free as when they had walked into the cabinet.

Now the applause came from the other side, with mocking cries of 'Darling, Darling!' Mr. Darling gave it up like a man. He had done his best. If anybody could do better, he was welcome to try.

Their success in Bangor was of course triumphant, as it was generally throughout the State, and wherever the people gave the phenomena a fair, or even unfair examination. An affidavit was drawn up, subscribed and sworn to by a number of leading and respectable citizens, who imagined that everybody would believe what they swore to, and of course they had the mortification of finding that their testimony had not the slightest weight with those who were determined that they would not believe, or whose minds were so constituted that they could not. It is said that belief is involuntary. It is certain that unbelief' or apparent unbelief, with strong and persistent denial, appears to be accompanied at times with great willfulness.

Mr. Darling, of Bangor, may have been converted, or have remained skeptical; but if he went away a believer, and expected any person who had not seen what he did, to believe it on his testimony, he was probably disappointed. The wife of his bosom may not improbably have said to him, 'My Darling, you are either a knave or a fool, or both together, to come and tell me such rubbish.' And she would have been considered a sensible woman, though indulging too much in her candour at the expense of her politeness.

FIG. 22. THE DAVENPORT BROTHERS IN THEIR CABINET.

The Fabulous DAVENPORT BROTHERS

CHAPTER ELEVEN
MORE WONDERS IN MAINE

A Riot and a Fight – "Capt. Henry Morgan, the Buccaneer" – Mr. Rand's Story – The Escritoire unlocked – Mrs. Rand's testimony.

These manifestations, as I may have mentioned, however triumphantly given, in spite of all the various tests to which they were submitted, were met everywhere with a more or less violent opposition. In large and orderly towns, the brothers were only denounced as charlatans, jugglers, and humbugs generally; in the smaller ones, and among ruder communities, they were sometimes assailed with open violence. Thus, while holding a séance in the town hall of the small seaport town of Orland, in Maine, Ira became conscious of an impending row, not as coming from the audience, but from 'outsiders;' and before they had far advanced in their operations, the doors were broken open by a rabble of drunken sailors and fishermen, who, it was afterwards said, had been hired by a zealous Methodist, with a hundred dollars, to drive them out of town.

The town-hall immediately became the scene of a desperate fight. Benches were torn up, windows smashed, women screamed or fainted, and all hands went in for a rough and tumble 'scrimmage,' in which the boys, of course, took part, and the assembly succeeded, at the expense of many broken heads, black eyes, and bloody noses, in beating off their assailants; but for that day, the manifestations were, of course, prevented, unless some took place during the melee.

The assaulting party was beaten off, but it might gather reinforcements and return; so they barricaded, armed themselves as well as they could, and waited. There was no second attack, and the assembly went to their homes.

"Well," I said to Mr. Ira Davenport, when he had got so far in the narrative of this affair, as I have substantially given it, "what happened then? Did you go away and try some less belligerent neighborhood?"

"No; we stayed there. 'Morgan' told us to go on."

"But a while ago it was 'John,' or 'John King,' who seemed to have the direction of your affairs."

"Yes, but at this time it was Henry Morgan, the buccaneer. We had some more séances, and from that time everything was perfectly quiet and satisfactory."

I am not sufficiently familiar with the life and character of Captain Henry Morgan to be able to say whether he was a likely person to manage such manifestations as were given in presence of the Brothers Davenport, but a bold buccaneer ought to be resolved in a fight. The things done require somebody, or something to do them, and that somebody or thing may call him-or it-self Henry Morgan, and we have no means of establishing an alibi, or in any way proving the contrary. This being the case, we will stick to the facts, and reserve the mooted point of identity for more mature consideration.

This visit or mission to the State of Maine was made in 1857. Among the persons with whom they became acquainted in this State was Mr. Luke P. Rand, who accompanied them on their return to Buffalo, and in their visits to various places. At Oswego, New York, in 1859, he published a pamphlet of sixty pages, containing his own observations and experience, connected with the manifestations. It is entitled 'A Sketch of the History of the Davenport Boys,' &c. He seems to have been — for I understand that he died some time ago — an honest, simple-hearted, zealous, religious man, and he quotes whole pages of Scripture to prove that whereas there were signs and wonders and marvels formerly, say from the creation down to a few centuries ago, there is a possibility of their occurring at the present day; though he would hardly go so far, I presume, as to claim that the beating on a tambourine by invisible hands, or by visible hands apparently not connected with living human bodies, was to be com- pared with a Scripture miracle.

I think Mr. Rand would have done better to have kept to his facts, of which he seems to have witnessed an abundance, and to have left alone both theories and Scripture. I am satisfied by internal and external evidence that he has made an honest statement of facts, and some of these I purpose to give, with the testimony of his wife, and others published in his pamphlet.

Mr. Rand, writing with great earnestness, and as far as I can judge with entire sincerity, says that 'scores and hundreds were permitted to feel the kindly and intelligent clasp' of a large and strong hand, growing out of space, or coming out of darkness, which he believed to be the hand of 'Henry Morgan,' and of other hands similarly produced, as in the case of Mr. Albro, already cited. Mr. Rand says, 'I have often felt, not only the clasp but the grasp of that hand, handling me as if I were a child, holding the grasp until the indentations of the pressure were clearly seen by the audience, when my hand was released from the spirit-hand, in full view, in the clear bright light. Often, within three seconds from the time we have seen the boys pinioned to their seats, beyond the possibility of release by themselves, has that hand, at a distance beyond their possible reach, clasped my own with a firm grasp, and thus been thrust forth into the full gaze of the audience. And many scores of others have felt the same grasp and had the same experience. . . The facts are so astonishing that we often find persons who are not only incapable of receiving the testimony of others, but unable also to rely upon the evidences of their own senses.

In the town of Milford, Maine, in the presence of twenty-five persons, a "secretary" (escritoire) was unlocked by invisible hands, and numerous articles taken out and distributed among the audience. In this case the key had been in the lock. The owner then placed the articles back, locked the "secretary," and placed the key in the hands of a gentleman present, selected for the trust. All persons in the room joined hands, so that each one was held by two others. The light was extinguished by one who was held, and we instantly heard the bolt of the lock slide, and the contents of the "secretary" were again distributed among our company, in perfect stillness.

A large spy glass was drawn out to its utmost extent, and brought far across the room over the heads of several persons, and placed, partly upon my head, and partly upon the head of a gentleman of Bangor, who sat next to me. The gentleman to whom the key was entrusted, held it in his hand all the time, and no person could have moved about the room, had there been such person, without being detected. This company was a selection of intelligent and candid persons, assembled there for the express purpose of testing these manifestations.

In the testimony of Mrs. Rand, as communicated to a newspaper of Oswego, New York, and afterwards published in this pamphlet, she says: "As one who has a right to speak of things she knows, will I make my solemn declaration. On or near the first of January 1858, I was called to attend a séance of these boys (Brothers Davenport) held in Bradley, Maine. A company of ladies and gentlemen were assembled, forming a double circle, the ladies being in the center, and the gentlemen in the rear; we all joined hands.

"Mr. Woodward invited us to sing; and we did so. Next a committee was chosen to tie the boys. When they were securely tied, the lights were extinguished, and sounds from the instruments in the box in which the boys were seated and tied, were heard. Tunes were played, in which could be distinguished the sounds of five different instruments — a guitar, tambourine, drum, violin, and bell. The bell was repeatedly rung outside the box, and touched some of the party on the shoulders and head, and then fell upon the floor. A hand was visibly protruded from a hole in the upper part of the box. The sounds were made to the last moment before the doors were opened, and the committee examined the boys, and reported that every knot in the rope was as they left it. It had taken the committee fifteen minutes to tie them."

* This exercise of singing is sometimes resorted to for the purpose, it is said, of harmonizing the circle.

"At Milford," continues Mrs. Rand – and here we come to some very curious experiences. I was invited by the presiding spirit, or what purported to be so," – observe that the lady means to be very careful in her statement – "to sit with the boys in the box. I accepted this invitation and was fastened to a seat between the boys by a rope around my wrists, and passing through an aperture in the seat that I might not be able to assist in the legerdemain. I saw the boys when I took my seat by them, and know they were fastened as securely as ropes and the strength of man could fasten them as only lions would need to be fastened for man to feel secure in their presence.

"Darkness! And as quick as that word can be spoken came a hand, large and strong, upon my head. Where did that hand come from? It was larger than the hands of either of the boys, and came quicker than they could have possibly been freed, had they ever so great dexterity. The audience were all seated with joined hands. Next, a large bell was drawn across my face. A guitar was placed in my lap, withdrawn, and replaced. A drum and other things were piled against me, and again the hand moved over my head, rested a moment on the back of my neck, when I distinctly felt the form of a wrist. Something was close to my hair, and a moment after, when the doors were thrown open, and the whole audience rushed to see what had been done, the ropes were all tied as strong as ever, but my comb was found twisted into Ira's hair. The doors were again closed, my comb was put back into my own hair, and the instruments were thrown around us.'

Mrs. Rand then quotes several passages of Scripture to show that miracles have been, and closes her testimony.

Mr. Rand accompanied the Brothers to Buffalo, and with them visited many places in New York, where he had some very extraordinary experiences, which I shall notice more particularly in their proper place.

I may also observe that here as elsewhere I have somewhat condensed the testimony of the witnesses, by throwing out superfluous expressions, but have in no way changed the purport of their language.

The Fabulous DAVENPORT BROTHERS

CHAPTER TWELVE
MORE PHYSICAL IMPOSSIBILITIES

A Bravo in the Cabinet – Jugglers and Conjurors – Domestic Manifestations – The necessary Conditions – Tables set by Invisibles – They eat Food like Mortals – Remarkable Testimony.

On their return from Maine towards Buffalo, the Brothers, accompanied by their friend Mr. Rand, arrived at Lowell, a manufacturing town in Massachusetts, often, from the number of its cotton mills, called the Manchester of America. Here they remained for four weeks, giving public and private séances, and creating, as everywhere, a great sensation. During this period a séance was arranged for twenty-five persons, and the boys were warned by their invisible confederates, this time by means of raps on a table, that there was a conspiracy to expose them. A man had been selected to enter the cabinet with them who had been a gambler and a bravo in San Francisco, where he had killed two men, and been half hanged himself under Judge Lynch, from whom he had been barely rescued. This dare devil was determined to fathom the mystery, and his friends stood by to assist him.

On being tied, not too securely, between the two boys, who were thoroughly fastened, he managed, by the aid of a dirk knife in his sleeve, to cut the rope and free his hands. At the instant he received a blow over the forehead, with a trumpet, which cut a deep gash, from which the blood spurted freely. He seized Ira, and found him tied securely as ever. He turned and grasped William, who was also closely bound. He called for light, and a dark lantern was thrust through the hole in the door, and by its light he saw that no one was in the cabinet but the two Brothers and himself, and that their fastenings had not been changed in the slightest degree. He opened the doors, and his friends seeing him wounded and covered with blood supposed he had been attacked and rushed forward to revenge him.

The bold, bad man was not a mean one. 'Stand back!' he shouted, 'these boys did not strike me — they did not touch me. Look for yourselves. There they are, bound exactly as you left them. Gentlemen, you can do as you like, but I have had enough of it.'

Another of the party, still unsatisfied, took his place in the box, to try the same game, but found himself so instantaneously seized by hands which he knew did not appertain to visible bodies that he became frightened and begged to be let out.

Going from Lowell to Boston, the Brothers Davenport found a man by the name of Bly pretending to expose them or their jugglery by cutting ropes and the aid of confederates. The brothers confronted him, claimed to be tested in the most thorough way by the persons who had seen the Bly performance and knew its methods, and were entirely successful. In eleven years, in America, where people are not wanting, at least, in shrewdness and inventive powers — in trickery, or the power of seeing into trickery — not only has no one ever advanced a plausible explanation on the hypothesis of fraud, sleight-of-hand, collusion, &c., but the most adroit conjurors — Mr. Herman, of New York, for example — have fully acknowledged that their art afforded no explanation. Indeed, they are as different as possible. Four persons out of five know how almost every trick of the jugglers is performed. They can be studied in books; their apparatus can be bought of the manufacturers, who instruct purchasers in the various tricks and illusions; they are advertised in the 'Times' newspaper.

Some jugglers, after doing certain tricks, explain the modus operandi. Juggling is a parlor amusement. But the things daily and nightly done in the presence of these young men, and in which it is made evident to everyone who has eyes and hands, and chooses to use them, that they have and can have no active agency, have never been explained on the hypothesis of legerdemain, illusion, or collusion, and it is quite certain that they never can be.

After leaving Boston, the Brothers visited Worcester, and Springfield, Massachusetts, Troy, Waterford, Saratoga Springs, Utica, and Rochester, in New York, and were joyfully welcomed home by their family and friends after their long absence. And here I may, as well as anywhere, give some account of the very peculiar manifestations, of what we may call a domestic character, which occurred at various times when they were at home, in the presence of their family and of familiar friends, when all the conditions may be supposed to have been favorable to their manifestations.

The first of these conditions appears to be darkness. Why darkness should favor these operations, or why light should hinder them, it may be difficult to explain: we may be content with the fact. Total darkness, it has been seen, is not always necessary; but the greater part seem to require at least a partial obscurity. For some reason, the belief that supernatural manifestations are more proper to night and darkness than to the open light of day, has existed always and everywhere.

Quiet, harmony, and the isolation of the persons who seem in some way necessary to the operation of the generally invisible forces, are readily obtained in a home circle.

In these family parties, when it was desired to give their friends an opportunity to see other than the usual manifestations, and when every precaution had been taken to secure the necessary conditions, and also to exclude the shadow of suspicion, or even of doubt, from the mind of any; when everything had been arranged, and the lights were extinguished, a curious performance would commence. The table would be drawn out into the centre of the room, the table-cloth spread, the dishes brought from the pantry, fifteen feet distant, the table set, tea made, bread cut, and the slices buttered, and then tea poured out for the party. While this was doing, there were heard noises like the rustling of women's garments. Once, when Mr. Davenport, Senior, was sitting tilted back on the hind legs of his chair in an American fashion, he was suddenly thrown over backward. Afterwards, a communication was rapped out by the alphabetic telegraph, in which a lady begged to apologize for the accident, caused, as she said, by the hoops of her 'crinoline' having accidentally caught under the raised leg of the chair in passing.

If one thing were more strange, or inexplicable, or incredible than another in all this history, I confess that I might hesitate at giving the following narration, which I have received from the lips of the Brothers Davenport, and which I find confirmed in the pamphlet of Mr. Rand. It is proper to say, also, that I have had from as credible people as I am acquainted with, scores of similar narratives. Such may be found abundantly in a recent work by the celebrated William Howitt, and also in a meritorious book by Thomas Brevior, which is quite a compendium of preternatural manifestations and experiences.

Mr. Rand also testifies to something which may be harder to swallow than the fact of tables and dishes setting themselves, and supper getting itself ready, or being got ready by invisible hands. It is, that these mysterious intelligences eat — eat like common mortals, and appear to relish their food, and have good appetites, and, it is to be hoped, good digestions. At all events, if we believe the testimony, the food disappears; and, hard as this may be to believe, it is not more difficult than what I have witnessed in London, and what has been witnessed by hundreds, as will be recorded in its proper place.

Mr. Rand, writing at Oswego, New York, in 1859, where he was with the Brothers Davenport, says: —

'Within the last few weeks a new order of manifestations has been introduced. Spirits [this is the name which Mr. Rand chooses to give to invisible intelligences, or mysterious intelligent forces, and it may be as good as another] have

DARK SÉANCE—THE DAVENPORT BROTHERS

spoken with audible voices, in the light, without a trumpet, as we have rode or walked by the way, and exhibited hands, placing them upon our persons, and handling us freely. [If Mr. Rand, by the plural pronouns, simply meant himself, this testimony would not be of much worth; as what only one person sees, hears, or feels may be readily referred to imaginary or other illusions; but I do not understand him as claiming to have seen or heard any such thing when not in the presence of the Brothers Davenport.] Spirits have also eaten food in our presence; cake, fish, boiled corn [maize], pineapple, and other fruits. We [here he clearly speaks of more persons than one] have usually placed the food upon the table, darkened the room, provided against any deception; then taking our seats around the table — near it or distant from it, as the case might be — the spirits have freely eaten, and talked to us the while. Six or eight ears of corn [green maize, boiled] have often been eaten in this way at one time, and in some instances much more, together with fruits and other food. Of this we have had proof, as the spirits have often brought the corn to us, and requested us to partake with them.

'On one occasion,' continues Mr. Rand, 'a party of gentlemen came to witness this, and brought thread to tie the Brothers Davenport. They were first secured firmly by ropes, then the thread was added; after which the boys' mouths were muzzled. Bandages were also put upon the mouths of all persons in the room. The pineapple was then sliced and placed upon a stool entirely removed from the boys, when it was eaten by unseen visitors, who were heard in their merry repast, and the rinds of the pine-apple were found dropped at their pleasure [sic] at the close. There are plenty of witnesses to these facts, whose names can be given to those who apply to Rufus Briggs, of this city (Oswego, New York). For the satisfaction of any who may wish for evidence on this matter, we give the names of a portion of the persons present when the Davenports were tied with ropes, and further secured with thread and muzzled, and yet food was eaten [disappeared ?] in their presence.'

The names given are —
'Philander Rathbux,
John Knapp,
Samuel Reynolds,
David Fairchild,
Rufus Briggs.'

It might be worthwhile for some person to write a letter to Oswego, directed to either of these gentlemen, enquiring if these things happened as here related.

Mr. Rand is satisfied that what he calls 'spirits' do really eat food like common mortals, and he makes the following statement in proof.

'An Indian spirit has often brought from the table to me an ear of corn (maize or Indian corn), inviting me to eat of the same with him, which I have often done. He has taken my hand, placed my fingers between his teeth, and given me sensible evidence of their reality. He has placed my hand upon his head, so that I could feel its form, and his long straight hair, most sensibly. And others have had this same experience, and the world will know that these are facts.'

I have no question of the perfect sincerity of this statement, but it will be doubted by many whether all necessary precautions were taken against deception. On the other hand, it does not appear that there was any disposition or motive to deceive. The pamphlet does not seem to have been written in the interest of the Davenports, or for any purpose but to enable Mr. Rand to give to the world what he seems to have believed were important truths.

As to the disappearance of material objects, as in this case, those who know most of matter will have least difficulty. Destroy certain forces, or suspend their operation, and all material forms become as nothing. Loose the attraction which holds in their places the atoms of a globe of steel, or the great globe itself, and they would become invisible gases. In truth, we know so little of matter, and it is so difficult to prove that matter exists, that the most advanced physicists of the present day are disposed to consider all material forms as nothing more than modifications of force. Abolish matter, and we have nothing left but force and its governing intelligence.

The Fabulous DAVENPORT BROTHERS

CHAPTER THIRTEEN
THE IMPRISONMENT IN OSWEGO

Mr. Rand and his Testimonies – Strong tests at Oswego – Prosecution and Imprisonment – An Astonished Jailer – The Prison door unlocked without visible hands – Declaration and Affidavit.

I now proceed to give some account of the adventures of the Brothers Davenport in Oswego, New York, and its vicinity, as contained in the pamphlet of Mr. Rand, their 'guide, philosopher, and friend,' from which I have made some extracts in the preceding chapter, including a small persecution, and a rather remarkable martyrdom. Mr. Rand had made the acquaintance of the Brothers Davenport during their visit to Maine, and appears to have become very familiar with the mysterious forces, powers, intelligences, or whatever they may be, who, or which, according to their own testimony, are engaged in the production of the astonishing phenomena which will be found imperfectly described in these pages.

Mr. Rand chooses to call these powers, forces, or intelligences, 'spirits' — I do not know upon what authority, and have some doubt of the strict propriety of the term, as applied to beings that have hands which grasp, teeth which bite, and who eat hearty suppers of boiled Indian corn and pineapples. This, however, is a mere verbal criticism.

"Words and names are not of much consequence, if we understand what is meant by them; and Mr. Rand has a right to use his own designations so long as he states the facts correctly and honestly to the best of his knowledge and belief, and that he does this I see no reason to question. He says: 'The boys came into our vicinity, and we were invited to attend their circles, and became deeply interested in the manifestations. The circles at which we made our first acquaintance with them were held in Orono (our residence), Old Town, and Bradley. I mention these places because the Davenports spent nearly a year at this locality, making it their home for the time – holding many circles, both in public and private, during their stay here, in the midst of a large circle of their friends, who had every opportunity of becoming acquainted with the boys, and the manifestations given through

111

them. We also made the acquaintance of the spirits; they seemed like familiar friends — they talked much with us and to us— they came to our homes, and talked familiarly with us and our children, often shaking us by the hand, often passing their hands upon our brows and upon our persons, handling and freely playing upon musical instruments, five and more, even, at the same instant of time, and giving the most unmistakable and absolute positive demonstration of their presence and power in a great variety of other ways and modes of communication."

I will give the remainder of the testimony of Mr. Rand, as to what he witnessed at public and private séances in the city of Oswego, and then condense from his very remarkable pamphlet the account of their persecution, arrest, trial, and imprisonment in Oswego, with the release of Mr. Rand from prison by supernatural, or if the word is preferred, preternatural agency, with the sworn affidavit of all the witnesses to this very striking manifestation, which is just as incredible, impossible, and true, as all the other phenomena described in this volume.

"At a large and stormy audience in the city of Oswego," says Mr. Rand, "a committee, selected from that audience, tied and worked upon these Davenport boys more than one hour, putting on all the rope we then had, about ninety feet, though we have often carried one hundred and fifty-feet, and twenty-seven feet of strong cord furnished by the audience. To this we submitted, to satisfy the audience; and then the younger boy's knots were firmly wound and secured by new and strong copper wire, bent and twisted on with forceps. This we also allowed for the test; and then the doors of the box were sealed with wax and private seals, and every avenue by which anyone could approach the box was guarded by sentinels. Then were the lights extinguished, and the older boy was untied in eleven minutes – every knot. He was taken out and held by the committee, and the younger boy examined, and the knots and fastenings found all secure. The box was again closed, and the younger boy left alone. He was released from his bonds of ropes, knots, and twisted wires in eight minutes."

To suppose the possibility of a slight youth of nineteen, with no instruments, and firmly bound with ropes and wires, hand and foot, on his seat and to his seat, shut up in darkness, and unaided, freeing himself, by first untwisting copper wires twisted on with forceps, and then untying more than a hundred feet of rope and cord, when it was not in his power to make the least movement toward such an operation, is, to speak very mildly, exquisitely absurd.

The next test, as described by Mr. Rand, ought also to be considered satisfactory – if people, in such a case, could be satisfied. He says:

"At a private circle of about forty persons, in the city of Oswego, the Davenport boys, with Wm. M. Fay, who took a seat with them, were all fastened at the extremes of a very long and large table, with strong fine cotton thread, wound closely round their wrists, and tied in many knots, each wrist of each boy being wound many times, and closely tied in many knots each time, and then the threads on either side of each lad carried out a few inches, tied in a knot at the end, and tacked down to the table by a common tack, and that knot and tack sealed with wax. This was faithfully done by a committee. All had an opportunity to look upon the knots and seals, and all knew it was utterly impossible for either boy to move his hand without breaking the threads. The instruments were then laid in the middle of the table, far beyond the possible reach of the boys. The audience were then all tied together by ropes and cords, so that no one could move without the knowledge of others, and then, on extinguishing the light, those instruments were taken up and borne about the room and over our heads, and thrummed and played by some intelligent hands other than our own. This was certain, as instantly on lighting the gas we found the boys, in every instance, firmly tied and immovably secure."

The William M. Fay here mentioned is a young man of about the same age as the Brothers Davenport, and appears to be endowed with, or attended by, similar powers. He was born in Buffalo, of German parents, and one of the first evidences he gave of being attended by extraordinary manifestations was, when playing with other boys, being raised bodily from the ground, and lodged in a neighboring tree, in sight of his companions. He joined the Brothers Davenport during their visit to Oswego; and his name will often appear in the future pages of this narrative.

While on this celebrated visit to Oswego, an important town near the eastern extremity of Lake Ontario, with water-power, mills, commerce, and a population of 17,000 inhabitants, the Brothers Davenport accepted an earnest invitation to visit a small village, named Phoenix, twenty miles from Oswego. At this place, while giving a private séance, they were arrested, at the instigation of some persons whom Mr. Rand describes as 'legal bigots and persecutors,' who, 'with fiendish exultation,' conducted them before the village magistrate, where they were charged with violating a municipal law which provides that persons exhibiting shows, circuses, menageries, &c., should procure a license. The Brothers had never thought of complying with this formality, licenses not being required for concerts, lectures, and similar entertainments. Their séance was a concert, so far as the playing on musical instruments by invisible, or very slightly visible, performers, was concerned; a lecture, as to the explanations of Mr. Rand; and as to the tying and untying of knots, moving of ponderable bodies by invisible forces, &c., it may have been considered as philosophical experiments. Only on the hypothesis that they were jugglers, or sleight-of-hand performers, could they be fined for neglecting to procure a license.

Mr. Rand undertook to defend his own case, and I do not see that his efforts disproved the proverb so dear to the learned profession of the law, which says that 'a man who pleads his own cause has a fool for a client.' He made a speech filled with scriptural quotations, and resting upon the facts of the case. He should have proposed a séance then and there, with the magistrate to superintend the tests and operations. They were fined thirteen dollars and thirty-nine cents – say, two pounds fifteen shillings – or in default, to suffer one month's imprisonment at the county jail in Oswego.

As this fine was considered by Mr. Rand and the Brothers Davenport – and, what was considerably more important to them, the intelligences who directed their movements, and who told them not to pay a farthing — a sort of religious persecution, they became, in a mild way, martyrs to the truth, and, refusing to pay the fine, were taken to prison. Of course, their friends were aroused; those who believed in them were indignant, and the general public was greatly excited.

On arriving at the jail at Oswego they were met by their friends, and the first thing done after entering the prison was to give a séance, for the benefit of the jailer, who was as curious as the rest of the world to witness the manifestations. His mode of procedure also, in choosing satisfactory tests, was highly original and effective; and here let me copy from the pamphlet of Mr. Rand, which was published on the spot, which appeals to a whole community of witnesses, and which has never, to my knowledge, been invalidated. The account says:

"The jailer, having expressed his willingness [to witness some manifestations], adjusted iron handcuffs to the boys' wrists, and made them fast to the iron bars in the door of the cell; a trumpet, furnished for the occasion, was then placed back into the cell, beyond the possible reach of the Brothers Davenport, their hands being fastened in an elevated position by the handcuffs to the iron bars of the cell doors, the boys standing in the cell. The cell was then made dark, by a cloth being put up at the bars of the door.

"Then the trumpet was taken from the back part of the cell where it had just been placed, and brought to the bars of the door, and beat upon them; and a voice spoke through the trumpet familiarly, holding an intelligent conversation with us who stood without the door of the cell, in relation to the circumstances under which we had come to the jail — stating to R. Briggs [the Eufus Briggs heretofore mentioned], who was present, that he [the voice] would not have their friends outside get excited, as if we were to be let out of the jail immediately: that there was a purpose to be executed in relation to our coming to prison, and that we were to remain there."

Was the jailer convinced by this manifestation? It appears not. He did not understand it, and, taking refuge in his ignorance, said: "It was a matter for scientific investigation!" Not bad for a jailer; but Mr. Rand was indignant at such an answer, and that any man could doubt that the power which brought the trumpet, to the cell door and then spoke through it was any other than an intelligent being. There was no question about the phenomena. The two young men were alone in the cell, fast handcuffed to the bars of the door; and the trumpet came itself, or was brought, and words were spoken. As to the words there may have been some chance for doubt; but I agree with the jailer that the trumpet, at least, required scientific investigation; though of what nature may be a question. Perhaps judicial investigation would be better.

While confined in this jail, at first in cells, and later in a larger and more comfortable room, they had a great number of visitors, and gave many séances, which there was no disposition to hinder, as they were not imprisoned for any crime, but merely for refusing to pay a fine, wrongly inflicted, as they believed, for a supposed disregard of a municipal regulation. About five or seven days before the expiration of their term they were directed to settle their affairs and hold themselves in readiness. This direction came from whatever intelligence held communication with them, and some of their friends were told that they might be expected to be set free in an unusual manner. The jailer became interested, and enquired why the mysterious forces, so worthy of 'scientific investigation' did not unlock their prison doors. Mr. Rand says that, from what he — the jailer — had seen, he seemed to believe that they could do it. However, he put a new lock on the door, determined to do his duty in every emergency.

The last night came. They were all together in the room, Mr. Rand and the two Brothers Davenport, and he took the boys by the hand and talked like a father to them. The jailer came to the door of the room at the usual locking-up time, and asked if they were all there. 'We answered promptly to the call that we were.' He put on a new lock which they had never seen.

"Then," says Mr. Rand, "immediately, sooner than we expected, a voice spoke in the room and said that I was to go out that night. I was told to put on my coat and hat and be ready. It was oppressively warm in our small room, with the window and door both closed, and I asked if I could be allowed to sit with my coat off, as I did not expect we should be released for more than an hour; but the answer was: 'Put on thy coat and hat and be ready.' Immediately, not more than twenty minutes from the time we were locked up, the door was thrown open, and a voice said, 'Now, go quickly. Take with you the rope (one which had been in the room), go to yonder garret window, and let thyself down and flee from this place; we will take care of the boys. There are many angels present, though but one speaks.'

"The boys came out with me into the hall, took up the lock which lay upon the floor, and for the first time examined it, and spoke of its being warm. They were told [by the voice] to return to the room, and the door was closed and locked again."

Mr. Rand, having made his way out of the jail, expected the boys to follow him. He told a friend whom he met that they were coming, and wrote the same to his wife, who was then in Massachusetts. It never occurred to him that the door was relocked. He says solemnly: 'It matters not to me what force these statements may have in the minds of others; I make them because they are true. Before God and man I make them, and shall make them while I exist; and, thanks be to God on high, I am not alone in this testimony.'

The boys, Mr. Rand came to think, were not allowed to go out, because people would not believe; and they might have been again imprisoned for making their escape. 'There are those,' he mournfully says, 'who cannot believe, who cannot entertain facts from human testimony. It is with them, as when, in a strange locality, the sun rises in the wrong place. They cannot make it seem right.'

Even the jailer was cruel enough to charge Mr. Rand, when he went back to the jail, with having deceived him, and not being in the room when he came, with a new lock and extra care, to lock them in for the night. This was a rather lame excuse for the jailer, for it was his most special business to have known that these prisoners, at least, were locked up safely. If the jailer, whose business it was to know, and with all his experience of the trumpet manifestation, and others, when he had himself manacled the boys to the cell door, could not believe that his strong lock had been unfastened and fastened again by that power which Mr. Rand believed "was nothing else than the strong spirit-hand of Henry Morgan," what credence could be expected of "outsiders" who had had no such experience? The more wonders – and the greater the wonders – proclaimed of these Brothers, the louder, of course, would rage the storm of abuse, and the stronger would be the accusations of jugglery and imposture. After all, there was no proof of the unlocking and relocking of the door, and the preternatural escape of Mr. Rand, but his own declaration and that of the only two witnesses, corroborated by the fact that the jailer ought to have known, and believed he did know, that he had locked them all three into the room with more than usual care. These declarations they made in the most solemn form possible, and under the sanction of an oath, taken before two magistrates, as follows:

"Declaration and Affidavit.

"Be it known to all people, that in the seventh month A.D. 1859, Ave, the undersigned were imprisoned in the common jail, in the city of Oswego, N.Y., on account of propagating our religious principles, and that after twenty-nine days of our confinement, at evening, when we were all in our prison-room together, as we had just been locked in by the jailer, we having truly answered to his call, a voice spoke and said: 'Rand, you are to go out of this place this night. Put on your coat and hat and be ready.'

"Immediately the door was thrown open, and the voice again spoke and said: 'Now walk quickly out and onto the attic window yonder and let thyself down by a rope and flee from this place. We will take care of the boys. There are many angels present, though but one speaks.' The angelic command was strictly obeyed.

"That this, and all this, did absolutely occur in our presence, we do most solemnly and positively affirm before God and angels and men.

'Subscribed and sworn before me, this 1st day of August, 1859.

(Signed)

'James Barnes,

Justice of the Peace.

'Ira Erastus Davenport.

'Luke P. Rand.

'Subscribed and sworn before me by

William Davenport, this 5th day of August, 1859.

'W. B. Bent,

'Justice of the Peace.

'William Davenport.'

Are we to believe that these three men have added to imposture lying, and to lying perjury? Or were they themselves the victims of some delusion?

No one is certain what the disposition was of the valet for the Davenports who was supposedly "scared to death."

The Fabulous DAVENPORT BROTHERS

CHAPTER FOURTEEN
TO THE MISSISSIPPI AND BACK TO THE ATLANTIC

Fastening a Committee – Sewed in Sacks – Social Science Congress in Michigan – Beating the Telegraph at Chicago – Bombardment of Fort Sumter – Dark Lanthorns in the Dark Circle* — A Fight with a Specter – A Confederate discovered – Washington and Baltimore – Riots and Prosecutions.

A dark lantern is a candle lantern with a sliding shutter so that it may conveniently be made dark without extinguishing the candle (archaically, dark lanthorn).

After a brief stay at their home in Buffalo, to which they returned after the events narrated in the last chapter, the Brothers Davenport commenced a tour westward by the southern shore of Lake Erie. At the beautiful town of Cleveland, Ohio, where their weird exhibitions were attended by large assemblages, an unusually hard-headed committee, in spite of the usual tests, persisted in the theory of legerdemain, and proposed on the next evening to bring tests which should satisfy everybody.

This being agreed to, a greater crowd than ever came to assist at the trial. The Brothers were bound with cords to their seats in the cabinet. Then their wrists were tied together with shoemaker's waxed thread. Next, silk tapes were fastened around their wrists and fingers and sealed with sealing-wax. The musical instruments were then lashed to the middle seat of the cabinet quite beyond their reach.

When all was completed the Brothers, accustomed to the shifts and subterfuges of committees, insisted upon a public acknowledgment that they were satisfied with the tests. It was made. 'Is there any loop-hole, any way to back out?' they asked. 'None whatever,' was the answer. The doors were closed and instantly the music began to play, the bell to ring, hands were protruded, and manifestations made of an unusually startling character: the doors were opened, and seals, tapes, and strings were unbroken. The committee, if not satisfied, was confounded.

At Akron, Ohio, the test demanded, as perfectly satisfactory, was that after being bound as securely as the ingenuity of the committee could effect it, the Brothers should be carefully and strongly sewed up in sacks; and this they also submitted to with the usual result.

Similar scenes, perpetually varied, but with the same general results, attended the visits to Columbus, the State Capital, Xenia, Dayton, etc.

At Lyons, Michigan, where they were invited to attend a convention of people interested in psychological phenomena – a sort of Social Science Congress, differing somewhat from that presided over by Lord Brougham – after gratifying large assemblies for three nights they were again prosecuted for giving performances without a license. The justice before whom they were taken proved to be a man of sense, and dismissed the charge, saying that the law did not apply to them, and if what they averred was true they should not be persecuted, while, if it was an imposture, persecution would only spread it the faster.

At the great lake city of Chicago, Illinois, they gave for some time séances limited as to numbers, alternating with large assemblies, with bindings by ship-riggers, flour tests, etc., such as have been described elsewhere.

This was in April 1861, and in the midst of a séance, a voice speaking through the trumpet announced the beginning of the bombardment of Fort Sumter, nearly a thousand miles distant. An hour or so later the same news came in due course by telegraph. Had the manifestation ended here it might be considered a lucky guess or a remarkable coincidence, but the news of the events of this famous siege came hour by hour, and day by day, and always in advance of the telegraph, owing to the time taken by the latter in repeating messages.

There were two excited crowds in Chicago filling the streets, greedy for news, one at the telegraph station, another at the rooms of the Brothers Davenport; and the news by the Davenport telegraph not only came sooner but was more accurate. This was notably shown when the electric telegraph announced that the Confederate floating battery had been knocked in pieces by the guns of Fort Sumter. The trumpet voice denied that any such thing had happened. Bets were made on the result, and when later news came the Davenports were found right, as usual.

At one of the smaller towns in Illinois one of the visitors, determined to know who really performed the wonders done in the dark circle, brought under his clothes a dark lanthorn, intending to open it when the instruments were flying about. The light was extinguished, but instead of the usual sounds raps were heard upon the table calling for the alphabet, and the fact of the presence of the dark lanthorn made known. Upon its being found and ejected the expected manifestations commenced.

The next night three dark lanthorns were brought by as many persons, with the idea that if one were suspected and detected the others, or certainly one of them, might remain. Light out, and, as before, raps for alphabet. Lanthorn! One was found and put out. Darkness again. Raps again. Lanthorn! A second one was found. The same process was repeated, and the last lanthorn put out, but not before it had burnt the clothes of the man who had so dishonorably tried to conceal it. Then everything went on as usual.

The result of striking a match or showing a light suddenly, while the musical instruments are circling rapidly in the air, I ought to say here, perhaps, is their instant release from the controlling power. They fly with more or less velocity in the direction in which the propelling force was acting at the moment. In this way the instruments are sometimes broken, and persons who may be in the way of their flight are seriously injured. This happens at times, but in a less degree, when the persons holding hands let go in the midst of a manifestation. A match was struck at Newcastle-on-Tyne, with such results as I have mentioned; but as a test, though dangerous, it was perfect, for while the instruments were seen to fall to the floor in different directions, no one was seen who could have directed their motions.

At Iowa City, west of the Mississippi, handcuffs were proposed instead of ropes, and accepted; but handcuffs are more liable to suspicion than ropes, and less satisfactory. A clever mechanician could make handcuffs which could be opened without the key, while ropes, knots, and seals everyone can more easily judge of.

At Davenport, Iowa, 'Lanthorn' was spelt out again, and as the person who had it would not avow himself, his name was spelt out by raps on the table. Of course this might have been contrived for effect, but it very certainly was not. It was here that a man brought a test of his own invention — plates of tinned iron, with holes for the thumb and fingers, which were tied in their places by twine; but, as often happens, when his test had been accepted, and had failed to detect the imposition he expected to defeat, he was still unsatisfied.

At Keokuk, Iowa, the mayor compelled them to pay a license-fee of twenty dollars a night. "If you were a party of Negro minstrels," said he, "I would give you a license for two dollars. I would ask you fifty if I could. I would rather have given a hundred than you should have come here; and I will give you a hundred out of my own pocket if you will go away." Why?

One night at St. Louis, Missouri, in the midst of the dark séance, a violent scuffle, accompanied by heavy blows, was heard in the open space in the middle of the circle, while the musical instruments were careering through the air. A light was struck; and on the floor lay a young man, almost senseless, with his head covered with bruises, and by his side lay a knife and battered trumpet. The Brothers Davenport were bound to their chairs, the circle was unbroken, except by the absence of this young man, who, according to his own story, being determined to solve the mystery, had rushed forward when he heard the sounds, armed with his knife. A strange contest ensued in which he was beaten by some antagonist whom he could not clutch, while every cut and stab he gave with his knife was at the empty air, and he was finally knocked down to all appearance with the trumpet that lay beside him.

At Louisville, Kentucky, on the Ohio River, an old steamboat captain tied the Brothers with tarred rope so brutally that the audience hissed him, and then put on iron handcuffs, but was no nearer the solution of the mystery.

Voyaging eastward to the Atlantic seaboard, the Brothers Davenport visited Philadelphia, in Pennsylvania, the second city in the United States. Here they met with violent opposition from several quarters—from the philosophers, the religious bigots, the spiritualists, and the rabble who cared for nothing but to make a row. It required fifty policemen to keep order. In spite of this the most extraordinary manifestations were given, and many curious tests resorted to.

One night a famous skeptic, in whose sagacity the people seemed to have great confidence, was chosen with remarkable unanimity as one of a committee to examine and report upon the manifestations. He had come fully prepared. He tied them with the greatest care, and then, to make his knots secure, wound them with annealed wire, which he made fast by twisting with a pair of forceps.

"Are you satisfied?" asked Ira.

"Yes, perfectly satisfied."

"Will you be satisfied if the manifestations take place as usual?"

"Yes, certainly."

"No, you will not; or if you are your friends will not, and before you leave this room somebody will charge you with being our confederate."

The man was indignant at such a supposition. He knew his popularity, and believed that if he could be satisfied everybody who knew him would be also. He was not long in finding the contrary. When the audience was passing out Mr. Ira heard him having high words and almost coming to blows with a man who accused him of having aided in what he believed to be an imposture.

At Washington, the Federal capital, the Brothers Davenport gave a series of séances at Willard's Hall, which were attended by most of the distinguished men connected with Congress and the Government. One night a flourishing personage got elected on the committee, who began by making a speech to the audience, telling them he had long wished for an opportunity to expose this gross imposture, by which so many even intelligent people had been deceived. At last he had the opportunity, and they would soon see one more humbug exploded.

Then he tied the young men until he was satisfied. The doors were closed. He was watching eagerly very near them. A hand came through the aperture, seized him by the hair, and pulled his head this way and that with more violence than was comfortable. The doors were thrown open, and it was evident that the only visible occupants of the cabinet were bound fast as ever.

The ambitious committee-man was not satisfied. He came next night with some hundreds of feet of tarred rope, and covered them from head to foot with a complete network. When it was fastened he took out twenty dollars in greenbacks, which he promised to give to the Sanitary Commission, if unsuccessful. The result was the same as before, and the commission twenty dollars richer by the operation.

In Baltimore, Maryland, the Brothers had large and orderly assemblies; they submitted to the most convincing tests, and the manifestations were more perfect, various, and powerful than in almost any other American city. This fact may, I believe, be scientifically accounted for.

In one of the towns of New Jersey a committee-man secretly daubed some of the knots in the ropes with printer's-ink. When the 'phantom hands' were pushed through the opening, one of them was seen playing for a moment round his face. The excited committee-man turned to the audience to explain the circumstance, when he was astonished by 'a most inordinate roar of laughter.' His face was completely smeared with the ink. The hands of the Davenports were not in the least blackened.

In visiting some of the wild and lawless western villages, ignorance and fanaticism, unrestrained by a police, sometimes caused disorders, and even riots of a threatening character, as well as more legalized forms of persecution. In Richmond, Indiana, for instance— where, from there being a large Quaker population, the Davenports expected to have a quiet time — there was a most violent opposition. When novel tests had failed — when creosote secretly rubbed upon the instruments could not be smelt upon the hands of any, and only violence was left to those who opposed the manifestations which they could not disprove, the lights were put out, benches smashed, women frightened, revolvers drawn, and, finally, preparations made to administer to the Brothers the favorite American remedy for any kind of heterodoxy ever since the Revolution of 1776: tarring and feathering.

The boys, their father, and Mr. Lacy (who then accompanied them as lecturer) were rescued from the mob separately by some courageous women, who, under the obscurity of night, took them away, making them pass for their protectors; and they all met, strangely enough, at the same house, some distance in the country, while a raging mob was searching for them, with yells and threats, until three o'clock in the morning.

As late as November 1860 they were threatened with violence, at the Armoury Hall, at Coldwater, Michigan. With a sword snatched from the wall in one hand, and a knife in the other, the elder brother kept the mob at bay, until they took refuge in the hotel, and when threatened there by a larger mob defended the staircase with a revolver, fortunately without the necessity of bloodshed. A vexatious prosecution for using arms in self-defense, and for giving an entertainment within two miles of a religious meeting, ended in nothing.

These prosecutions, some of which have been alluded to, notably the one attended by imprisonment and the release of Mr. Rand at Oswego, were troublesome, costly, and vexatious. There were eleven in all, a few of which resulted in small fines, and when these were resisted, in imprisonment.

During the height of the spiritualism fervor, it was common at séances, to see floating musical instruments and spirit hands writing messages.

The Fabulous DAVENPORT BROTHERS

CHAPTER FIFTEEN
AT THE NEW YORK COOPER INSTITUTE

Immense Audiences – Report of the New York Herald – Report of The World – Another Scene from the Herald – A Sporting Circle – Mayor and Aldermen – A Séance in Brooklyn – Testimony of Mr. Tice.

The séances given by the Brothers Davenport at the Cooper Institute, New York, in May 1864, were the culmination and crowning triumphs of their ten years' American experience. The Cooper Institute – the gift of Mr. Peter Cooper, a wealthy merchant of New York, to the city – contains a very large free reading-room, library, picture-gallery, and school of art. The lecture-room is one of the largest in America, and, being centrally situated, is used for the largest public meetings.

This immense room, seating more than three thousand persons, was densely crowded, night after night, to witness the manifestations. Full reports were given in the New York papers, from which I select, with some condensation, an editorial notice, and a full and evidently very fair report from the 'New York Herald,' and a fuller report, written in a humoristic and sensational style, but pretty correct in its details of facts, from the leading Democratic organ, the 'New York World.'

From a leader in the 'New York Herald,' May 4, 1864:

A NEW ERA IN HUMAN DEVELOPMENT—THE DAVENPORT BROTHERS.

As the world grows older it grows wiser. Human development has made greater advances in every direction within the past fifty years than during the five thousand years before. Old things are now passing away; everything is becoming new. Systems of science, religion, philosophy, government – all are being revolutionized. We are in a transition state from darkness to light, and every day brings us nearer to the grand new era of the future.

Here, for example, are the Davenport Brothers. They do the most wonderful things in public and private. Perhaps their performances are more astonishing in a private parlor, where deception appears impossible, than in a public hall, where there may be room for a suspicion of trickery. These brothers make musical instruments float about the room. They cause spectral arms and hands to become visible and tangible. They raise chairs and tables from the floor to the ceiling. They illuminate the room with balls of blazing fire.

While these phenomena are occurring the Brothers remain seated, their hands and feet firmly tied and incapable of motion, even if any sleight-of-hand or sleight-of-foot could suffice to perform such modern miracles. Yet the Davenport Brothers do not attribute these wonders to spiritualism. They say that the power to produce such manifestations has been bestowed upon them; and it is perhaps the same occult power, differently developed, as that shown in the telegraph and the steam-engine. It may be a physical power, or a mental power, or a moral power, or a combination of them all, but certainly it is as yet inexplicable.

From a report in the 'New York Herald,' May 1864:

THE DAVENPORT BROTHERS— MORE WONDERFUL MANIFESTATIONS, THE WHEAT-FLOUR TEST, ETC.

The performances of the Davenport Brothers at the Cooper Institute continue to attract general attention and large audiences. Last evening there was a very full and fashionable house, and the manifestations were unusually satisfactory. This was undoubtedly the result in a great measure of the good order maintained by the spectators, almost all of whom were too intelligent to interfere with their own enjoyment by unnecessary vociferation. Those who made the most noise were those whose opinions are of the least consequence.

Upon the suggestion of Mr. Lacy, who said that there had been some talk about wires and electricity, glass tumblers were placed under the feet of the stools upon which stands the magic cabinet or closet. The closet was carefully examined inside and out, and was found to contain nothing and to have no visible connection with any apparatus. The Davenport Brothers — two very intelligent and gentlemanly persons—then came forward, and were warmly welcomed. These gentlemen were securely tied, hand and foot, by the committee, and fastened to the seats in the closet. The committee reported themselves perfectly satisfied thus far, and certainly we have never seen better tying than that accomplished by the Fire Marshal. The lights were turned down.

Half-a-dozen musical instruments – a guitar, banjo, tambourine, violin, trumpet, and bell – were placed in the closet by the committee. The two side doors of the cabinet were closed and locked, also by the Messrs. Baker.

Then the center door was pushed to, and in less than a second it was bolted upon the inside and the trumpet thrown violently out of the hole in the door. The committee rushed to the closet, the lights were turned up, and there sat the Davenports bound as before. The astonishment of the audience may be imagined.

DARK SÉANCE—THE DAVENPORT BROTHERS

Those who were skeptics a moment ago now began to doubt their own conclusions and joined in the general applause.

The manifestations then followed in the regular order, the audience remaining very quiet and watching everything critically and intelligently. The committee seemed to be extremely impartial, and briefly reported the results of their examinations. A full chorus of instruments playing a jig was heard inside the closet: the doors were hastily opened, and the Davenports had not moved. Spectral hands and arms appeared at the closet window: the doors were opened, and the Davenports were still bound. While the doors were partly open the instruments were flung out and a hand was seen to strike Fire- marshal Baker.

Still the Davenports were tied. Then, the doors being closed for three minutes, the Brothers were discovered perfectly unbound. In four minutes more they were bound again, better than the committee could have bound them, as these gentlemen candidly acknowledged. Then Judge Baker entered the closet and sat between the Davenports. The doors were shut: the manifestations continued; and when the lights were again turned up, the Judge was revealed with a tambourine on his head, and reported that the Davenports had not moved a muscle. The Fire Marshal then tried the same experiment and made the same report. All of the manifestations were repeated several times, to satisfy the most distrustful. It was especially noted that in every case the inside bolt of the center door was heard to shoot into its socket in less than a second after the door was closed. This destroyed the theory that the Davenports untie themselves.

By way of finale, Mr. Lacy suggested that wheat-flour should be placed in the hands of the Messrs. Davenport while they were still tightly tied. This was accordingly done by the committee, and any of the flour that had fallen within the box during the operation was neatly brushed away. The doors were then closed for the last time, and still the manifestations continued. Noises were heard, an open hand was shown at the window, and the trumpet was thrown out. The doors were opened, and there stood the Davenport Brothers, unbound and holding the wheat-flour in their hands. The committee failed to find any of the flour about the closet or upon the clothes of the Davenports; and yet they could not have avoided spilling some of it had they unclosed their hands ever so little.

For such wonders, and for those performed by Mr. Fay in the room above, the hypo- thesis of legerdemain or jugglery does not seem a reasonable explanation. No modern juggler has ever performed such deceptions, if they are deceptions; and during the many years that the Davenports have appeared in public no one – not even the professors of Harvard College – has detected them in their "impositions," as some people call the manifestations.

The following description of another of their famous séances, from the 'New York World' is in some respects more graphic and particular, and records occurrences more remarkable, if possible, than the one from the 'Herald.' It is also a good illustration of the American style of reporting, which is in newspapers somewhat like pre-Raphaelitism in Art.

From the 'New York World':
THE NEW SENSATION THE DAVENPORT BROTHERS AT THE COOPER INSTITUTE.

The Davenport Brothers, known throughout the country, appeared last evening at the Cooper Institute; and it was announced by advertisement that startling wonders, mysterious displays, and unaccountable manifestations would take place in their presence. The fame of their feats of diablerie (reckless mischief) had preceded them, and the large hall was crowded.

The Wonderful Closet.

Upon the center of the platform a plain closet, with three doors opening in front, from six to eight feet broad and eight to ten feet high and two or three feet through, was placed upon three stools with four legs each. The closet was entirely disconnected from either the platform below or the column behind, which it did not touch.

A Preliminary Explanation.

At eight o'clock the musicians retired, and Mr. Lacy, the agent, appeared on the plat- form. He made a few remarks, in which he said that they did not come here to force any religion or philosophy on the audience, but simply to show them a series of startling, mysterious, and wonderful manifestations, for which they could account as they thought proper. One of the conditions necessary to this was darkness, and therefore this closet was used; so that the young men might be in the dark, and yet the manifestations might be witnessed by the audience.

Choosing the Committee.

He desired that a committee of two should be chosen by the audience, to examine all the manifestations and see if there was any deception. By vote of the audience. Colonel Olcott and Rev. G. T. Flanders were selected as a committee. Colonel Olcott is a candid and intelligent gentleman, well known to many citizens. Rev. Mr. Flanders is the present pastor of the Second Universalist Church, which meets in the hall of the Historical Society building, and is well known to the public as an eloquent preacher, and is respected in the community as a candid, educated, and unimpeachable gentleman. He came to the platform with much reluctance, and after many calls.

These gentlemen then examined the closet in every part. The doors being thrown open, two seats were discovered, one on either side. The doors being shut, an opening of less than a foot square, in the shape of a diamond, remained near the top. The closet was pronounced simply a plain affair, with no springs, traps, or machinery in any part, and the seats were securely fastened. The carefulness of the gentlemen in looking: under and over and inside and around the article excited considerable laughter but gave satisfaction.

The Davenport Brothers now appeared on the platform. They looked remarkably like each other in almost every particular, both quite handsome and between twenty and twenty-five years old, with rather long curly black hair, broad but not high foreheads, dark keen eyes, heavy eyebrows, moustache, and 'goatee,' firm-set lips, muscular though well-proportioned frame. They were dressed in black with dress-coats, one wearing a watch-chain.

They are tied.

The committee examined them, they in the closet, one on each side; and the committee were a considerable time in tying them in every possible way with small ropes. Their hands are bound behind them, their feet bound together around the ankles, below and above the knee; they are tied to the sides of the closet so that they cannot stand up, and Colonel Olcott also ties his man about the waist.

Mr. Flanders stated, for himself and his colleague, that these gentlemen were tied in the most complicated manner possible. With respect to those he had tied he would defy any man with both his hands to untie the snarl and complication of knots in half an hour. He would state that he had never witnessed performances of this character before, and had no opinion in regard to them. He was not accustomed to make up his mind either for or against anything he knew nothing about. He had never seen these two gentlemen (the Davenports) that he was aware of, and had only heard of them by rumors through the newspapers.

A Tyer of Knots Pronounces his Decision.

A gentleman in the audience said a friend of his, acquainted with tying knots, would like to see if the men were tied securely. The tyer of knots examined the men carefully.

A Voice: "What does the professor say?"

Tyer of Knots: "The knots seem to be sufficiently complicated at any rate."

Whether they are professionally as well done as an expert might do them deponent sayeth not.

Look Out!

The gas was partially shut off; not, however, but that everything was plainly visible. A bell, trumpet, guitar, fiddle, and banjo were placed between the Brothers, out of reach of each, in center. The committee closed the two side doors, and as Mr. Olcott was closing the middle one he was . . .

Struck in the Face!

. . . by what appeared to be a man's hand, and many of the audience saw the hand. How was that? The doors were opened, and there sat the two men quietly tied. They were examined and were secure. Rev. Mr. Flanders then proceeded to shut the doors, and was quietly adjusting the bolt of the middle door, when he suddenly withdrew it, and turned about with a start.

Mr. Flanders — 'I will state to the audience that, on reaching to adjust the bolt, my fingers were severely grasped.'

Hardly were the words out of his mouth, when, rap! Thump! Out of the opening the heavy trumpet right against and over Mr. Flanders' head on to the platform. (Little screams from the audience.) Mr. Lacy, the agent, opened the doors and turned on the gas as quickly as possible, and the two men were sitting, each on his side, calm and fast.

Colonel Olcott: "I will state that this trumpet was thrown out with such force that the mouth is bent."

Mr. Flanders (with his hand to his forehead): "I'm afraid it was bent on my skull." (Laughter.)

While the doors were being shut again a hand passed quickly out twice before the middle door, and the audience saw it. Then a bell was thrown out of the opening, and the doors being suddenly opened the two men were sitting still and secure.

Whispers: "There's no humbug about that!"

"Oh, oh! Did you see the hand?"

The doors were shut, and a hand appeared plain and palpable at the opening, shaking its fingers.

The agent looked into the middle door, and a hand caught him by the beard. It had a man's wristband and coat-sleeve.

Mirabile Dictu (Wonderful to Relate)

The doors were closed and the committee took seats. Tremendous knocks were heard at the back, side, front, and top of the closet. Two hands — not ghostly and shadowy, but plainly flesh and blood — appeared out of the opening and shook the fingers. The guitar and the violin were heard, as though being tuned. Mr. Flanders stood on one side, and Mr. Olcott on the other, so that there was no part of the closet but what was visible as disconnected from the platform or column.

Suddenly a band of musicians seemed to be playing inside the closet; there was the violin, the guitar, and sometimes the banjo or bell. A very quick jig was struck up and continued a little time, and while it was playing a hand came at the opening. Finally the spirits were disgusted with the music, and pitched the banjo violently out of the opening, so that it passed beyond the platform against a gentleman's head. The spirits were evidently excessively disorderly — they were mad, and there was no method in their madness. First they slammed the sides of

DARK SÉANCE—THE DAVENPORT BROTHERS

the closet as though they would knock it sky-high, so to speak, then they played spasmodically on the instruments, and, wildest of all, they must dash a banjo against a quiet gentleman's head with a force greater than Dan Bryant exerts in his most hilarious efforts. The doors were opened quickly, and the young men were discovered sitting, apparently in meditative mood, tied fast. It was noticed, however, that they were in perspiration, but the closet was close.

The Severest Test.

Mr. Flanders then sat in the closet between the two young men, one hand tied to each man, so that any motion of body or limb would be felt by him.

The doors were shut and dead silence reigned. There was heard the sound of voices in the closet; then came a great racket — it seemed to be a wreck of matter and a crash of worlds; the instruments were tuned.

The doors being opened, there sat the young man and Mr. Flanders smiling, with a banjo on his head. He was untied, and coming out took a bell out of his bosom.

Relating his Experience.

He said, while in the closet, what had occurred had been so incredible, that he was justified in a degree of hesitation in making the statement. He felt hands over his face, upon his breast, back, shoulders; his nose was held tightly, his ears pulled; he was struck with instruments, and all the while he had his hands on the young men's legs, and his fingers stretched so as to touch their bodies, and they were immovable. Of course there was no deception here, and, as he should not like to be suspected of collusion, he should be glad if some other person would take the same place.

The Spirits Tie and Untie Knots

When the doors were opened again the ropes were lying in a pile between the young men, and they walked out free. They were shut up again, and in four minutes the doors were opened and they were securely tied, but not as they were at first. The ropes first used were recognized as the same now on the young men.

Again the young men were shut up, and there was knocking and music, and appearance of hands and arms; some swore that it was often the hand of a lady.

A Voice: "Show us their faces."

The Agent: "Faces not infrequently appear."

Voice: "Let's see one then."

The Agent (philosophically): "They are not mine to show."

Voice: "Can't you catch that hand?"

Acting on the suggestion, both of the committee grasped the hands as they appeared.

Voice: "Were the hands cold?"

131

DARK SÉANCE—THE DAVENPORT BROTHERS

Mr. Olcott: "No; they were warm and moist."

Mr. Flanders said he had tried to hold it, but though his grip was very strong he could not do it.

Once, while the middle door was open, the trumpet, in full sight of the audience, shot into the air in the direction of Mr. Olcott's head.

The 'World' also gives a report of a private séance, or dark circle, with Mr. Ira Davenport and Mr. William M. Fay, accompanied by the same kind of manifestations as those which have so much astonished the savants, the literati, and the highest circles of English society.

The following extract from a report in the 'New York Herald,' giving an account of the closing scenes of another séance at the Cooper Institute, is not, I am assured, an exaggeration:

"The brothers now re-enter the cabinet, and in a few minutes, apparently without earthly assistance, the doors are opened, and the youths appear more firmly tied than ever. Mr. Bradbury so reports. Mr. Conklin says, vaguely, 'I can't see how that's done.' A gentleman proposes that, as the Brothers might slip their hands out of the ropes and in again, that thread, instead of cord, be used to tie them. There was at this time indescribable confusion among the audience. Mr. Conklin is urged to get into the box with the Brothers and find out the deception, if he can.

"Get into the box, Conklin."

"That's it; go in, Conk."

"Go in, Conk."

Mr. Conklin looks imploringly at the audience; he is evidently terribly confused. A lull in the cries and noises enables him to be heard.

"Gentlemen," he cries, "be men and ladies." This speech was hailed with another general outburst of merriment, in the midst of which Mr. Conklin enters the miraculous cabinet, and is last seen before the doors close sitting between the Brothers, with a hand on the shoulder of each. As the doors closed the uproar among the audience was redoubled. 'Goodbye, Conklin," cries a stentorian voice at the back part of the hall; "I smell brimstone," cries another; "How — are — you — Conklin?" ejaculates still another voice.

And now the audience are hushed in silence, as strange voices inside the cabinet are heard. There is a drumming on the guitar, and the bell is rung. In a few moments the doors are opened, and Conklin comes forth like a ghost from a sepulcher. The Brothers are seen still tied fast, and apparently unchanged in their position in the slightest degree. The audience are clamorous for a report of Conklin's experience while with the goblins.

He says, "I had a hand on the shoulder of each. They did not move a muscle, or I should have felt it; and, by the Eternal! I don't believe they did move. But I got a crack on my head from the violin — that I know."

(Boisterous laughter.) Once more are the doors shut, and in the shadowy darkness a long white spectral human arm is seen slowly moving through the aperture. The audience is hushed. A sensation is created. There is something supernatural in the appearance of this ghostly-white arm. But the inevitable Conklin is dauntless — he is not scared. He rushes to seize the arm, and a sturdy red hand at the end of it seizes his own hand and drags the unfortunate man's arm clear into the aperture with a grip that made him wince with pain. Conklin acknowledged that that was a hand, "and a mighty powerful one, too." And now a terrible racket is heard in the cabinet; the spirits seem to have broken loose, and are raising a miniature pandemonium. Thundering, rapping, tumultuous shaking of the doors and sides of the cabinet, loud bell ringing, the clanging of musical instruments, and other noises of almost every sort create a disturbance lasting some minutes. Ever and anon the spectral arm appears. The audience become infected with the tempest of discordant sounds, and help along the infernal din by all kinds of cries. Once when the mysterious arm appeared, a masculine voice cried, "Stick your knife in that arm, Conklin," (Sensation.)

Conklin was no such brute. There were vociferous cries of "Open the door," "Open the door," "Oh! Let 'em rip," "Order," "Order," "Order!"

Mr. Lacy appeals to the audience to be quiet. The ghostly hand spasmodically rings the bell at the aperture. "Look out for your head, Conklin." A regular shindig is struck up; the violin is played vividly, the tambourine is banged savagely, the bell is rung vociferously, and every few moments that strange white arm is thrust out and in the aperture, like the arm of a corpse through a new-made grave amid gleams of moonlight. "Oh, humbug!" ejaculates a hardened skeptic near us.

"You're a philosopher," deprecatingly observes a careful and deeply-interested watcher of the entire phenomena. The cries to "Open the door" now became unanimous and boisterous all over the house. Mr. Lacy finally opened the doors, and out came, pell-mell, the guitar, trumpet, tambourine, and we don't know what else; while the Brothers were seen still tied as tight and fast as ever, and sitting as composedly as if nothing had happened.

Conklin, perfectly dumbfounded, exclaimed, "Gentlemen, this is beyond my comprehension!"

During their triumphant season at New York, so fully and vividly reported by the leading journals of that city, they were invited by Fay to visit Mr. John Morrissey, a well-known sporting man and prizefighter — perhaps the most successful and popular member of what used to be called the 'Fancy' in America. He fought Heenan; he backed other champions: he has his horses on the race course;

DARK SÉANCE—THE DAVENPORT BROTHERS

he used to keep a faro bank; he speculates in stocks and gold in Wall Street.

A Minor Digression:

Engraving circa 1860
Member of the U.S. House of Representatives
From New York's 5th district
In office
March 4, 1867 – March 4, 1871
Preceded by
Nelson Taylor
Succeeded by
William R. Roberts
Personal details
Born
February 12, 1831
Templemore, County Tipperary, Ireland
Died
May 1, 1878 (aged 47)
Troy, New York
Political party
Democratic
Occupation
Boxer, Gang leader, and Politician
Religion
Roman Catholicism

John Morrissey (February 12, 1831 – May 1, 1878), also known as Old Smoke, was an Irish American bare-knuckle boxer and a gang member in New York in the 1850s and later became a Democratic State Senator and U.S. Congressman from New York, backed by Tammany Hall. Morrissey began his bare-knuckle boxing career after a confrontation with a man known only as "Chroel" who was notorious for troubling his fellow townsmen. Although Morrissey was on the bitter end of his first bare knuckle bout, his display of bravery and fortitude earned himself the respect and historical acknowledgment of his peers.

Early life

Morrissey was born in Templemore, County Tipperary, Ireland in 1831. In

DARK SÉANCE—THE DAVENPORT BROTHERS

1833 his parents immigrated to the United States and settled in Troy, New York.

Desperate to escape poverty, he worked as a cargo thief and also as a collection agent for Irish crime bosses in the area, and before he was 18, he had been indicted twice for burglary, once for assault and battery, and once for assault with intent to kill. Along with his criminal and ferocious fighting abilities, Morrissey also displayed driving ambition, teaching himself to read and write while working as a bouncer at a South Troy brothel. After spending two months in jail, Morrissey left Troy for New York City.

During a fight with a gang member named Tom McCann, Morrissey was pinned on his back atop burning coals from a stove that had been overturned. Morrissey endured the pain as his flesh burned, fought off McCann, and got back on his feet. Enraged, Morrissey beat McCann senseless as smoke from his burning flesh rose up from his back. The event earned him the nickname "Old Smoke," which stuck with him through the rest of his life.

After two years in New York, Morrissey sailed to San Francisco, seeking fortune during the California Gold Rush. While he didn't have any luck in that endeavor, Morrissey became a renowned gambler and made a fortune winning gold from prospectors. It was also during this time that Morrissey appeared for the first time in a professional prizefighting ring. He knocked out George Thompson in the 11th round, earning $5,000. This success encouraged him to return to New York to fight the American Champion, Yankee Sullivan.

The Champion

Morrissey returned to New York and challenged Sullivan repeatedly until the latter finally agreed. Due to the violent nature of the sport, boxing was illegal in most places during the 1850s. The first boxing rules, called the London Prize Ring rules, were introduced by heavyweight champion Jack Broughton in 1743 to protect fighters in the ring where deaths sometimes occurred. Under these rules, if a man went down and could not continue after a count of 30 seconds, the fight was over. Hitting a downed fighter and grasping below the waist were prohibited. Fights usually lasted for 20-30 rounds. Rounds continued until one fighter touched the ground with his knee, or simply fell down.

The fight between Morrissey and Sullivan was scheduled for October 12, 1853, in the hamlet of Boston Corner, which was then in Massachusetts, but out of reach of its authorities, and thus a good location for the illegal match. The fight took place in a field, and was supposedly viewed by over 3,000 spectators. Sullivan dominated the match for most of the fight, but Morrissey held his own, and the tough Irishman would not quit, though his face became distorted and unrecognizable. In the 37th round, more than an hour after the start of the fight, Sullivan lost after he knocked out Morrissey. There was a dispute over the rules. Sullivan had left thinking he'd won but was disqualified.

DARK SÉANCE—THE DAVENPORT BROTHERS

Dead Rabbits

Morrissey became involved in Democratic politics in New York City and a rivalry with William Poole, also known as "Bill the Butcher". Poole was an enforcer for the Know-Nothing Party, leader of the Bowery Boys, and a boxer. In 1854, Morrissey was hired to prevent Poole and his gang from seizing ballot boxes and rigging an election. As a reward for having stopped the ballot rigging, Morrissey and his gang, the Dead Rabbits, were permitted by Tammany Hall to open a gambling house without police interference.

One of Morrissey's friends, Lew Baker, shot and fatally wounded Bill the Butcher at a saloon on Broadway in 1855, following Morrisey's loss to Poole in a boxing match eight months earlier. Morrissey and Baker were indicted for the murder, but the charges were dropped after three trials resulting in hung juries.

Morrissey then retired from boxing at the insistence of his wife, and returned to Troy, New York. Morrissey's business ventures were unsuccessful, and he returned to boxing in 1858 to defend his championship in Long Point, Ontario, against fellow Troy, New York native John C. Heenan. The fight lasted 11 rounds, with Morrissey knocking out Heenan, for several minutes, to defend his title. Heenan claimed the title on Morrissey's retirement from boxing in 1859.

Saratoga

After establishing a successful gaming house in Saratoga Springs, New York, Morrissey created the Saratoga Race Course with the help of William R. Travers, John R. Hunter, and Leonard Jerome. He also established "The Club House," a casino in Saratoga that attracted such notable guests as Chester A. Arthur, Rutherford B. Hayes, and Ulysses S. Grant, as well as Commodore Cornelius Vanderbilt, John D. Rockefeller, and Mark Twain.

Politician

After his retirement from boxing, Morrissey focused his attention on gambling establishments, owning stake in 16 casinos at one point. In 1866, he ran for Congress with the backing of Tammany Hall and served two terms (1867–1871) in the House, in the 40th and 41st United States Congress. As a Congressman, he always looked out for the interests of the Irish, and was known to use strong-arm tactics to accomplish his legislative goals, at one point declaring that he could "lick any man in the House." He eventually grew tired of the rampant corruption within Tammany Hall and left the House after his second term. He eventually testified against William Tweed, which helped put the notorious boss in prison. Morrissey was elected as an Anti-Tammany Democrat to the New York State Senate in 1875 and was re-elected in 1877, sitting in the 99th, 100th and 101st New York State Legislatures.

Morrissey contracted pneumonia and died on May 1, 1878 at the age of 47. The state closed all offices and flags were flown at half-mast. The entire State Senate attended his funeral in Troy, and 20,000 mourners lined the streets to pay their last respects. He was buried in St. Peter's Cemetery, just outside of Troy. At the time of his death, Morrissey's estate was valued at more than $2 million.

Legacy

• In 1996 he was elected to the International Boxing Hall of Fame.

• Morrissey was featured on a portion of the History Channel documentary, "Paddy Whacked, The History of the Irish Mob" as the first Irish mob boss in American history.

• Prizefighter Johnny Morrissey is the hero in a popular Irish ballad called "Morrissey and the Russian Sailor." Though the ballad has several variations, most versions include some phrases that connect the song's hero with the historical John Morrissey: his Irish birthplace in Templemore, County Tipperary; his status as a champion fighter, signified by a prize belt; his defeat of Thompson/ Thomson and of 'the Yankee,' among others. The main story in the ballad, however—an heroic prizefight against a Russian sailor in Tierra del Fuego—does not seem to be historically documented. One version of the song was printed as a broadsheet by E.C. Yeats's Cuala Press in 1911; a digitized image of it has been posted by Villanova University Library. There are a number of other ballads written about Morrissey including "Morrissey and the Black," "Morrissey Again in the Field," and "The Fight at Boston Corners." Three of them are documented in the book, Songs of England, Ireland and Scotland: A Bonnie Bunch of Roses by Dan Milner (Oak Publications).

• He is an ancestor of Joseph D. Morrissey, an American politician and former lawyer currently serving in the Virginia House of Delegates.

•

(To continue:)

The Brothers Davenport were naturally curious to see so distinguished a character, and they aver that many clergymen have treated them with less politeness and kindness than was shown to them by Mr. M. and his friends, and on other occasions by publicans and sinners. The object of the visit was to arrange for a private séance for Mr. Morrissey and his friends. It was readily agreed to. A sailor was brought by one party, who spent an hour and a half in tying the Brothers with tarred rope, until they were covered as with a net, and heavy bets were made that they would or would not be untied. This was the only manifestation they cared for. Everything was conducted with as much scrutiny as the pending interests demanded, but also with a fairness that would have shamed more pretentious people. When the lights were put out a variety of manifestations were given. Then the knots were all untied in fifteen minutes, to the satisfaction of winners and losers.

A private séance was also given to the Mayor and Common Council of the

DARK SÉANCE—THE DAVENPORT BROTHERS

City of New York, who will, I trust, pardon me for having given precedence to the more piquant if less dignified one attended by Mr. John Morrissey and his respectable confreres.

I close this long but I believe interesting chapter with the following statement, published in the New York papers:

The Brothers' Hands Blacked

We have had furnished us a statement made by Mr. Thomas S. Tice, an unbeliever, respecting certain tests applied by him while the Brothers were exhibiting in Brooklyn. Mr. Tice acted as one of the committee on the occasion referred to.

Mr. Tice's Statement,

"I took a piece of chamois skin well filled with lampblack, previously prepared for the purpose, and, unknown to the Brothers, while examining the cords that tied their hands, I smeared them over as well as I could, even rubbing the black upon the wrists, so that if it were their hands that appeared at the aperture it would show the smearing I gave them. I was at the side of the cabinet when a hand appeared at the opening which I did not see; but I immediately enquired if there was any black upon it, when it was stated that the hand was a beautiful clean white hand and without any trace of black upon it, and there were at least a dozen people in the front row watching to see if they could detect any black upon the hand whatever.

"Again, after both of us that were on the committee had been enclosed with them, a hand appeared at the opening — as clean and perfect a hand as could be. In fact the hand looked quite fleshy, and as if it belonged to some young lady, and not like the Brothers' hands, with veins and sinews showing very plainly; and, in conclusion, I will only add that I cannot account for the mysteries that appear in connection with the Brothers and their wonderful cabinet.'

The Fabulous DAVENPORT BROTHERS

CHAPTER SIXTEEN
VISIT TO ENGLAND

Character of the English — Past and Present Beliefs — The Mission of the Brothers Davenport — Their Confederates — The first Séance in London — The Press in a Difficulty , and How they Got out of it — Report of the 'Morning Post'— 'The Times'—'The Herald.'

After the ten years of strange and wonderful experiences in America, here truthfully but briefly and imperfectly recorded, and while a sanguinary war is raging over their native land, the Brothers Davenport, after a visit to the British-American Provinces, elsewhere spoken of, received and obeyed the direction given them to cross the Atlantic to their ancient fatherland, the birthplace of their mother, and in which the dust of their ancestry reposes, to continue in Britain and in Europe a mission in whose beneficent purposes they have an undoubting faith, and which may carry them around the world.

England, the country in which they would naturally first continue the work so long and faithfully pursued in America, is probably one of the most incredulous, materialistic, practical, and impracticable countries in the world. Hard, scientific, unimpressible, and unimaginative, devoted to precedent and respecting authority, the English people, as a rule, have long since adopted, and are now firmly settled in, the belief that there is and can be nothing beyond the range of ordinary experience. Two centuries ago they believed in witchcraft, and burned or hanged wizards and witches in abundance. Three centuries ago they believed in miracles — that is, they believed that miracles might be, and often were, worked in the later as well as in the earlier Christian centuries. That faith still exists over a large part of Europe; but in England it died out after the Reformation, and has not been revived. To an Englishman at this day a miracle, such as his ancestors three or four hundred years ago believed in with an earnest and lively faith, and such as the people of three-fourths of Europe still believe in, seems an utter absurdity. It is opposed to his science, and it shocks his common-sense. It is stuff and nonsense. In the days of Shakespeare, the ghost of the Royal Dane in Hamlet, the dread specter of the murdered Banquo in Macbeth, and the terrible vision that froze the blood of Richard III., were very real things; now they are matters of ridicule, and at the most appeal only to some childish remnant of traditional superstition.

The Englishman has long since made up his mind that what he calls the laws of nature are, in this steam-engine-driven and gas-enlightened age, never violated: the Society for the Diffusion of Useful Knowledge and the 'Penny Encyclopedia' settled all that long ago.

If the Brothers Davenport have really any mission — any proper and worthy business — in England, it is to meet on its own low ground, and conquer by appropriate means, the hard materialism and skepticism of England. The first step to knowledge is to be convinced of ignorance: small things often lead to great results.

The fall of an apple or the swing of a pendulum may suggest an investigation into the most profound laws of the physical world. If the manifestations given by the aid of the Brothers Davenport shall prove to the intellectual and scientific classes in England that there are forces — and intelligent forces, or powerful intelligences — beyond the range of their philosophies, and that what they consider physical impossibilities are readily accomplished by invisible and to them unknown intelligences, a new universe will be opened to human thought and investigation.

I say, if they have any real mission; for to come here as mere jugglers, doing tricks by sleight-of-hand and aid of confederates, denying that they are so done, would be not only a mercenary, base imposture, but, in their case, the most infamous of falsehoods, and the most horrible of perjuries. If they say falsely, they and those who are with them, that they have no voluntary agency in the production of the phenomena described in these pages; if they are trying to palm off as preternatural or supernatural, the results of mere trick and collusion, they are the most base and infamous wretches in the world, compared with whom a common forger, an ordinary felon, is a man of honour and a gentleman. I cannot put this case more strongly than I wish to put it, or than it ought to be put.

Penal servitude for life at Norfolk Island would be a mild punishment for so detestable an outrage.

In good faith, as I believe with no shadow of doubt, the Brothers Davenport embarked from the city of New York on the 27th of August, 1864, bringing with them, in consequence of a nervous debility in Mr. William Davenport, a reinforcement in Mr. William M. Fay, who is not to be confounded with one H. Melville Fay — said, upon I know not what kind of authority, to have been detected in attempting to produce similar manifestations, or what might pass for them, in Canada. They were accompanied by Mr. Palmer, widely known as an impresario or busi-

DARK SÉANCE—THE DAVENPORT BROTHERS

ness manager in the operatic and dramatic world, to whom, as an experienced agent, was confided the business and pecuniary portion of their undertaking — a matter of such obvious necessity that it needs neither apology nor explanation. To these were added Mr. J. B. Ferguson, a gentleman of education and position, formerly a clergyman of Nashville, the capital of Tennessee, where he was highly respected and esteemed.

Mr. Ferguson was born in the valley of Virginia, but emigrated early in life west of the Alleghenies. He is now forty-seven years old, and is greatly esteemed by those who know him best as a man of integrity and honor, of high religious principle, purity of character, deep thought, and eloquent expression. Distinctively American, of the southern and western type, with striking American peculiarities, he has yet, I believe, made a very favorable impression upon Englishmen.

In the war that has convulsed his native country, and desolated the State in which he was born and in which he resided, he has taken the part of a peacemaker, and in that capacity has visited Richmond, and once before crossed the Atlantic.

It is very unlikely that such a man, holding such a character, standing in such a position, so gifted, honored and beloved, would lend himself to a mean and miserable imposture. In another chapter, Mr. Ferguson has given his own statement of the motives which have induced him to accompany the Davenport Brothers, to watch over them, and be the intellectual manager of the séances, in which powers and forces unknown to and unrecognized by science are demonstrated by incontrovertible facts.

This party arrived safely at Glasgow, Sept. 9th, and on the 11th reached the great metropolis. Their first private séance was given at the residence of Mr. Dion Boucicault, the well-known dramatic author and actor — author of 'London Assurance,' 'The Young Actress,' 'Colleen Dawn,' 'Streets of London,' and a score of entertaining and delightful comedies and dramas, in which it is hard to say whether his merits as dramatist or actor were more conspicuous.

I speak in this special manner of Mr. Boucicault as a matter of justice, because he has shown a moral courage equal to his ability, and because I shall be indebted to his hand for one of the clearest descriptive statements of the nature of these manifestations that has ever been written.

This first and very important séance, given Sept. 28, 1864, was attended by several gentlemen connected with the leading daily newspapers of London, and other distinguished men of science and letters. It would have been difficult to select a company better able to examine the phenomena presented, or better qualified to make a proper report to the public. In the case of the production of a new farce, the opening of a donkey-show, or a prize-fight for the belt of the champion

141

of England, the reports of these gentlemen, who stand high upon the staffs of their respective journals, would have been published in the usual form; but in this case, where occult powers and hidden forces of the universe were in question, every daily paper excepting the 'Morning Post' published the accounts which were given as anonymous communications. This is not at all to be wondered at.

Considering the obstinate incredulity of the public mind, it is wonderful that the editors of these leading organs of public opinion published them at all. It may be supposed that they thought the facts reported to them too marvelous to be vouched for, but also too striking to be passed over in silence.

I propose to copy from these reports so much as may be pertinent to the case and interesting to the reader, taking the liberty to condense, by omitting superfluous portions, unnecessary repetitions ; and first the article from the 'Morning Post,' which appears to have been written by one of its editorial staff.

From the London 'Morning Post,' Sept. 29, 1864:

'Extraordinary Manifestations,

'Yesterday evening, in the front drawing-room of a house in the immediate neighborhood of Portland-place, a select number of persons were invited to witness some strange manifestations which took place in the presence, if not by the agency, of three gentlemen lately arrived from America. The party consists of two brothers named Davenport, twenty-four and twenty-five years of age, and a Mr. Fay, a gentleman born in the States, but we believe of German origin. They are accompanied by Mr. H. D. Palmer, a gentleman long and favorably known in New York in connection with operatic matters, and by a Dr. Ferguson, who explains the nature of the manifestations about to be presented, but who does not venture to give any explanation of them.

'It should be stated at the outset that the trio, who appear to be gifted in so extraordinary a manner, do not lay claim to any particular physical, psychological, or moral power. All they assert is that in their presence certain physical manifestations take place. The spectator is, of course, at liberty to draw any inference he pleases. They invite the most critical examination (compatible with certain conditions to be observed), and those who witness the manifestations are at liberty to take all needful precautions against fraud or deception.

'The party invited to witness the manifestations last night consisted of some twelve or fourteen individuals, all of whom are admitted to be of considerable distinction in the various professions with which they are connected. The majority had never previously witnessed anything of the kind. All, however, were determined to detect, and, if possible, expose any attempt at deception. The Brothers Davenport are slightly- built, gentleman-like in appearance, and about the last persons in the world from whom any great muscular performances might be expected. Mr. Fay is apparently a few years older, and of more robust constitution.'

The writer proceeds to describe the cabinet, and says the bolt of 'the middle door was shut by some invisible agency from the inside.' The Brothers are securely tied. 'Instantly on the center door being closed the bolt was secured inside, and hands were clearly observed through the opening. A gentleman present was invited to pass his hand through the opening, and it was touched by the hands several times.' Music was heard; the doors flew open; the Brothers are seen to be firmly secured; the doors are 'closed by persons who, when doing so, were touched by invisible hands, and the noise of undoing the cords was distinctly heard.'

'After an interval of two minutes, the Brothers were found securely bound with the same cords, the ends of the rope being some distance from their hands.'

A gentleman sits in the cabinet with his hands tied to the knees of the two Davenports, whose hands were bound behind their backs, and to the bench, and their feet securely fastened. The gentleman stated that 'the instant the door was closed, hands were passed over his face and head, his hair was gently pulled, and the whole of the musical instruments played upon, the bells violently rung close to his face, and the tambourine beat time on his head. Eventually the instruments were thrown behind him and rested between his shoulders and the back of the cabinet.' A gas-burner and two candles were burning.

Here are the facts — two Davenports and a witness in a box scarcely larger than needed to contain them, and all securely bound — yet observe what happened:

A dark circle was then formed, the Brothers bound to chairs, and the whole company, including Mr. Ferguson and Mr. Fay, taking hold of hands. 'The instant the lights were extinguished the musical instruments appeared to be carried all about the room. The currents of air which they occasioned in their rapid transit were felt upon the faces of all present. The bells were loudly rung; the trumpet made knocks on the floor, and the tambourine seemed to be running round the room jingling with all its might. At the same time tiny sparks were observed as if passing from south to west.'

Several persons were lightly, and one (the representative of the 'Times,') severely struck with the passing instruments. Lights were struck from time to time, and the Brothers always found securely bound.

Mr. Fay was now bound to one of the chairs, with his hands firmly tied behind him. As soon as the light was extinguished, a whizzing noise was heard. 'It's off,' said Mr. Fay, meaning his coat, and on striking a light, his coat was no longer on, but lying on the floor, and his hands were still tied together behind him!

Astonishing though this appeared to be, what followed was more extraordinary still. Dr. Ferguson requested a gentleman present to take off his coat and place it on the table. This was done, the light was extinguished, a repetition of the whizzing noise was heard, and the strange coat was found upon Mr. Fay, whose hands and feet were still securely bound, and his body tied almost immovably to the chair. Several other manifestations were made, and some while the Davenport Brothers and Mr. Fay, instead of being bound, were held by those present, and all with similar results.

This manifestation of the taking off a man's coat, and putting on another man's, both garments being intact, with the wrists closely bound together behind the back, and the person securely tied to a chair, is undoubtedly one of the most astounding ever given. It is simply what is called a physical impossibility. It is as if two links of a chain should be separated without a fracture and then restored to their places. That it was done on this occasion, and has been done scores, perhaps hundreds of times, there is no doubt whatever.

All this was done, it will also be observed, not in the presence of ignorant and credulous persons, but in a select company, which included some of the sharpest minds in England; not in a prepared theatre, but in a gentleman's drawing-room, where there could have been no deception had it been in any case possible.

After giving the details, which I have condensed, because they will be still more minutely given in other statements which are to follow, the writer in the 'Morning Post' makes the following observations:

"The séance lasted more than two hours, during which time the cabinet was minutely inspected, the coats examined to ascertain whether they were fashioned so as to favor a trick, and every possible precaution taken to bind the hands and feet of the persons whose presence appeared to be essential to the development of the manifestations.

"It may be asserted that all the illustrations above enumerated can be traced to clever conjuring. Possibly they may, or it is possible that some new physical force can be engendered at will to account for what appears on the face of it absolutely unaccountable. All that can be asserted is, that the displays to which we have referred took place on the present occasion under conditions and circumstances that preclude the presumption of fraud. It is true that darkness is in some cases an essential condition, but darkness does not necessarily imply deception. But, putting aside the cabinet manifestations, there is abundance left to excite curiosity and challenge the attention of the scientific. Learning, we know, is not a limited quantity; it is inexhaustible for all mankind, and here is a field for the investigation of the scientific world. In the present state of knowledge upon the subject of occult forces, dependent more or less upon the will, all that can be said is, that the manifestations of Messrs. Davenport and Mr, Fay appear to be altogether inexplicable.

"In a little time we believe it is their intention to give séances at the Egyptian Hall or some other suitable place, when the public will be afforded an opportunity of witnessing some of the astonishing feats of which we have given an outline. For the present it is sufficient to say that they invite the strictest scrutiny on the part of men of science, and that, whatever be the theory involved, they repudiate any active agency in the production of the extraordinary manifestations which take place in their presence. It is perhaps well for them that they were not in the flesh a century and a half ago, as, in the then state of human knowledge and social enlightenment, they would unquestionably have been conducted to Smithfield, and burnt as necromancers of the most dangerous type."

The writer of this article, in the most fashionable and aristocratic journal in England, no doubt conferred with the gentlemen of the press and other cool and careful observers then present, and has given their ideas and observations as well as his own. It has every appearance of being a fair, candid, and intelligent statement, and the editor of the 'Morning Post' did not shrink from the responsibility of giving it a suitable place in his journal.

The 'Times' — 'the leading journal of England, Europe, and the world,' 'The Thunderer,' the paper that more than any other can make and unmake fortunes and reputations, which wields so great a power that it may be hoped its conductors never forget that great power involves a corresponding responsibility — the 'Times ' is said to have been represented on this occasion by one of its ablest writers, but its account of the séance is 'From a Correspondent.' It may seem strange that the 'Times' did not publish a report of the personal observations of one of the most trusted and matter-of-fact writers on its staff, but it is well to be wary of impossibilities.

The 'Correspondent' of the 'Times,' September 30th, says: "I was present at a séance, at the house of Mr. Dion Boucicault, whose party comprised several persons known in the literary and artistic world. Having arrived rather late, I missed some of the earlier 'experiments,' which seem to have been extremely curious.

"When I entered the room devoted to the 'manifestations,' I found it occupied by a number of persons who attentively listened to a strange discordant concert held within a wardrobe placed at the end furthest from the door. When the sounds had ceased the wardrobe was opened, and three compartments were discovered, two of which were occupied by the Brothers Davenport, bound hand and foot with strong cords, like the most dangerous malefactors. The center compartment held the musical instruments, and on each side of this sat the corded brothers. The ostensible theory is that the Davenports, bound as they were, produced a combination of noises, compared to which the performance of the most obtrusive German band that ever awakened the wrath of a Babbage is the harmony of the spheres. The cords are examined, the wardrobe is closed, the instruments are replaced, and presently, through an aperture in the center door, a trumpet is hurled with violence. The wardrobe is reopened and there are the Brothers Davenport corded as before.

"A change takes place in the manner of the performance. Hitherto the brothers have remained incarcerated in this box, while the audience are at liberty. They now leave the wardrobe and take their place in the middle of the room, where they are firmly bound to their chairs. The gentle- man who officiates as their lecturer or spokesman even offers to drop sealing-wax on the knots, and requests any one of the company to impress it with his own seal.

"On the evening of my visit this offer was not accepted, but the fault, if any, lay with the investigators. When the lights had been extinguished, and as we were all seated round the room with hands joined, at the request of the lecturer, a most extraordinary "manifestation" took place. The air was filled with the sound of instruments which we had seen laid upon a table, but which now seemed to be flying about the room, playing as they went, without the smallest respect to the heads of the visitors. Now a bell jingled close to your ear, now a guitar was struck immediately over your head, while every now and then a cold wind passed across the faces of the whole party.

"Sometimes a smart blow was administered, sometimes the knee was patted by a mysterious hand; divers shrieks from the members of the company indicating the side on which the more tangible "manifestations" had taken place. A candle having been lighted, the brothers were seen still bound to their chairs, while some of the instruments had dropped into the laps of the visitors. I myself had received a blow on the face from a floating guitar which drew enough blood to necessitate the employment of towel and sponge.

"A new experiment was now made. Darkness having regained its supremacy, one of the brothers expressed a desire to be relieved of his coat. Returning light showed him in his shirt-sleeves, though his hands were still firmly bound behind his chair. It was now stated that he was prepared to put on the coat of any one of the company willing to "loan" that article of attire, and an assenting gentleman having been found, the coat, after a short interval of darkness, was worn in proper fashion by a person for whom it had not been designed by the tailor.

"Finally, the brothers desired a release, and one of the company, certainly not an accomplice, requested that the rope might fall into his lap. During the interval of darkness a rushing sound as of swiftly drawn cords was audible, and the ropes reached the required knees, after striking the face of the person in the next chair!

"Such are the chief phenomena. To sum up the essential characteristics of the exhibition, it is sufficient to state that the brothers, when not shut up in the wardrobe, are bound while the candles are alight, perform their miracles in the

DARK SÉANCE—THE DAVENPORT BROTHERS

dark, and on the return of light are found to be bound as before. The investigators into the means of operation have to ascertain whether the brothers are able to release themselves and resume their straitened condition during the intervals of darkness, and whether, even if this is practicable, they can, without assistance, produce the effects described." — Times, Sept. 13.

A clear, brief, evidently honest statement by a man who would have exposed the slightest indication of imposture had there been any to expose.

The 'Morning Herald' and 'Standard' were represented at the party of Mr. Boucicault, it is stated, by one of the able writers of their regular staff, but the report, following the prudent example of the leading journal, is given in a communication 'to the Editor,' over the signature of 'Incredulous Odi.'

Having given a careful statement of the facts, it will be sufficient to copy a few of this clever writer's observations, and his "views of a puzzle which, whether it be physical or metaphysical, is likely to cause much and various speculation ere it be finally, if ever, solved."

Mr. 'Incredulous Odi' was there at the beginning. He examined the cabinet and found it too simple in construction to admit of any concealed machinery. One of the gentlemen engaged in tying the Brothers Davenport was a nautical gentleman, and profound in the matter of knots.

He had no doubt of the perfect rigidity of his fastenings, nor had the other gentleman, or any of the company who examined the complicated ligatures, which, passing through holes perforated in the bench, and connecting the ankles with the wrists of the patients, served to render all free motion, at any rate of arms or feet, an impossibility.

"Dr. Ferguson told us that he would advance no theory or explanation of what was about to happen, and begged us not to discuss the causes of what we saw or heard, but content ourselves with the attitude of simple and candid observers. Now, let me say what did happen, so far as my own observation is concerned. As the doctor had told us, the bolt of the middle door was heard to be drawn from inside; hands then appeared at the lozenge- shaped aperture, one from each side of the cabinet, as it appeared, and jigged in front of the curtain, which was thrust slightly back. The hands were in a semi-obscurity, the gas by which the room was lighted having been slightly lowered, and the arms belonging to them not being visible from the smallness of the aperture, they looked ghostly enough to elicit a set of little awestruck ejaculations from the ladies present."

But this 'Incredulous Odi' is not content with stating the facts. He thinks it necessary to offer a theory by way of accounting for them. He thinks that if the brothers, bound in the cabinet and watched by a third person sitting between them, could have got only partially loose, without the use of their hands, they might have shown the hands, played on three or four instruments, etc.! He suspects that Mr. Fay may have moved and played upon the guitar while in close contact with himself and the 'Times' correspondent.

He says:

"Granting that Mr. Fay and his companion could move at all, bound as they were — and since the chairs to which they were bound were not fastened to the ground, this seems an easier supposition than in the case of the cabinet — there is no reason why they should not by the act of their own bodies do all that was done — viz., chuck about hand bells, whisk guitars rapidly enough round to cut people's noses, trundle tambourines along the ground, take off and put on coats, remove watches out of hands holding them out, and place rings on the wrong man's finger (the new science is fallible even in its native darkness), especially to a quiet observer like myself it was clear there was time enough allowed to do all this naturally and he found in one's seat again when the signal was again given for light. I am not going to adventure an exact explanation of how this is to be done, as the modus operandi is at present an immature conception in my brain, but I have a shrewd guess at it. I will only say that Mr. Fay is a very strong-built man, and could carry Mr. Davenport, a very light weight, in any conceivable position; adding, that I should like to be entrusted, during this performance, with the candle and Lucifer borne by Dr. Ferguson, unrestricted by the promise not to re-illume the former till I was requested."

To anyone who has seen how these young men are bound in their chairs, with their wrists firmly knotted behind their backs; who has heard the guitars ringing and whirling through the air like a flight of swallows, and seen the candle lighted instantly, and examined the ropes with which they were tied, this kind of theorizing is more wonderful than the phenomena it tries to explain.

It is needless to give further extracts from the notices of this famous séance, which spread the news of the arrival of the brothers Davenport and accounts of the wonders wrought in their presence over the world.

The Fabulous DAVENPORT BROTHERS

CHAPTER SEVENTEEN
"STILL THE WONDER GREW."

Private Séances — Report of 'Master of Arts' in Daily Telegraph — The Morning Star — A London Minister — The Morning Post — Tests that ought to be satisfactory.

To the remarkable opening séance described in the last chapter succeeded others at private houses, and at one of the smaller salons of the Queen's Concert Rooms, Hanover Square; but all were private in the sense that they were attended by persons of scientific, literary, or social distinction, who were specially invited.

One of them, at the residence of Mr. S. C. Hall, well known in the world of literature and art, where the cabinet was not used (which is the 'apparatus' referred to below), was attended by, among many others, a well-known man of letters, whose very clear and excellent account of what he heard and saw was in due time published by the 'Daily Telegraph,' as a communication from a 'Master of Arts,' following the prudent example of other leading journals.

This account of the séance is so frank and so vivid as to deserve to be given entire, and whether written by editor or correspondent, is evidently a clear and truthful statement.

'The Brothers Davenport.

'(To the Editor of the 'Daily Telegraph.')'

'Sir, — I was a witness, on Friday evening of last week, to some of the manifestations which were exhibited by, or rather occur in the presence of, the young Americans who have recently come over here. It is well known that they intend to give public séances among us, and the more ordinary of these manifestations will soon therefore become familiar. There are, nevertheless, circumstances about a private sitting which make it especially useful for previous criticism, since it takes place in a locality and amid a society where deception must be more difficult, while inspection is naturally closer and freer than at a public hall.

'In the circle, for instance, to which I was invited, the guests were mutually known, and bent upon the sharpest investigation. The host was a man of letters, of a character for truth and gravity which it would be impertinence to eulogize; the scene was an apartment crowded to profusion with delicate works of art, and therefore most awkward for any rough conjuring resources; and finally, the apparatus employed, I understand, elsewhere, was by the nature of the place excluded here. These are conditions which cannot be repeated in public; I therefore offer you. Sir, as a contribution to the decision which such strange phenomena await, my own observations, stripped of bias, theory, or opinion, and made as I should make them in the witness-box of a court of justice.

'Custodem quis custodiet? (Quis custodiet ipsos custodies — Who will watch the watchers?) However — who will testify to the witness ? He may be in turn an impostor — may be incapable of calm observation — may be a headlong generalizer — and those with him may have been severally and collectively, like himself, fools or knaves. True, that is possible; but what is not possible is to find evidence not open to these astute objections. I pass them by, therefore, as the inevitable fate of anonymous testimony. My name will weigh, however, with you, I think, for sincerity and ordinary intelligence and with regard to an acquaintance with the resources of legerdemain, a long knowledge of jugglers and snake-charmers, with their budget of tricks, has at least blunted the edge of my wonder upon that score. For my fellow-guests, they too were not people upon whom deception could be easily played. Officers of the army and navy, a colonial baronet, a well-known sculptor, a public writer, and others habituated to keep their wits about them, made up, with ladies, the circle of twelve or fifteen present.

'The party was completed by the two Brothers Davenport, a Mr. Fay, and a Mr. Ferguson. There is nothing very marked about the first two gentlemen; the Davenports are quiet young men, of mild and agreeable address; so also is their companion, Mr. Fay, though he is more English or German in appearance. The spokesman of the party, indeed, Mr. Ferguson, seems a decidedly "remarkable man," as those who encounter him in metaphysical discussion will probably acknowledge. I pass, how- ever, from metaphysics to what I saw, heard, and felt. We sat in a half-circle round the side of the drawing room — Mr. Ferguson being at one end, and one of the Davenports at the other; in the middle the second brother and Mr. Fay placed them- selves upon two ordinary chairs, with a small table between them, on which were laid a guitar, bell, tambourine, and trumpet; while about twelve yards of clothes-line, in two pieces, lay at hand. It was then requested that some of our party should secure each of the sitters hand and foot to the chairs with the cord. Mr. Davenport was operated upon by a captain of one of Her Majesty's vessels of war, a distinguished Arctic navigator (Captain Inglefield).

As a yachtsman, I must here plunge so far into technicalities as to say that each ankle of Mr. Davenport was roundly seized up by this gentleman with a "clove-hitch," as also each wrist — the wrists being fastened to the bar of the chair behind, and the legs made secure by passing the line round and round the foot-bars, and up to meet the wrist-rope, when both were joined with a "bread-bag knot." Sailors well know that a "bread-bag knot" can only be imitated by those who comprehend exactly the trick of turning a "reef-knot" into it; in fact, it is the old boatswain's trap to catch a thief at his biscuit-store. Mr. Fay was made fast less scientifically, but very sufficiently, and the circle was formed in front of the captives. We were specially warned to keep our hands joined while darkness lasted, and the gentlemen at each extremity of the semicircle were duly grasped and held by their neighbors. The lights were then extinguished, and in an instant there commenced a medley of noises from tambourine, guitar, and bell. These sounded in all parts of the apartment, now high, now low, now here, now there — simultaneously be it observed — and the passage of them through the air could be heard and felt, immensely rapid, and accompanied by no foot-fall on the floor. The knees, forehead, and feet of those in the circle were every now and then rapped by the instruments in a manner boisterous but harmless, and exclamations of amusement or surprise on our part mingled with the curious Babel.

The guitar especially passed and repassed with what was more like flight than ordinary motion, at times violently strummed, at others as gently thrilled as an Aeolian harp. At the end of all this a signal for light was given by taps, and, the apartment being instantly illuminated, the prisoners were discovered exactly as they had been last seen, the instruments lying about, or upon the knees of those present. The captain's sailor-like fastenings were precisely as he had left them, and were declared to have been untouched after our closest examination. The same was the case with Mr. Fay. Hands were then joined, and the lights were once more extinguished; whereupon the same curious and vivacious sounds, motions, and playful rappings re-occurred; and hands, or what appeared such — soft, warm, and well-defined — grasped the joined hands of some, or touched the knees and heads of others. This interval was very brief indeed, and then a sound was suddenly heard of rope being swiftly whisked apart.

The light was struck again, and Mr. Davenport was found perfectly free, with his rope festooned about the neck of one of the guests. The whole space of this interval did not appear at all sufficient for the task of thus disentangling the captive in toils.

After discussing this marvel or trick, the circle was re-formed, the rope placed on the floor, and the lights re-extinguished. To the same discordant music, and with the same rustling noise, the rope was now heard to be taken up, and in a very short time Mr. Davenport was shown to us more tightly bound than before, in the old position, with a perfect roll of hitches on wrists and ankles and the chair-bars. Again darkness was made, and it was desired that the dress-coat worn by the prisoner should be removed. Certainly — no sooner said than done; for with a "swish " something was heard to fly towards the circle, and Mr. Davenport appeared bound exactly as before, but in his shirt-sleeves, the coat lying between two of those looking on. We had been requested previously to assure ourselves of the integrity of the second set of knots by sealing them; this was not done, but an India-rubber band was twisted in a very peculiar way over the principal knot, and band and knot, so far as the sharpest of us could judge, were absolutely intact after the experiment. We had either witnessed, therefore, a feat which laughs at the law of "the continuity of matter," resembling that of turning the skin of an orange inside out without breaking it, or we have been duped. You, sir, must take your choice, as we did, of the alternatives.

This was performed with Mr. Davenport's coat, which may give "Wizards of the North and South" the right to smile at what they could certainly, with some important preparation beforehand, counterfeit. But afterwards the coat of one of the gentlemen present was taken off and laid on the table, and, with the same "swish" in the dark, it was instantly and accurately adjusted to the back and arms of Mr. Davenport; his wrists being still bound together and still fastened behind him to the chair-back; the knots also being again ascertained to be, so far as could be judged by the closest inspection, unviolated. Again, Mr. Editor, I must present you with the dilemma, upon the horns of which we were tossed; either we had witnessed an annihilation of what are called material laws or we were the dupes of genuinely clever conjuring.

The last is the explanation, I have perceived, of some professional prestidigitators, naturally alarmed for their trade; but, though the "coat-changing trick" is common enough among the "Houdins" and "Andersons" of Europe and Asia, it remains to be seen if they can accept the conditions of it which I have attempted to describe. If they can, it is doubtless prestidigitation which we witnessed, and the darkness is a shield of tricksters, not an atmospheric condition absolutely demanded by the subtle laws of some new and unexplained force. As a candid reporter of the proceedings, I must confess that the verdict of "conjuring" was not that which was pronounced by my companions. But then almost everyone was in the habit of seeing and hearing "manifestations," at home or in private residences, of a kind daily familiar now to them, whatever, and whencesoever they may be — familiar, indeed, I understand, to thousands of persons, but very little spoken of except among the initiated.

These would make, however, a bead-roll most surprising to the esoteric, comprising, it is whispered, distinguished statesmen, authors, scientific men and clergymen, who form together a curious and quiet society — either the embodiment of a mutual and colossal self-deceit, or the silent heralds of a social revolution which must shake the world,

I shall neither report to you the astounding accounts which were given to us of what "had occurred" in the same way, nor the explanations attempted in the conversations that followed. My wish has been simply to present here what was seen, heard, and felt to happen in a private drawing-room, and among intelligent and careful observers, with serious reasons for detecting a trick, if trick could be detected. It only remains to add that the cords upon Mr. Fay's hands and feet had been all this while so tightly tied, that the tension was painful, and another minute's gloom was therefore resorted to to free him, upon which the cords were instantly thrown loose and fastened about Captain Inglefield's neck, in a knot which sailors call the "hangman's" — an intricate slip-knot, which gives upwards, but not downwards. A voice then called through the speaking trumpet "Good night;" and the puzzling "manifestations" of which I offer you a perfectly sincere, and I think an exact account, were concluded. The problem is very simple. The "wizards" have only to perform exactly the same things, and whatever more can be done, under the conditions which the Brothers Davenport dictate and accept, and the public will agree with their view of what at present is not easily explained.

'I am, Sir, yours, etc.

'Master of Arts.'

To this testimony, which speaks for itself, I shall add a few brief extracts from that of other competent observers without tasking the patience of the reader by copying entire articles.

In a communication to the 'Morning Star,' written, it is said, by Mr. W. E. Hickson, for eleven years editor and proprietor of the 'Westminster Quarterly Review,' occur the following observations:

The moment Mr. Ferguson took away his hand the middle door was pulled to and fastened from within, and at the next instant the distinct form of a large human hand appeared at a diamond-shaped aperture of the door; sounds were heard among the musical instruments; the doors flew open, and the trumpet and bells were thrown out on the floor. By whom? Not certainly by the two bound prisoners, for, if free, there had hardly been time for them to rise from their seats. Was it possible that the projecting forces required had been obtained by electric and chemical agency? This experiment was repeated several times with similar but not quite the same results. Once the two bells appeared outside the aperture ringing violently without any hand to hold them, and sometimes different hands appeared — two, in one instance, together.

And what were these hands? Mr. Ferguson was asked might they be touched. Permission being accorded, two gentlemen approaching the aperture were patted by the hands, and I succeeded in just touching one of them, or something palpable, before it receded backwards, vanishing or melting in the darkness. The brevity of the interval of their appearance, too short for serious examination, was the unsatisfactory part of this experiment.

DARK SÉANCE—THE DAVENPORT BROTHERS

Who carried the guitar? Not Mr. Ferguson, for his hands were joined to ours; not Messrs. Davenport and Fay, for they remained tied to the chairs, and the position of their feet, which we had marked with pencil, showed they had not stirred. If a confederate in list slippers, no footfall could be detected, and no chance was given us, with our legs stretched out, of tripping him up as he passed.

The coat test, however, and indeed all the manifestations, have yet to be better tested than, under the circumstances, they could be by me, or anyone witnessing them only for the first time. I will say of them only that the general result of what was seen, heard, and felt by all, was, in spite of the ludicrous mixed up with it, more startling and perplexing than I had conceived, calculated to produce certainly a profound impression on many minds, and that, if jugglery be at the bottom of it, those by whom it can be exposed cannot too early explain the deception in the interests of the public.

Another correspondent of the 'Morning Star,' the Rev. Jabez Burns, after describing the preparations of binding, etc., and stating that the knots were covered with sealing-wax, and sealed with the crest of a gentleman present, says:

The guitar was now touched with phosphorus, and when the lights were extinguished we saw the luminous spots on it, on the table. Shortly it rose and moved around and above us, and we could distinctly trace it by the phosphorescent light it emitted. In passing close to me it struck the foot of a young gentleman whose hand was linked with mine, and left the phosphorus light on the leg of his trousers. In the course of the experiments the coat of one of the Davenports was removed, and afterwards they were uncorded, and the rope of one thrown into the lap of a person who sat near me.

Now such are the actual occurrences, without rhetorical garniture, and literally as they were seen by myself and all present.

I had expected that Dr. Ferguson would be in connection with the closet, but he never went near it during the experiment, one of the gentlemen being invariably between him and the closet. I cannot conceive of any exhibition being more open and straight-forward, and if there should be a conjuror able to repeat these tricks, as they are called, I shall be glad to be one of a committee to record it.

The 'Morning Post' of October 6, 1864, contains an article, not published as a communication, which says:

The theory of the Americans [Brothers Davenport] is that, by whatever agency they are untied, they themselves are passive agents in the matter, and that their own hands in no way contribute to their release. An ingenious test was applied, a few evenings since, at a séance which took place at the Queen's Concert Rooms, Hanover Square, to prove the value of the assertion. To show that the uncording was not affected by the hands of the Americans, some flour was procured, and after the process of pinioning had been completed to the satisfaction of all present, the fingers of the brothers were covered with the substance, and they were required to hold a quantity of it firmly in their hands, clasped and locked firmly one in the other. They were at the time dressed in ordinary evening costume, and it would have been impossible for them to have untied the ropes, and subsequently tied them again, without being covered with the flour.

'The result was, however, as the Americans predicted it would be. When the doors of the cabinet were thrown open, they were found with their limbs untied, and in precisely the same positions in which they had been left, but with no portion of the flour on their clothes. The doors of the cabinet were subsequently closed, and after an interval of two or three minutes were thrown open, when the brothers were found tightly pinioned hand and foot, and clutching the flour as before.'

The reader, in the earlier chapters of this biography, may have had a faint suspicion that the writer had what the phrenologists used to call 'the organ of credenciveness,' largely developed. Will the testimony of so many of the most accurate observers, and able writers of the leading journals of London convince him that every statement contained in this volume is not only made in good faith, but is supported by good evidence?

If what some of the ablest writers in England assert is to be believed, then all here stated may be believed; for when we pass the limit of ordinary possibilities, we have no guide but the observation of facts. It is no longer a question of what is probable or possible, but of what is true.

The piano jumped so violently and shook us up so roughly that we were thankful to get off it.   See page 36.

CHAPTER EIGHTEEN
IMPORTANT SÉANCE

Nobility, Savants, and Men of Letters — Second Séance at Mr. Boucicaut's — An admirable Description — Needless Disclaimers — The true Philosophical Method.

I COME now to the most important, clear, and authoritative statement yet made in this volume:

On the night of October 11th, 1864, a very distinguished company assembled at the residence of Mr. Dion Boucicault, to witness the manifestations which are given in the presence of the Brothers Davenport. It consisted of Viscount Bury, M.P., Sir Charles Wyke, G.C.B., Sir Charles Nicholson, Ambassador to Mexico, the Chancellor of the University of Sydney, the Speaker of the House of Representatives of Queensland, Mr. Robert Bell, Mr.Robert Chambers, LL.D., Mr. Charles Eeade, D.C.L., Capt. Inglefield, the Arctic navigator, two physicians, and several writers of the daily press, whose names will be found in the following luminous and admirable report of the proceedings by Mr. Boucicault.

'The Davenport Brothers.

'To the Editor of the "Daily News."

'Sir, — A séance by the Brothers Davenport and Mr. W. Fay took place in my house yesterday in the presence of Lord Bury,

Sir Charles Nicholson,

Sir John Gardiner,

Sir C. Lennox Wtke,

Rev. E. H. Newenham,

Rev. W. Ellis,

Capt. E. A. Inglefield,

Mr. Charles Reade,

DARK SÉANCE—THE DAVENPORT BROTHERS

James Matthews,
Algernon Borthwick,
I. Willes,
H. E. Ormerod,
Mr. J. W. Kate,
J. A. Biestock,
H. J. Rideout,
Robert Bell,
J. N. Mangles,
H, M. Dunphey
W. Tyler Smith, M. D.
E. Tyler Smith,
T. L. Coward,
John Brown, M. D..
Robert Chambers,
and
Dion Boucicallt.

'The room in which the meeting was held is a large drawing-room, from which all the furniture had been previously removed, excepting the carpet, a chandelier, a small table, a sofa, a pedestal, and twenty-six cane-bottomed chairs.

'At two o'clock six of the above party arrived, and the room was subjected to careful scrutiny. It was suggested that a cabinet to be used by the Brothers Davenport, but then erected in an adjacent room, should be removed into the front room, and placed in a spot selected by ourselves. This was done by our party, but in the process we displaced a portion of this piece of furniture, thus enabling us to examine its material and structure before we mended it. At three o'clock our party was fully assembled, and continued the scrutiny. We sent to a neighboring music-seller for six guitars and two tambourines, so that the implements to be used should not be those with which the operators were familiar.

'At half-past three the Brothers Davenport and Mr. Fay arrived, and found that we had altered their arrangements, by changing the room which they had previously selected for their manifestations. The séance then began by an examination of the dress and persons of the Brothers Davenport, and it was certified that no apparatus or other contrivance was concealed on or about their persons. They entered the cabinet, and sat facing each other. Captain Inglefield then, with a new rope provided by ourselves, tied Mr. W. Davenport hand and foot, with his hands behind his back, and then bound him firmly to the seat where he sat. Lord Bury, in like manner, secured Mr. I. Davenport.

'The knots on these ligatures were then fastened with sealing-wax, and a seal was affixed. A guitar, violin, tambourine, two bells, and a brass trumpet were placed on the floor of the cabinet. The doors were then closed, and a sufficient light was permitted to enable us to see what followed. I shall omit any detailed account of the Babel of sounds which arose in the cabinet, and the violence with which the doors were repeatedly burst open and the instruments expelled; the hands appearing, as usual, at a lozenge-shaped orifice in the center door of the cabinet.

'The following incidents seem to us particularly worthy of note: While Lord Bury was stooping inside the cabinet, the door being open, and the two operators seen to be sealed and bound, a detached hand was clearly observed to descend upon him, and he started back, remarking that a hand had struck him. Again, in the full light of the gas chandelier, and during an interval in the séance, the doors of the cabinet being open, and while the ligatures of the Brothers Davenport were being examined, a very white, thin, female hand and wrist quivered for several seconds in the air above.

'This appearance drew a general exclamation from all the party. Sir Charles Wyke now entered the cabinet, and sat between the two young men — his hands being right and left on each, and secured to them. The doors were then closed, and the Babel of sounds recommenced. Several hands appeared at the orifice — among them the hand of a child. After a space, Sir Charles returned amongst us, and stated that while he held the two brothers several hands touched his face and pulled his hair; the instruments at his feet crept up, played round his body and over his head — one of them lodging eventually on his shoulders.

'During the foregoing incidents the hands which appeared were touched and grasped by Captain Inglefield and he stated that to the touch they were apparently human hands, though they passed away from his grasp. I omit mentioning other phenomena, an account of which has already been rendered elsewhere.

'The next part of the séance was performed in the dark. One of the Messrs. Davenport and Mr. Fay seated themselves amongst us. Two ropes were thrown at their feet, and in two minutes and a half they were tied hand and foot, their hands behind their backs bound tightly to their chairs, and their chairs bound to an adjacent table. While this process was going on, the guitar rose from the table, and swung or floated round the room and over the heads of the party, and slightly touching some. Now a phosphoric light shot from side to side over our heads; the laps and hands, and shoulders of several were simultaneously touched, struck, or pawed by hands, the guitar meanwhile sailing round the room, now near the ceiling, and then scuffling on the head and shoulders of some luckless wight. The bells whisked here and there, and a light thrumming was maintained on the violin. The two tambourines seemed to roll hither and thither on the floor, now shaking it violently, and now visiting the knees and hands of our circle — all these foregoing actions, audible or tangible, being simultaneous. Mr. Rideout, holding a tambourine, requested it might be plucked from his hand; it was almost instantaneously taken from him. At the same time Lord Bury made a similar request, and a forcible attempt to pluck a tambourine from his grasp was made, which he resisted.

'Mr. Fay then asked that his coat should be removed. We heard instantly a violent twitch; and here occurred the most remarkable fact. A light was struck before the coat had quite left Mr. Fay's person, and it was seen quitting him, plucked off him upwards. It flew up to the chandelier, where it hung for a moment, and then fell to the ground. Mr. Fay was seen meanwhile bound hand and foot as before. One of our party now divested himself of his coat, and it was placed on the table. The light was extinguished, and this coat was rushed on to Mr. Fay's back with equal rapidity. During the above occurrences in the dark, we placed a sheet of paper under the feet of these two operators, and drew with a pencil an outline around them, to the end that if they moved, it might be detected. They of their own accord offered to have their hands filled with flour, or any other similar substance, to prove they made no use of them, but this precaution was deemed unnecessary; we required them, however, to count from one to twelve repeatedly, that their voices constantly heard might certify to us that they were in the places where they were tied. Each of our own party held his neighbor firmly, so that no one could move without two adjacent neighbors being aware of it.

'At the termination of this séance, a general conversation took place on the subject of what we had heard and witnessed. Lord Bury suggested that the general opinion seemed to be that we should assure the Brothers Davenport and Mr. W. Fay, that after a very stringent trial and strict scrutiny of their proceedings, the gentlemen present could arrive at no other conclusion than that there was no trace of trickery in any form, and certainly there were neither confederates nor machinery, and that ail those who had witnessed the results would freely state in the society in which they moved, that so far as their investigations enabled them to form an opinion, the phenomena which had taken place in their presence were not the product of legerdemain. This suggestion was promptly acceded to by all present.

'Before leaving this question, in which my name has accidentally become mixed up, I may be permitted to observe that I have no belief in what is called Spiritualism, and nothing I have seen inclines me to believe in it — indeed, the puerility of some of the demonstrations would sufficiently alienate such a theory; but I do believe that we have not quite explored the realms of natural philosophy — that this enterprise of thought has of late years been confined to useful inventions, and we are content at least to think that the laws of nature are finite, ascertained, and limited to the scope of our knowledge. A very great number of worthy persons seeing such phenomena as I have detailed ascribe them to supernatural agency ; others wander around the subject in doubt; but as it engages seriously the feeling and earnest thought of so large a number in Europe and America, is it a subject which scientific men are justified in treating with the neglect of contempt?

' Some persons think that the requirement of darkness seems to infer trickery. Is not a dark chamber essential in the process of photography? And what would we reply to him who should say, "I believe photography to be a humbug; do it all in the light, and I will believe otherwise, and not till then?" It is true that we know why darkness is necessary to the production of the sun picture; and if scientific men will subject these phenomena to analysis, we shall find out why darkness is essential to such manifestations.

'I am, etc.

'Dion Boucicault.'

326 Regent Street, Oct. 12, 1864.

I have given this clear and authorized statement of facts entire, as it appeared in many of the London journals, because I did not wish to take the liberty of condensing in the slightest degree so remarkable a document. Otherwise I should have taken the liberty to omit — and, had I been consulted in the matter, should have advised Mr. Boucicault to omit — the first few lines in the last paragraph but one. He had given the facts as they were witnessed by himself and the distinguished party of gentlemen he had invited. They were all satisfied that there had been, and could have been, no deception, no collusion, no imposture whatever in the manifestations.

What are called physical impossibilities — what are usually denominated miracles — occurred at every stage of the proceedings. They could not distrust themselves or each other, and they took the most thorough means of preventing the possibility of their being imposed upon by the Brothers Davenport, Mr. Fay, and Mr. Ferguson. Where, then, was the necessity of a personal disclaimer as to a matter, theory, or belief, of which there was, so far as appears, no question whatever? Or why did not Mr. Boucicault go further, and assert that he was not a Methodist, or Mormon, Roman Catholic or Buddhist, nor a believer in Fetishism or Mumbo Jumbo?

The report is complete, and every one must agree that it is admirably written, so far as it is a report, down to the two concluding paragraphs. Mr. Boucicault fails only, where many men of genius have failed, when he comes to personalities which had better be left out of the case altogether.

It is also to be regretted that Lord Bury became so nettled by the chaffing of

DARK SÉANCE—THE DAVENPORT BROTHERS

'Times' correspondents as to consider it necessary to make a petulant answer, which had, how- ever, the merit of being also a witty one. He says: 'One of your correspondents, who informs us with superfluous candor that he is "no conjuror," proposes, for the sake of fair play, to bind me and Captain Inglefield hand and foot, and throw us into the Serpentine. I should like to say a few words first.'

Lord Bury proceeds to say that he refused to sign a paper which referred the manifestations to some mysterious agency, and said that 'all the Brothers Davenport could reasonably expect from us was, that we should state in society the simple truth — viz. that we had failed to detect any evidence of trickery or collusion.'

Of course this was all that could be asked of any committee whatever. Lord Bury and the gentlemen present at this séance are not asked to tell us how these things are done. Of course they know no more about it than the rest of us. What we require of them is very clearly indicated — it was to tell us what was done, and that it was not done, so far as twenty-four gentlemen, as well qualified for the purpose as any other two dozen in the United Kingdom, could judge, by trick or collusion, fraud or jugglery.

Further these deponents say not, and further no one can reasonably expect them to say.

In the case of the toads enclosed in solid limestone, what could they do more? They would first examine the stone as it lay in the quarry; they would see it split open. The toad, waking from his sleep of ages, drags himself out of his hole in the rock, and the cavity which contained him is examined. If Lord Bury were on a scientific committee, should we expect him to tell us how the toad came to be enclosed in the solid rock, or how it had managed to survive its incarceration of thousands of years?

Not at all. We might take his theory for what it was worth: but what we should want first of all would be assurance of the facts, and that there was, as far as he and the committee could judge, 'no trick or collusion.'

Still I must say that the lovers of truth, without regard to theories, are indebted to Lord Bury and all the gentlemen who attended this séance, and more than all, perhaps, to Mr. Boucicault, for an exhibition of so much candour, moral courage, and genuine philosophy, which I cannot but think more in character for English gentlemen than the sneers, ridicule, and flagrant abuse of a portion of the press of this metropolis.

The Fabulous DAVENPORT BROTHERS

CHAPTER NINETEEN
AUDI ALTERAM PARTEM

The Press in Opposition — Ugly Trash for Bedlam — Common Conjuring — Fantastic Tricks and Farthing Candles — Miserable Trifling — Grotesquely absurd and stupidly meaningless — Reverend Dobbs — Tedious, dull, and vulgar — The Secret not worth knowing — Human Nature and an Awful Warning.

Having given so much of the testimony of the London newspaper press and its correspondents respecting the earlier séances of the Brothers Davenport in England, it may be considered but fair, and it will certainly be amusing, to hear the other side.

The 'Standard' of October 1, 1864, in its leading leader, begs 'to suggest that it was all, from beginning to end, a piece of flagrant jugglery.' It thinks 'it is astonishing to find respectable journals defacing their columns with this ugly trash.' It gives all the particulars, notwithstanding, in its largest type and most conspicuous column, and then says: — When a "floating guitar" has drawn blood, while the Brothers re- main bound to their chairs, the remedies which irresistibly suggest themselves are those of Bethlehem Hospital.' To what are we coming, or rather to what are we going?'

'But what, after all, is the social use of these enchanters? They do nothing for us. They cannot trace a pickpocket, or find a lost watch, or reclaim a missing relative. . . . We discard Magus, and we had hoped not to hear of him again, duplicated by the Brothers Davenport, with their changing of coats, their miraculous appearance in shirt-sleeves, and their apparatus of ropes, which we trust will be some day more efficaciously employed.

'Really, an intellectual poison and intoxication have come into fashion on these bewildering subjects, and the public have been dosed so often and so powerfully that we wish this experimental physician who prescribes such mysterious drugs would cut short his visit.'

It is pretty evident that this writer tries to think the manifestations are vulgar jugglery, but he finds it hard to keep to that opinion. He suspects they are real, and is a little afraid of them.

The 'Spectator' thinks it looks like 'a common case of conjuring managed by a secret entrance into the apartment behind the cabinet.' But as the room is alight, and the committee passed behind the cabinet or surrounded it, such an explanation will not answer. When persons sit in the cabinet between the brothers, no such aid would be possible.

The 'Herald,' October 4, says: 'An attempt is being made to palm off these Brothers Davenport as phenomena. They themselves accept their ludicrous reputation, though as yet we have heard nothing of their doings more extraordinary or dignified than the tricks of a common juggler in the street, of a Chinese theatre, or of a strolling company of Japan. . . . We trust that public curiosity will not encourage the sham. It means, if anything, that spirits — powers hovering between earth and heaven — help a man off with his coat, tinkle a muffin-bell, play upon banjoes, touch people's knees, rap them on the knuckles, and play a hundred fantastic tricks, which cease immediately upon the lighting of a farthing candle. It is too much!'

It is also 'too much' to be begging the whole question in this fashion. The first thing to be decided is, are these things done, and not by the Davenports or other human agency? Who or what does them, and why they are done, will then be the questions next in order. It is not philosophical to say of any phenomenon, 'If this occurred, it must have been from such a cause, which is absurd — therefore it never happened.' So many improbable things happen that we have the proverb, 'Truth is stranger than fiction.'

While some of the journals are content to be flippant and sarcastic, the 'Daily News,' of October 8, is tremendously indignant. In its solemn view of the subject, 'it is both surprising and deplorable that persons of education and standing should not only countenance but welcome and applaud such efforts, and that influential organs of opinion should be found ready to give them indirect encouragement, if not positive support.'

The 'Daily News' asserts that their tricks are vulgar jugglery, such as are commonly performed on both sides of the Atlantic. Then it scolds educated and respectable people for encouraging such impostures. Then it is a reaction from skepticism. Finally, 'such miserable trifling with noble emotions is not only utterly unworthy of any serious and manly mind, but must, in the nature of the case, lead to most injurious results. To divorce any emotion from its true objects and ends is to abuse and degrade it, and to do thus with regard to emotions that lead us beyond the world of sense tends directly to dry up the most sacred springs of belief and action.'

And all this outburst of eloquence and morality about a party of common jugglers, who are doing tricks with which everybody is familiar! It reminds one of the thunder-clap that astonished poor Moses when he had stolen into a dark corner of a chop-house to eat his bit of bacon.

The 'Saturday Review' would be expected of course to have something very spicy or very savage on so exciting a subject. It could not keep its various nicknames of 'Saturday Reviler' etc. otherwise. It says: 'As to the phenomena themselves, anything so grotesquely absurd and stupidly meaningless has not yet been produced, even in the dreary annals of spiritualism.'

And then, losing its usual pointed vivacity, it goes off, like the 'Daily News,' into a solemn sermon about 'the world of spirits' — as if that had anything to do with the case whatever!

The 'John Bull' has heard a story of a 'Reverend Dobbs,' in Canada, who tied and untied knots, and declared himself ready to do whatever the Davenports did if they would only lend him their apparatus — the apparatus consisting of a walnut-box, some half-inch ropes, and a few not very costly musical instruments!

The 'London Review' suggests "that until the Brothers can be seen bound while the manifestations are occurring, people will believe they have something to do with them," but as thousands of people have seen the manifestations, and the Brothers fast bound without so much as a second intervening, this goes for very little.

The 'Morning Star' says: "We give an opinion which we know is not shared by some highly intelligent and candid men who were present at last night's performance (the Press séance), when we say that it appeared to us tedious, dull, and vulgar. If the exhibition were an avowed display of conjuring cleverness it would be but a poor and vapid entertainment. Only those who believe it to be performed by some supernatural or extra-natural power can feel any genuine interest in it."

This is to a certain extent true. If the manifestations were deceptions, by legerdemain, machinery, and the aid of confederates, they would be very poor and worthless, and the whole London press would have made itself very contemptible by taking so much notice of them.

The 'Globe' is rather of this opinion, and talks in a superior manner of "two baker's dozens of accomplished gentlemen engaged in a dark room in trying to find out how conjurors perform their tricks! What a satire on this enlightened age! We say, let the brother conjurors make their money; but if they are to be put to the test, let the test be applied, not by men of science, but by a board of conjurors under a competent chairman. We should then soon know the secret — a secret not worth knowing."

It has been stated in some of the London papers that the Brothers Davenport were watched closely for a week by Mr. Hermann, one of the cleverest prestidigitators and conjurors in America, without being able to get any clue to the secret, and that he became perfectly convinced that no kind of jugglery had anything to do with it. The suggestion, however, is not a bad one. There are no doubt respectable manufacturers of conjuring apparatus and performers in London, who, associated with two or three men of science and a couple of sharp detectives, might find out the 'secret not worth knowing.'

It is useless to continue quotations which are to the same purport, and when we have no guarantee of the wisdom or even of the sincerity of the writers. If the leading writers of the leading papers of London, stating simply matters of their own observation — what they saw and heard — felt obliged to assume the mask of contributors, as if not sufficiently shielded by being anonymous, or if the editors of these leading and powerful organs of public opinion thought it necessary thus to disown the members of their respective staffs, what could be expected of periodicals in a less independent position?

On the whole, 'human nature' enters about as largely into the composition of the gentlemen of the press as elsewhere. The press is 'free' to do what is for its interests, and it is 'independent' of whatever will not affect its circulation and influence. Nowhere probably is the press less purchasable, or less capable of being directly influenced by base and mercenary considerations; but there is the great public of readers, whose tastes and prejudices must be consulted.

The case of a celebrated monthly magazine has been an 'awful warning' to the whole English press. Some years ago it published a perfectly fair statement of facts, as observed by one of its favorite contributors. The result is said to have been the loss of three thousand copies of its circulation, to say nothing of unmeasured ridicule and abuse. Even in free England it is not always profitable to tell the truth. This magazine has repented and recanted. A few months ago it laid down the rule that a man ought not to believe what he considered improbable on any amount of testimony, that of his own senses included — a safe rule for magazine editors, no doubt, if not a wise one for the general public. First make up your mind what you will believe and what you will refuse to believe, and then 'so much the worse for the facts,' when they happen to be against you.

The Fabulous DAVENPORT BROTHERS

CHAPTER TWENTY
A PERSONAL STATEMENT

What I think of the Brothers Davenport, and what I saw at a Séance at the Hanover-square Rooms.

This may be as good a place as another to give my individual testimony respecting the Brothers Davenport, and the phenomena which occur in their presence.

The young men, with whom I have had but a brief personal acquaintance, and whom I never saw until their arrival in London, appear to me to be, in intellect and character, above the average of their young countrymen. They are not remarkable for cleverness, though of fair abilities, and Ira has some artistic talent. The manifestations seem to have been quite as extraordinary ten years ago, when they were boys of fourteen and fifteen years, as at the present time. The young men seem entirely honest, and singularly disinterested and unmercenary — far more anxious to have people satisfied of their integrity and the reality of their manifestations than to make money.

They have an ambition, without doubt, which is gratified in their having been selected as the instruments of what they believe will be some great good to mankind, and they are not free from the personal tastes and vanities common to their age, and from which only a few of the very wisest of us are entirely exempted.

I have elsewhere given my estimate of Mr. Ferguson, the gentleman who exercises a friendly and almost parental care over them, and who attends them to state the conditions of the manifestations. Of the purely business relations of Mr. Palmer I need not again speak.

The séance I am about to describe took place at the Queen's Concert Rooms, Hanover Square, on Friday evening, October 28, 1864. The company consisted of fifty-two persons, the larger portion of whom had secured admission by payment. The rest — members of the Press, and some who had attended previous séances — were invited. It was desired that Captain Inglefield should be one of the tying and trying committee, but he declined, on the ground that he had done his best on two or three former occasions, but his knots were all untied, and he was naturally discouraged.

Two intelligent and sufficiently skeptical gentlemen were chosen, and proceeded to tie the two brothers in and to the slight cabinet, which could be seen over, under, and on each side, and by the committee behind. It was at no time possible that any person could approach it in any way, or for any purpose, unseen by the audience: concealed machinery was equally out of the question.

After the binding twenty persons, perhaps, examined the ropes and knots. The side doors were then shut and fastened. The middle door was then pushed close, and the bolt inside was instantly heard to shoot into its fastening; the trumpet was thrown out of a small opening near the top of the door, and the middle door thrown open from the inside. In two seconds — as quickly as possible — the other doors were opened, and the Brothers seen to be firmly bound, precisely as they had been. Who threw out the trumpet? Hands were shown at the opening, and the bell held out and rung, and then dropped on the floor. Instantly the open doors showed the Brothers bound.

There was not a moment's delay — not time to untie or tie one of twenty knots. Whose were the hands, and who rang the bell? Most certainly neither of the Davenports, and as certainly no other person.

One of the three doors was closed, and from behind it hands and portions of arms appeared. The closed door was flung open instantly, and the young men were seen bound as before. Once a feminine hand and two-thirds of a bare arm was reached through the hole in the middle door, and the whole interior was exposed in a moment, with the same result as before.

What hands and arms were those? Certainly not those of the Davenports, and as certainly there was no other person in the cabinet, or near it.

The doors were again closed, and a rattling and drawing of ropes was heard for nearly four minutes (three minutes forty-eight seconds), with the ringing of the bell and other noises. The doors were opened, and the young men stood up free, while the thirty or forty feet of small rope with which they had been bound lay coiled between them.

Had they unbound themselves? Their wrists were firmly knotted together; their hands cannot pass through a rope-ring considerably larger than their wrists, and they could in no way reach the ends of the ropes. On other occasions they have held their hands full of flour, had the knots sealed, and submitted to similar tests innumerable.

The doors were closed again, and after a noise of rattling and whishing of ropes, lasting about two minutes, they were found to be bound more thoroughly and securely than before. A large portion of the audience went upon the platform to inspect this new binding. Who did it? The hands were firmly knotted together, and fixed in their position; the feet were immovably fastened. They were bound to their seats, and the ends of the rope were entirely beyond their reach. It is certain that they did not tie themselves, and it is equally certain that no other visible person was in the box.

Several musical instruments were now placed in the cabinet between the Brothers, but not within their reach. The doors were scarcely closed before we heard the tuning of the violin, the keys turning while the strings were snapped. That takes two hands. Whose? Then a rude concert commenced — the violin being played with the bow; the tambourine rumbled, the guitar thrummed, and the bell joined in the accompaniment. The music was not of a high order, but three common rustic tunes were played in good time and tune, lasting in all some ten or fifteen minutes. Then, while the instruments were still sounding, the middle door suddenly flew open, the instruments came tumbling out, the side doors were instantly opened, and everyone saw the Brothers Davenport bound hand and foot, with no indication that they had made the slightest movement. The committee reported the knots perfect. People got upon the platform to look for themselves.

Now, who made the music? Certainly not the Davenports. Provided they could have got out of their fastenings, which I believe impossible, they had not two seconds from the time we heard the instruments all playing, before we saw them securely and elaborately bound, so that the committee could not see even the slightest change. Well, who made the concert? It required four pairs of hands; but here were but two, and they securely fastened!

It was stated by one of the committee that Mr. William Davenport's pulse was raised to 130, while Mr. Ira Davenport's was not affected. The fact of Ira's pulse not being affected perceptibly, shut in the close box, proves that he did not unbind and bind him- self, or take part in the rapid and violent concert. The different state of William's pulse, under the same conditions, would indicate some difference of temperament, or constitutional susceptibility.

The assembly was next seated in a semi-circle of two rows, one close behind the other. In the centre, some ten feet removed from the nearest persons, was an oblong table and two chairs, one on each side of the table. Mr. Ira Davenport was firmly bound to one chair, by a gentleman selected from the company, and Mr. Wm. M. Fay to the other. Their feet were made fast, and their hands very firmly tied behind them. Sheets of white paper were placed under their feet, and marked round with a pencil. Everybody took hold of hands, so that each person was held by two others. Wm. Davenport was held by a gentleman at one end of the semicircle, and Mr. Ferguson, who held the candle and matches for relighting, was held by Captain Inglefield at the other.

The instant the light was extinguished, and before the quickest-footed per-

DARK SÉANCE—THE DAVENPORT BROTHERS

son could have entered the room, the bell and musical instruments on the table were in commotion. A guitar flew around in the air above our heads like a bat or swallow, twanging as it went, its course and motion being easily distinguished by the sound. It went much higher than a man could reach, and it was not thrown in right lines, but flew in curves or circles, ringing as it went, and plainly fanning the air upon our faces with its rapid motion. The sound was not so sharp as that made by the fingers or thumb, but loud and full. After a few moments the instrument rested on the floor, a match was struck, and everyone was satisfied that neither Mr. Davenport nor Mr. Fay had moved. Their hands were tied behind them, their feet had not stirred from the pencil-marks.

Now, who made the flying music? Not the Davenports, nor any person in the company, for they were all secured too firmly, had they been able to do it. By some power the twanging ringing instrument was made to fly round the room over our heads more like the flight of a swallow than anything to which I can compare it. Again and again after these sounds the candle was lighted, and each time the fastenings found secure.

Then Mr. Fay was unbound by some invisible power, while Mr. Davenport remained bound; next Mr. Davenport was unbound, while Mr. Fay was bound ; then both were found again more securely bound, if possible, than at the beginning.

And now came the crowning marvel — a thing so utterly astounding that I should not hope to be believed had I been its only witness. While both were firmly bound to their chairs, several feet apart, and the company secured by each other, a slight rushing or whishing sound was heard, and the light called for. Mr. Fay's coat, which he had on the moment before, was lying on the table, and he sitting in his shirtsleeves, with his hands still firmly tied together at the wrists behind him, and also to the chair. The coat was examined, and no rip or rent discovered.

How can a man take off his coat, or how can it be taken off, with his hands tied together behind him? I only know, as some hundreds of persons in London know, that it was done!

It was asked if some gentleman would lend his coat for a few moments. A stout beaver-cloth coat was proffered and laid upon the table. The candle was blown out, and in a few moments relighted. The borrowed coat was found completely and properly put on Mr. Davenport, over his own, while his hands were seen to be firmly and very tightly tied behind him, and bound to the back of the chair. I felt and examined the knots, as did many others: there was no mistake, or possibility of a mistake.

How was this done? To say that in those few moments Ira Davenport was unbound, put on the coat, and was again tied, is absurd. It was the same when the knots were sealed with sealing-wax or his hands fastened with sticking-plaister.

DARK SÉANCE—THE DAVENPORT BROTHERS

There was not time even to untie him had there been confederates to do it. He could not have untied himself. It is perfectly evident that these coats went on and off, in direct violation of what we know as physical laws, by the same power that had done all the things which may seem less wonderful or less impossible, but of which we can give no better explanation ; and they show that this power has a control over material substances of which we are unable to form the least conception.

I am sensible that my account does not differ essentially from several others, but there were particular points which I wished to press upon the notice of the reader.

There is one more. If what I have written be true, and every cool observer present will confirm every word, the whole matter deserves the most earnest investigation of men of science. It is more interesting than the gorilla: it is of more importance than a new gas, a new metal, or a newly-discovered planet.

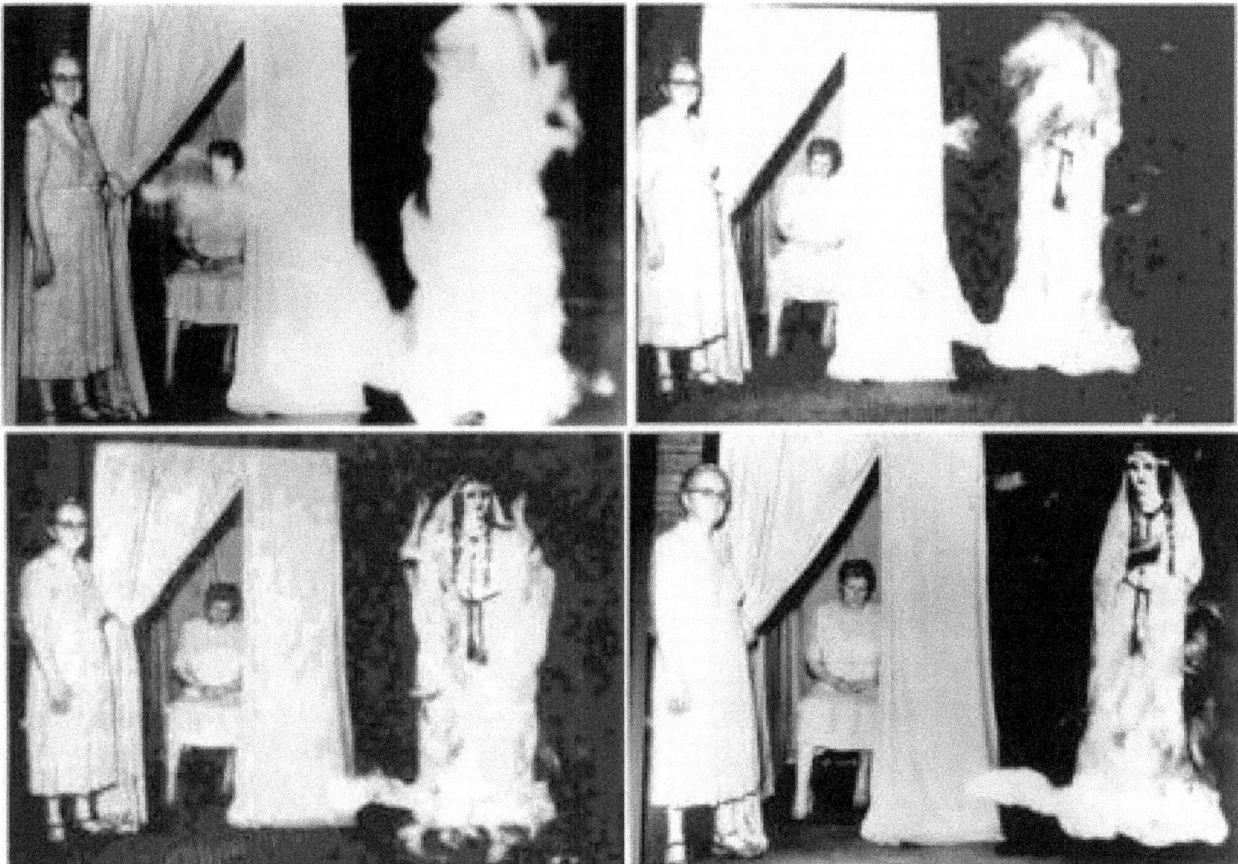

Here is shown a "full materialization" of an "Indian Spirit Guide."

171

DARK SÉANCE—THE DAVENPORT BROTHERS

Here a spirit hand appears to be tipping the table.

The Fabulous DAVENPORT BROTHERS

CHAPTER TWENTY-ONE
'AND THE MAGICIANS DID SO WITH THEIR ENCHANTMENTS.'

The Professors, Excited — Duty to Expose Imposture — Professor Anderson — Mr. Tolmaque — Challenges Quibbled out of — The Magicians resort to Tricks — Rope-tying in Demand — A Ten Years' Contest — Testimony of an Amateur.

In the 'Dark Ages' the marvels done in presence of the Brothers Davenport would have been referred by a large majority of the people to necromancy or witchcraft. In these enlightened days all those who do not care to examine ascribe them at once to legerdemain, and the mechanical deceptions of professional jugglers or so-called conjurors. Of course at this day, and in this country, no one out of the nursery believes in magic as it was anciently believed in everywhere, and still is over the Eastern World.

Most people have been amused and, per- haps, astonished at the tricks of our modern magicians, who fry pancakes in hats, make cards or money dance, pour all kinds of liquors out of a single bottle, shoot gold watches into the center of uncut oranges, and so on. These tricks are amusing and, until we know the modus operandi, they are surprising. It is not strange that those who cannot account for the Davenport manifestations, and who also know but little about them, should class them with such performances.

It is not strange, either, that as soon as the various 'professors' of these magical arts found the phenomena attending the Brothers Davenport noticed in the leading papers of England as their amusing but not especially wonderful performances were not likely to be, they should endeavor to take advantage of this kind of publicity, and of the excitement these wonders had produced. And if the 'professors' believed that the Davenports were mere jugglers like themselves, they had also a right to be indignant, as would everyone, that they were gaining notoriety, and perhaps money, under false pretenses. I cheerfully admit that it would be the right, and perhaps the duty, of every magician in England to expose such a base and infamous deception, and they could not do it too speedily.

DARK SÉANCE—THE DAVENPORT BROTHERS

The Brothers Davenport had scarcely appeared in London before Professor Anderson, then performing at St. James's Hall, declared that they were 'very clever young artistes, who have been performing the rope-tying trick, bell-ringing, trumpet -flying, and changing coat experiments, all of which my son is exhibiting at the present time in America, by natural agency only.' Then came 'M. Tolmaque, Prestidigitator,' declaring that he could do the same things as the Davenports in the same manner and offering to show a committee how they were done if the Davenports would do the same.

An 'Officer of the Army' offered to take off his jacket without removing his coat; but when he was required to have his hands tied together, like the Davenports, he respectfully declined.

The Brothers Davenport met the statement of Professor Anderson fairly and squarely, as follows:

30S Regent Street, Oct. 6, 1864.

'Sir, — Having read your letter in the 'Morning Post' of Saturday last, we beg to accept the challenge made or implied in that communication. We are ready to appear before a party of twelve or more gentlemen, specially chosen as capable of fairly investigating the phenomena we present. You shall be present, and shall have every facility given yon to examine the empty room and the instruments we use. You shall then explain, to the satisfaction of the gentlemen present, the legerdemain you have stated we employ, or produce, if you can, in your own person the same results. Should you succeed, by legerdemain, in performing or imitating those results, or be able to detect and expose imposture, we shall then be ready to acknowledge that your accusations are justly founded. But if you fail — as we are well assured you will do — we shall require you to retract publicly the accusations you have publicly made against us.

'We are, etc.

'Brothers Davenport.

'To Professor Anderson,

'St. James's Hall.'

The Professor denied that he had given any challenge! It would be impossible for even a professor of legerdemain to back more coolly out of a difficulty.

A similar letter was sent to 'M. Tolmaque, Prestidigitator,' and he also declined the encounter in the same manner.

These two magicians did not so with their enchantments.

Finally, to cover the whole ground, the following letter was written, and, like the others, published in the 'Morning Post' (Oct. 8, 1864):

DARK SÉANCE—THE DAVENPORT BROTHERS

London, Oct. 4, 1864.

'Sir, — The séance which took place in your house, and in the presence of yourself and friends, last Wednesday evening, has given rise to much discussion, in which we have been pronounced by some not only jugglers but impostors [say jugglers, and therefore impostors]. Two professed conjurors have publicly announced that they can produce, by legerdemain, all the phenomena we have exhibited. We accept the challenge, and shall feel obliged if a committee of gentlemen of character and position can be found, selected from such as are quite free from any prejudice in the matter. A séance shall then take place in a room which may be examined beforehand, and with instruments to be furnished by the committee. We are prepared to produce there certain phenomena in the presence of these gentlemen, and in the presence of the two conjurors; and when we have done, the conjurors shall be required to attempt to produce the same, under the same conditions, or shall expose, to the satisfaction of the committee, the fraudulent means we are stated to have employed: but this they shall do by the exercise and exhibition of legerdemain (or, if they please, by machinery), and not by any occult power of the nature of that we possess, and which they might use in secret and then repudiate, for we do not pretend that we have the exclusive possession of the power we employ.

'We trust, sir, in fairness to us and to those who believe in our honesty, that the test will be fairly and strictly applied, and the result, whatever it may be, made public.

'We make this offer in all sincerity and good faith, and we hope it will be met and dealt with in the same spirit.

'We are, yours truly,

'Ira Erastus Davenport,

'William H. Davenport,

'William M. Fay.

'To Dion Boucicault, Esq.'

This fair and open challenge, which has simple good faith written in every sentence, and which, in the latter portion, shows the extent of it in a very curious manner, met with no response from the magicians.

A correspondent of the 'Morning Post' asks of M. Tolmaque, who gave an exhibition of tying and untying himself, very clever, no doubt, but not at all to the purpose. 'Can he, dressed in black, and holding powdered chalk or flour in his hands, effect both the phenomena of tying and untying the ropes, as exhibited by the Brothers Davenport, and in the same space of time, without dropping any of the flour from his hands? Can he produce visible and palpable hands, distinctly and unequivocally human to outward sight and touch, ending at the wrist, without wires or rods or human arms connected with them?

'The writer offers to pay any sum he may name to any prestidigitator who can do these things, on condition that, failing, he will give a quarter of the sum to some charity.

Professor Anderson, instead of accepting any of these offers, challenged the Brothers to do their 'tricks' in his theatre, in full light, instead of darkness; knowing perfectly well that total darkness in some cases, and partial obscurity in others, was usually an indispensable condition and, so far as can be known, one of the laws of the phenomena — as much so, perhaps, as in the camera obscura. If the things done in the absence of light could be done in its presence, the cabinet and ropes, sealing-wax, flour, straps of diachylon, and all other tests might be dispensed with, though it may be doubted if people would more readily believe.

M. Tolmaque declined the challenge, on the ground that he would have nothing to do with works of darkness.

Mr. Palmer was not quite satisfied with the 'backing out' of the prestidigitators. He was nettled, perhaps, that a portion of the press persisted in declaring that the magicians had solved the problem and exposed the cheat, when they had refused the fairest opportunities to do so, with all the glory that would have attended such an achievement. Mr. Palmer therefore, on the 22nd of October, published the following: 'If M. Tolmaque or any other person will, by legerdemain, produce precisely the same phenomena as those to which the Brothers Davenport give rise, under precisely the same conditions, to the satisfaction of a majority of the noblemen and gentlemen who were present at the séance held last Friday evening at the Hanover Square Rooms, I will pay £100 to any of the dramatic funds that may be selected; the party of course attempting, should he fail, to pay a like sum to the same institution.'

The dramatic funds are vainly watching and waiting for that hundred pounds; but the response of M. Tolmaque is a curiosity. He writes ('Morning Star,' Oct. 24):

'I, M. Tolmaque, prestidigitator, hereby inform Mr. Palmer that as long as he sails under false colors I will not answer him, or any of his friends, on the subject of the Brothers Davenport.

'M. Tolmaque'

And this, I believe, ended the pretenses of the magicians, who, not being able to do so with their enchantments, gave curious experiments of their own, and untied knots at the music-halls.

This feat of untying knots is old and familiar enough, and is just what the Brothers Davenport do not do. To prove this they allow the ropes to be sealed: to prove it they hold both their hands filled with flour or other white powder; to prove it they have been sewn up in bags, enclosed in wooden tubes, and subjected to all the tests mentioned in these pages, and a hundred beside. What they wish to show is that they neither untie nor tie themselves, and that they do none of the remarkable things done in their presence.

The same power or powers that show the hands without arms, or hands and arms where no bodies are visible; which play on the instruments; which hurl the guitar sounding through the air; which remove a coat from, or put one upon, a man whose hands are bound securely together — the same power ties and unties the Brothers Davenport, when they are placed beyond the aid of confederates, and equally prevented — by the flour test, for example — from doing it themselves.

Mr. Palmer might very safely have offered the magicians themselves a thousand, or ten thousand, pounds to do one of these things by jugglery, under the same conditions.

The tyings and untyings at the theatres and music-halls may be ingenious tricks enough; but it is very absurd to compare them with what is seen at the séances of the Brothers Davenport.

It should be observed that this conflict with the conjurors is not a new thing with the Brothers. It began ten years ago, when they were but children, and when the phenomena were quite as extraordinary as they are to-day. They have been watched by the cleverest jugglers, who failed to discover the semblance of trickery. They have everywhere challenged every kind of test, and the most searching examinations. No magician has ever ventured to accept their standing challenge to exhibit the same phenomena under the same conditions.

Observe, also, that the so-called magicians never interfere with each other — never challenge each other. Each does as well as he can, and no one ever attempts to expose another's tricks. They do all they can, however, to throw discredit on the Davenports, not because they can but because they cannot do the same or even similar things. The London press, while giving credit to the skill of Professor Anderson, has very frankly declared that his pretended imitation or exposure of the Davenports is simply absurd. There is not the least resemblance.

When Professor Anderson's coat is taken off his back while his hands are securely fastened behind him with cord, or tape and sealing-wax, or copper wire, or diachylon plaster, or by wires passing through holes in his thumb and finger-nails, or by several of these means in combination, under the inspection of a competent and impartial committee, he may talk about 'an exhibition after the manner of the Brothers Davenport.' On this matter the following extract from a communication in the Newcastle Chronicle (Nov. 7, 1864) is to the purpose. The writer, after describing the favorable impressions made upon him by the Brothers and their companions, so different from what certain of the London papers had led him to expect, says:

DARK SÉANCE—THE DAVENPORT BROTHERS

"I have only this remark to make. I have seen nearly all the greatest conjurors of the present day. I have been behind the scenes, and assisted in making the necessary, preparations for a wizard's entertainment. I have seen both M. Tolmaque and Mr. Redmond do their rope-trick, and I know how it is done. I can honestly declare that what the Davenports do as far surpasses Anderson, Tolmaque, and Redmond, as these gentle- men can surpass such a clumsy amateur as I am. I am totally at a loss to account for the Davenports' feats by any known principle of legerdemain. If what they do is conjuring, all I can say about it is, that it is the cleverest conjuring I ever saw or heard of."

CHAPTER TWENTY-TWO
THE TESTIMONY OF MR. FERGUSON

Six Months with the Brothers Davenport — Séance in a Railway Tunnel — Convincing Manifestations — Personal Explanations.

The Rev. J. B. Ferguson, late of Nashville, Tennessee, who has already been mentioned as having accompanied the Brothers Davenport to England, and who has been engaged as director and lecturer, so far as explanations are required, at the séances given in this country, has, at the request of the present writer, given an account of his experiences with them in the following statement:

"On the night of the 26th April, 1864, in company with a friend, I attended the exhibition of the Brothers Davenport at the Cooper Institute, New York. On the night succeeding, in company with five of my friends from the Southern States, I attended another exhibition at the same place. I had been for years familiar with phenomena and experiences of a similar character to those represented as attending the Brothers; and from the knowledge of this fact, my Southern friends were anxious that I should accompany them.

"Of the Davenports themselves personally, or as representatives of the 'wonders' associated with their names, I knew nothing. Of course I had often seen their names in public prints, but my attention to what was said either in their favor or to their disparagement had never been sufficiently attracted to secure any conviction respecting them. Accordingly, on my way to their proposed entertainment, in reply to a question of my friends, I remember to have stated that, if the Davenports were not jugglers or deceivers, and were really instruments through which man's allied nature to the invisible or spiritual world was reflected, we should receive evidence such as no candid man could refuse to accept. I also expressed a hope that one of my friends, who was a skeptic in the saddest sense, would receive the tangible proof of what he had heard me assert and defend for fifteen years.

"When we came to the place of meeting — the large lecture-room of the Cooper Institute, the largest in New York city — we found some thousands assembled. The entertainment — for such it may properly be called — opened, and a committee was chosen to secure the young men in the cabinet and report to the audience what occurred. I need not describe the manifestations, or their effect on the audience, as the New York papers gave graphic reports at the time, and have indulged in tiresome repetitions since. It is enough to say that I was convinced that the Davenports were no jugglers, and that the displays of power through them admitted of no explanation according to any known estimate of natural laws.

"I called upon the Davenports in private, and attended their public entertainments for eleven days and nights. My skeptical friend, after the closest scrutiny, admitted that there was no clandestine mechanism or arrangement of machinery, and no sleight-of-hand in what he had so doubtingly and thoroughly examined. He is a man of the first eminence at home and abroad in discovery, and in the application of discovery in the most intricate and difficult mechanics, and in mechanical skill has few equals.

"When the Davenports appeared at Brooklyn, near New York, it happened that their representative before the public was absent; and they, through their friends, invited me to introduce them to the public of the city of Brooklyn. In that city, at the time, I was solicited to meet the representatives of a highly respectable religious society, with a view to becoming their pastor. I, however, consented to introduce the Davenports in "the City of Churches." I did this in a spirit of candid enquiry and experiment respecting a subject which I hoped might prove of interest. I did so knowing that, however desirable it might be that I should become the pastor of the church above mentioned, my action in this matter would put an end to all hope of such pastoral charge being entrusted to me. I did so because I was fully convinced that the phenomena which occurred in the presence of the Brothers was a part of the supra-mundane evidence given to this age — evidence not to be measured by the conventional restrictions of time and men, however respectable the time or however religious the men.

"When I saw and knew, for myself and not by another, that the evidences given through the Davenports were true, I accepted a proposition to accompany them to England and Europe — if, after three or four months' experience with them before the public, I should find the work such as I could perform without detriment to them or to myself. Accordingly, I spent three months in the interior towns and cities of New York State and New England, and a month in the chief cities of Canada. During this time they were brought before every class of the communities they visited; every conceivable form of fastening and other methods of 'test' and trial were submitted to — such as being held by the hands and feet while the manifestations of force were witnessed, the use of sealing-wax, and many other devices — and always with complete and undeniable success. Indeed, it were impossible for me by any use of language too strongly to state this fact.

DARK SÉANCE—THE DAVENPORT BROTHERS

"During this time I resided with them at the same hotels, and we often occupied the same suite of apartments. I travelled with them, in the unavoidable intimacy of traveling companionship, over thousands of miles of the widespread territory referred to, and consequently must have had every opportunity of detecting fraud, if fraud there were to be detected. But it becomes me to say that I never detected any, nor the appearance of any. When they were, to all appearance, sound asleep, some of the most marked of the manifestations have occurred. In traveling by rail, when entering a dark tunnel, I have, to a mental wish, received them in tangible and unmistakable forms; and this experience has been repeated in England. For example, upon our arrival at Liverpool, when we had taken our seats for London, immediately upon leaving the former city, amid expressions indicative of the natural anxiety of young Americans in their first observations and experiences as strangers in a strange land, on entering the tunnel near Liverpool, one of our party, I think Mr. Fay, said, 'I wonder if John came with us over the sea?'

"The question was instantly answered thus: I was grasped by a strong hand, and so was each one of the company. At the same time that I was thus grasped, my face and hands were gently felt by seemingly human hands. I confess the evidence was so palpable and satisfactory as to distinctness of touch, responding to my wishes, that I feared some one of our party was the operator. I pleasantly charged them with it, when each solemnly protested he was the recipient of similar evidences, and had not moved, not even desired to do so. I then desired mentally that I should be met by an evidence of such a character that it would admit of neither doubt nor denial. As we entered another tunnel I changed my position in the railroad carriage, so that no one of my party could touch me without my knowledge. In response to a mental wish I was touched, my face manipulated, and my person distinctly handled, when I knew positively that no one visible was near me.

"Of the satisfaction given by such an evidence I need not speak; no words can do it justice. I state the fact, and leave it to the appreciation of all who have the desire for similar evidences. I could give many other instances of force guided by invisible intelligence. On extinguishing the light in my room, I have had my chair instantly lifted and placed upon my head, with the legs upward, and the cushion resting on the top of my head. A voice — not mine, not that of anyone present — has directed me to feel the position of those present. I did so while the chair held itself, or was held, firmly where it was placed. In distinct vocal tones I was invited to be seated, the chair being at the same time taken from my head and placed properly, that I might comply with the invitation.

"I might record a volume of such and similar manifestations. But with respect to all these evidences, expressions, or demonstrations from the invisible world, I have one remark to make; I wish it to sink deep into the minds of my readers. These are not given in response to mere curiosity, idle wish, or selfish desire. They have come when and where they were needed, and where there was a degree of good faith in the individual to use the evidence for universal good. The rule with me is, that whenever and wherever the mind is ready for an ascent in actual progress, evidences are given that transcend all our existing standards of truth and good.

"For six months I have traveled with the Davenports, and in various conditions, advantageous and disadvantageous, I have witnessed the evidences of the power that attends them. I have seen them subjected to every form of scrutiny that skepticism could devise. I have seen their professed friends, with anxiety, caused by a bigoted and sensuous denial, return to the Davenports with fresh doubts, to be met and reassured by evidences that admitted of no denial. I can truthfully say that no time, place, or condition of the most diverse and promiscuous audiences, or the most select companies, bas ever prevented the manifestations, though they have been rendered less satisfactory in various ways. The anxiety caused the Brothers by aimless discussion, captious criticism, and obstinate denial is a very unfavorable condition.

"I have seen them associated with persons who only wished to make gain of their gifts, and whose methods of presenting them to the public were calculated only to produce distrust, and to place the evidences of the power attending them on a level with ordinary jugglery. I have seen these persons confounded, most unexpectedly to themselves, by the evidences of truth, wisdom, and power attending the manifestations.

"Through the most painstaking ordeals, the severest scrutiny, the most searching analysis these evidences have passed. They have ever come forth more clear, more satisfactory and convincing to all honest enquiry. Many of my own friends, utterly unconvinced, and looking upon me with profound astonishment that I should be so duped as to become insensible to the charms of respectability and, I may add, to the attraction and use of the 'almighty dollar,' have witnessed these evidences, and have either become silent, or have acknowledged that no duty could be more sacred than the one I have assumed. In the presence of doubt, distrust, and odium, my own arm has at times become weak and my heart faint.

"This state in me has been met by proofs of a superior recognition and protection be- yond the power of mortals to order or deny. Hence I can say, in presence of men and of the Great Unseen though not Unknown Power who governs all human action that these evidences are all and much more than is claimed for them by those through whose agency they are brought before the mind. These evidences are entirely above and beyond the capacity of those through whom or by whom they are given, physically, intellectually, and morally. True, the mental capacity of the Messrs. Davenport is fully equal to, if not above, the average of their countrymen, or men of their age and opportunities. Physically, they are sound, healthy, active men. Morally, I know them to be honest candid men, with manly moral courage, decision of character, perseverance, and self-reliance under difficulties and dangers that would have appalled many who have presumed to disparage them without knowledge of their character, or from inability to account for these wondrous manifestations.

"I feel it a duty I owe to truth to say, that I know these men as well as men usually know each other. I know also that it is thought that persons who are made the instruments of such or kindred manifestations are liable, more than others, to disease of both body and mind, and it is often more than hinted that their morality is far beneath the common standard. This is not true of the Davenports. And when it is considered that for three years they gave free exhibitions, and for over seven years they have made these exhibitions the business of their lives, and are today men of clear heads and sound healthy bodies, we are forced to the conclusion that the manifestations through them are perfectly consistent with the laws or conditions of mind, physical organization, or true moral responsibility. Indeed, in a somewhat varied field of observation upon men and manners, I know of no men of like mind and opportunities who are their equals, certainly none their superiors, in all that tends to sound judgment, perseverance in the path of duty, or capacity to meet the diverse fortune or serious responsibilities of life.

"Such manifestations are not confined to these persons; I meet them in degrees everywhere. I have had similar experiences and demonstrations in my own person for years. I have met them in others in the most calm and serious periods of my somewhat eventful life. I am sure that no man can give to them an honest and unbiased attention without being satisfied that they transcend our existing estimates alike of benevolent purposes and of material law.

"I have no reason to doubt that persons through whom supra-mundane manifestations have been given have mingled trickery and fraud with what was really above them. Human nature is frail. Curiosity on the part of the public, and an eager desire for notoriety on the part of those who are for the time being ministers to this exacting curiosity, have been too powerful temptations to the weak and foolish. It has of course been said that the Davenports have descended to tricks. I can only speak for the time I have known them. Since my connection with them I know that they have not so descended, nor needed to descend. It is to the fact of entire sincerity that I attribute their untarnished success in the New World and in London and England. They are mortal, and subject to temptation, like all of us; but as regards these evidences they can have no inducement to fraud any more than a man with a million of pounds has occasion to steal. They need not to invent tricks when genuine phenomena constantly attend them. Whenever they have sat for the manifestations they have been presented in such form as to be convincing.

DARK SÉANCE—THE DAVENPORT BROTHERS

"There is only one exception to this statement in England, and that occurred at the meeting of the representatives of the press, (October 25, 1864), in London. Even then evidence was given in one form though withheld in another. There were dictation and interruption on that occasion which proved sufficient to derange the conditions of manifestation partially. But on that very evening I witnessed manifestations, in the presence of the Davenports and Mr. Fay, after the Press séance, and elsewhere, transcending all I had seen during my connection with the Brothers. Lessons of wisdom on all that had transpired were given in an audible voice, and much was anticipated, for them and for myself, that no mortal vision could then descry.

"The evidences of intelligence, of wisdom, of prophetic information and warning, of insight as to events that are as yet to occur, and which always do occur when thus fore- told — the protection and guidance and care unfailing attending the mission of these men and all who are connected intimately with it are to me equally powerful and convincing evidences as the manifestations of force or power. I do not undervalue those evidences of power that shock the materialist into belief. I know what immortality is worth as a motive to man in producing a living hope, and I know that these evidences are evidences of hope to all — yes, one mighty all — despite all the denials, vain efforts at explanation, and seeming misapplication that a diversified appreciation and culture may make of them. I know they are true, and will outlive all our standards of adaptation and application.

"I know they reveal the Godlike in man. I know they are the culmination of the movements of all the nations, tribes, and peoples of a common humanity. I know they reveal a unity in all human diversity. They will go on in increasing power, as our age and time shall unfold to receive them. They wall stay the desolating hand of selfish and sectarian animosity. They will lay low the vain conceptions of those who seek not beyond the gratification of personal desire and self-aggrandizement. They will assure us that God lives in all: and as spirit is above form, right above wrong, so will they rise above the murky mire and the clodded earth, which too often weigh us down beneath all that would adorn and beautify man as one and undivided in the Spirit that gives him life and destiny. However faint the scintillations, they come as the sparkling forms of thought divine to illumine the midnight of human erring; and they make us know that there is no hour so auspicious with hope, no day so bright, no achievement so good but that its equal will come to each, and bring the conscious reflection that through the deepest penury and want, and the most trying scenes of human care and responsibility, we are ever ascending, under the mighty hand of progress, that spans all time, to a good no language can either express or measure, under the benign rejection of the evidences of a hope to man universal, which are so signally marking our age or time.

"I present, dear Sir, to you this my honest and unwavering testimony to the nature and character of the manifestations that ever attend these deservedly celebrated young Americans.

"J. B. Ferguson,

"Of Nashville, Tennessee."

The peculiar relation of the writer of the above statement to the Brothers Davenport gives him a right to speak warmly in their behalf, and the zeal and enthusiasm with which he engages in their work, and his ideas of its importance and consequences, are evident. Those ideas are his own, and for them he is alone responsible.

At a Dark Séance in France, one lady bounded from her chair and cried,
"Wait! I will ask him to untie!"

The Fabulous DAVENPORT BROTHERS

CHAPTER TWENTY-THREE
MORE FACTS AND EVIDENCE

Mr. Coleman's Statement — He talks with 'John King' and sees Divers Marvels — Astounding Phenomena — Mr. Howitt's Testimony — Facts and Tests — Genius and Science nonplussed.

Mr. Benjamin Coleman, of No. 51 Pembridge Villas, Bayswater, a gentleman well known upon the London Stock Exchange, and who has been a careful observer of extra-natural phenomena in both hemispheres, has prepared an account of his observations at several public and private séances of the Brothers Davenport, from which I have been permitted to select the following facts, not contained in the previous chapters, or more circumstantially related.

Of the Brothers Davenport, Mr. Coleman says: 'Under ordinary circumstances, it would have been a sufficient guarantee of the respectability of the Davenports, that they were associated with a gentleman of the high character and intellectual acquirements of Mr. J. B. Ferguson, whose past history and great sacrifices for the cause of truth is well known to me.'

While in America, Mr. Coleman was assured by Professor Mapes, an eminent chemist and engineer, that 'John King' had conversed with him in an audible voice for half an hour, and had given his hand a most powerful grasp. "I am now enabled," says Mr. Coleman, "to corroborate this extraordinary fact, for I, too, have conversed with 'John King.'"

It was at a private séance, at which were present only the Brothers Davenport, Mr. Ferguson, and Mr. Coleman. He says: "The lights being extinguished, we sat a short time in silence, when a startling bang was made upon the tambourine, which instrument, with the guitar, were instantly placed upon my knees. A hand gently caressed me on the head, and a stream of phosphoric light passed across the spacious room, which was succeeded by another rising from the floor to the ceiling, A voice then spoke to me through a trumpet which was brought within a few inches of my face; and in a clear, distinct and sonorous voice, I was thus addressed:

"How are you, Coleman?"

"Oh!" exclaimed both of the Davenports, "that's 'John' — that's 'John' — we have not heard him speak for a long time. Keep him in conversation, Mr. Coleman."

"I then said, 'You appear to know me, John.'

"Yes; I know you in spirit."

"Have you ever seen me before?"

"Yes; I saw you in America."

"Do you think, John, that you will be able to convince the skeptics in this country?"

"Yes; we have power enough to make them surrender. There is a lady standing by your side."

"What is her name?"

"Kate."

At this moment one of the Davenports said, "I hope you will be with us to-morrow night, John (the night of the press séance).

"Certainly, certainly!" Then turning in an opposite direction, as I could easily detect by the sound, the voice said "How are you, Ferguson?"

After a few words more, the voice turned again to Mr. Coleman, a hand passed over his head, and patted him kindly on the shoulder, and the voice said, "I must go now; good night."

"Skeptics may save themselves the trouble," says Mr. Coleman, "of suspecting illusion, ventriloquism, etc. I know it was a reality. I am sure that a voice addressed me, and that it was not the voice of a mortal.

"At a séance at the house of a friend, the coat of Mr. Fay was removed from his back in an instant, and my friend's coat put upon him in the same space of time, Mr. Fay's hands being firmly tied together behind him, and the knots of the cord sealed. On the same occasion, the still more bewildering fact occurred of Mr. Ira Davenport's waist- coat being removed while his coat remained, his hands being bound behind his back. The waistcoat lay at our feet, with his watch in the pocket and the chain hooked in the button-hole, just as he had worn it a moment previously, the waistcoat remaining buttoned."

Mr. Coleman confesses himself staggered by this phenomenon. It must be a trick. But how could it be done in an instant, and with the hands tied and the seals unbroken? He says: "On a subsequent occasion I saw the same phenomenon when the wrists were secured with soft copper wire, in addition to the rope, which made it impossible to slip the hands, and for more perfect security, at other times, when the natural hands would have been required to play on musical instruments, etc., sticking-plaster was put around the hands, which were also filled with flour.

DARK SÉANCE—THE DAVENPORT BROTHERS

"I saw at another séance Mr. Fay tied to his chair, with his hands fastened behind his back, and after several coils with inter- mediate knots around his person. Captain Drayson of the Royal Observatory at Woolwich fastened the final knot beneath the seat of the chair, and placed a legible seal in wax on this final knot, which of course embraced the two cords of the rope. After the usual manifestations, Mr. Fay requested the in- visible operators to untie him and leave, if they could, the seal unbroken. We heard the untying of the rope, and in a minute or two Mr. Fay was set at liberty, when, to our amazement, the first knot remained [with the seal intact] every intermediate knot was taken out, leaving a plain knotless rope with a loop at the end. This remarkable fact was made evident to all present, numbering some thirty or forty persons, who eagerly examined the rope and were obliged to accept the palpable fact, inexplicable as it appears to be.

"On another evening, the lights being extinguished. Sir Henry de Hoghton asked that Mr. Fay's coat should be taken off. He had scarcely uttered the words when Mr. Ferguson struck a brilliant light, and I saw the coat leaving the body of Mr, Fay, and all could see it in its flight in the air until it reached and rested on the knees of Sir Henry, who was sitting in the center of a large semicircle some ten or fifteen feet from either Mr. Fay or Mr. Ira Davenport, who were both tied hands and feet to their chairs. Sir Henry de Hoghton then took off his own coat, and placing it on his knee asked that it should be put upon Mr. Fay. We instantly heard a rushing sound, and in less time than it takes me to say it — in fact not more than a second or two — Sir Henry's coat was found not on Mr. Fay, but on Mr. Davenport, over his own coat, which had not been removed.

"Let the incredulous smile and the savants shake their heads; these astounding facts remain and are unimpeachable.

"Benjamin Coleman.

"London, 51 Pembridge Villas, Bayswater."

A very remarkable statement, which, standing alone, would go far to send a man to a lunatic asylum, but which is supported by such abundant testimony, and is susceptible of such easy proof, that a less solid and reputable man might make it with safety.

But let the reader consider a moment one or two of these facts. Can he conceive of a man's waistcoat being taken all buttoned from his body, without removing his coat, and while his hands are bound together behind him? Can he conceive of a dozen well-tied knots in a doubled rope being untied, while the last knot that secured all the others remains intact with its seal unbroken?

Mr. William Howitt, the well-known and delightful author of so many thoroughly English books, has published a statement respecting the Brothers Davenport, from which I am able to make only brief extracts. Mr. Howitt says:

189

DARK SÉANCE—THE DAVENPORT BROTHERS

"Having been familiar with the career of the Davenports in America for the last ten years, in fact, ever since they were boys — having read the testimonies of the most respectable American journals, and knowing that thousands of the acutest and most honest of the distinguished men of America had satisfied themselves of the bona fide nature of their manifestations, I did not even require to see them myself to be quite certain that they were genuine. I knew that every ingenuity, every test which a most wide-awake and ingenious people could apply, had been applied in their case. I knew that they had gone, through all these years, over the length and breadth of the North American continent, through all that rowdyism, vulgarism, learned ignorance, journalistic conceit, lying, menace and browbeating violence could do and show."

Mr. Howitt says that he saw these manifestations at the Hanover Square Rooms, and was satisfied of their genuineness, and, with his usual frankness and independence, he did not hesitate to declare his convictions.

To give a full account of all the remarkable phenomena that have occurred in this metropolis alone, during the brief stay of the Brothers Davenport, would require a volume. At one séance in a private mansion, one of the instruments, whirling through the air, knocked a large and costly vase from the mantel-piece. It was heard to fall upon the fender with a crash and shiver, as if it had been dashed into fragments. No one doubted that such was the case until a light was struck, and it was found standing upon the hearth, whole and uninjured.

The tests which have been applied have been almost as remarkable as the phenomena produced. At a séance at the residence of a distinguished man of letters, a clergyman twice broke the circle and rushed into the center of the room, expecting to find either the Davenports untied or to detect their confederates. In each case he found them both firmly bound in their chairs, and no other person.

These facts are very well known to almost all the writers of the London press. They would be confirmed personally by nine out of ten of the writers for the most respectable journals. The time will probably come when they will be willing to publish to the world their genuine convictions. It is remarkable that even those who have honestly and frankly stated the facts have offered no theory to explain them. No mechanician, no advent in legerdemain, no man of science, has attempted to show how one of these marvels has been accomplished. A score or two of the very cleverest men of England, some of whose names have been given, have had the best possible opportunities to investigate the whole matter. Had there been fraud, deception, or delusion of any kind, they could not have failed to detect it.

The Fabulous DAVENPORT BROTHERS

CHAPTER TWENTY-FOUR
WHO, AND WHY?

By whom are the Manifestations Produced, and for What Purpose? Examination of Evidence — Conclusion.

When any person has become convinced by testimony which he cannot doubt, or, if that be not sufficient, by the evidence of his own senses, that the phenomena described in these pages are real, actual, unquestionable facts, the next thing in order is to ask how, or rather by whom, are they produced? If the Brothers Davenport, as they solemnly aver, have no direct and voluntary agency in producing the manifestations, and there is no collusion, no deception, no jugglery or fraud about them, by what or by whom are they accomplished ?

Are they the result of some subtle element, like magnetism and electricity? Most certainly not. These natural forces act according to certain laws, and do not possess intelligence. Electricity may rend trees and rocks, produce light and heat, propel machinery or convey messages, but for these last operations it requires to be guided by some intelligence out of itself. Electricity or galvanism will not tie or untie ropes, nor play on musical instruments, nor take off or put on the coats of persons whose hands are securely tied together, much less hold conversations and communicate information.

What we see exhibited at every stage of this history, and in all the phenomena, is force, governed by intelligence. We cannot conceive of an active intelligence, or an intelligent force or power, except as an individualized being, in some respects like ourselves. In all these manifestations there are evidences of the actions, and consequently of the existence, of intelligent beings, having some faculties similar to our own, usually invisible, but with the power of taking on, under certain conditions, a partial visibility. Hands and arms are often seen — perhaps oftener felt unseen, and not seldom both seen and felt. Sometimes, but rarely, larger portions of forms, very human in their appearance, are visible. These hands, arms, portions of bodies, seem to be formed in space out of no visible material; but visibility, it must be remembered, is only an accident of matter, not an essential property. They also melt away, sometimes to the sight, often to the feeling, into invisibility and intangibility.

Men have at different times and in different countries believed in the existence of many kinds of beings having these properties of intelligence, force, and of being visible or invisible at will, or according to varying conditions. The belief in the gods and demigods of the old mythologies of India, Egypt, Greece, and Scandinavia, was once common, if not universal. So has been the belief in fairies, brownies, the "good people," spirits, goblins; also in angels and demons; good and bad spirits of a high order of intelligence; and it has been only in very recent times that many persons have doubted of the continued existence of human beings, and that they sometimes appeared, after being separated from the body, or in some way made their presence known to the living.

Now, it must be admitted by those who have attended the séances of the Brothers Davenport, that very wonderful and very astounding manifestations do take place.

It must be admitted that the Brothers Davenport do not produce them; and also that no living men, by trick or skill, can or do produce them.

We cannot conceive of any blind force in nature producing manifestations of intelligence, or speaking, playing on musical instruments, and exercising mechanical ingenuity — in some cases in defiance of the common laws of nature.

We are forced to the conviction that these things are the work of intelligent beings; and it is also certain that they are usually intangible, invisible, and not subject to material laws, and that they can exercise powers over matter, of which we can form no distinct conception.

The next question is — who, or of what nature, are these beings?

The character of the manifestations is not such as to indicate that they are the work of a high or superior order of intelligences. We cannot suppose, for example, that angels would be engaged in producing such phenomena.

We cannot reasonably attribute them to a high order of wicked spirits. There are no evidences of transcendent intelligence joined to transcendent malice. They are sometimes called diablerie; but I see no evidence, so far as the Davenports are concerned, of such demoniac complicity.

The only real clue or positive testimony we have, as to the beings who produce the phenomena described, is the declarations of the beings themselves. They are the only witnesses we can examine: theirs is the only testimony we can take.

Their testimony is that they are human beings like ourselves. They do not say that they are better than we are, or wiser. They say that, by the fact of no longer having bodies composed of the grosser forms of matter, they have certain advantages over us in respect to sight, locomotion, &c. In many cases they declare their identity with persons who have lived upon the earth, and they convince many persons of this identity.

The Brothers Davenport, from the beginning of their remarkable experience, have had, by various means, communications from the intelligences which produce the manifestations. They are as familiar with an audible voice which speaks to them as with the phenomena commonly witnessed. They have a familiar acquaintance with two or three of these intelligences, who profess to be human beings in a different stage of existence. These voices, and these verbal communications, have been heard by many persons besides themselves, and by some in this country.

I give these facts, as they have been substantially given elsewhere in the course of the narrative, that all the important facts may be placed before the reader.

This being the testimony of the very powers or forces which claim to produce the phenomena, we are to decide whether they, speaking of themselves, are worthy of belief. So far as I know, their testimony, is unimpeached. There is no witness to the contrary. There is no other hypothesis even which will bear examination. If the operations performed are those of intelligent beings, and those beings are not what they declare themselves to be, what are they?

I am not putting forward a hypothesis, but simply recording the testimony or explanation given by the manifesting power, as one of the facts of the manifestations. It is no theory of the Brothers Davenport. They do not advance any. But they afford in some way, not clearly known to physiologists and psychologists, the means — some normal element, perhaps, or nerve aura of a peculiar character — by which the manifestations are made; and one of those manifestations is the declaration, true or false, that they are made by human beings in another state of existence.

To this statement it is objected by certain theologians, that men, when they leave the body, go at once either to a place they would not leave for such a purpose, or to a place they could not. To this, it may be replied, that other theologians recognize the existence of intermediate conditions, and of future states, as various as men's characters and actions.

Another objection is, that the manifestations are trifling, coarse, vulgar, and not in accordance with our views of the nature and conditions of men in another state of being. To this, it may be replied, that we know very little of that state, and that as men differ very greatly in culture and tastes in this world, we do not know that they suddenly change their natures, or become wise, dignified, and good, by getting rid of their bodies. Reasoning of the other life from this, we should expect changes to be gradual, and not rapid. Growth and progression appear to be the law of the universe, as regard both matter and mind.

As to the manifestations, they are certainly very human, or they would not attract so wide and deep a human interest; and, a priori, one would say they were more likely to be produced by human beings than by any others we know of; and if it can be shown that they are not produced by human beings in the body, it is not a very unreasonable supposition that they may be produced by the same sort of beings out of the body.

When we come to this point, and possibly before, we are met with that wonderful question, Cui bono? (who benefits?) It looks very wise in Latin, and is pertinent enough in English. What is the object, and what can be the benefit of these manifestations?

If they were only facts in physical science, and had no other significance, they would be of greater interest than any facts of recent observation.

If they are ever so coarse manifestations of the existence of intelligences, ordinarily hidden from our senses, their use in overthrowing a coarser materialism is evident: if they give us palpable evidence of the existence of a universe of which we were in doubt, and of a life in the future, in which millions have no faith whatever, they are not useless.

These and similar manifestations seem to me to be rude and elementary lessons, adapted to ignorance and false science worse than ignorance; the first steps to the recognition of a higher life.

THE END